After Evil

After Evil

Neil Jackson
As told by
Jane Carter Woodrow

HODDER &
STOUGHTON

First published in Great Britain in 2009 by Hodder & Stoughton
An Hachette UK company

1

Copyright © Jane Carter Woodrow and Neil Jackson 2009

The right of Jane Carter Woodrow and Neil Jackson to be identified as the Authors of the Work has been asserted by them in accordance with the Copyright, Designs and Patents Act 1988.

A CIP catalogue record for this title is available from the British Library

Hardback ISBN 978 0 340 99243 2
Trade Paperback ISBN 978 0 340 99244 9

Typeset in Monotype Sabon by Ellipsis Books Limited, Glasgow

Printed and bound by CPI Mackays, Chatham ME5 8TD

Hodder & Stoughton policy is to use papers that are natural, renewable and recyclable products and made from wood grown in sustainable forests. The logging and manufacturing processes are expected to conform to the environmental regulations of the country of origin.

Hodder & Stoughton Ltd
338 Euston Road
London NW1 3BH

www.hodder.co.uk

Dedicated to the memory of Emily Jackson and to all the other victims of Peter Sutcliffe including, importantly, the victims' children and families.

Jane Carter Woodrow, 2009

This book is dedicated to my brother Derek and to Mum.

Neil Jackson, 2009

Contents

Author's Note

I think Neil has a very important story to tell. And in all my years of working with victims of violent crime, his is the one that has affected me the most.

But first let me tell you how I came to meet Neil and hear his story.

I have a background in criminology, and as an author and writer for television and film. I have written crime dramas and drama documentaries for the BBC and ITV, whilst also conducting extensive research into prisoners and their families. It was these two strands of my life that eventually led me to look at the indirect victims of violent crime, and to Neil's story in particular.

I began my research by looking at the dependent children of women in prison in the late 1980s and early 1990s for my PhD whilst studying at the Institute of Criminology at Jesus College, at the University of Cambridge. Although several thousand women pass through the prison system each year in the UK, nothing was known about what happened to their children at this time. What I found was that most children had chaotic lives (often even before their mother's imprisonment) and were frequently traumatised by the experience. These children were very much the forgotten victims of crime.

This, and further research I have undertaken, led me to

conclude that there were many untold stories hidden behind the bold facts and figures regarding the effects of crime on men, women and children. And, while academic research can be of enormous value in shaping policy on offenders and victims, it can never really shed light on the individual trauma and emotional destruction visited on the families, and particularly on the children, left behind.

I began to wonder how much more difficult it must be when the perpetrator of crime is high profile. This led me to the Yorkshire Ripper case. Although much is known about Peter Sutcliffe, very little is known about his victims, particularly the children of the women he murdered, who not only had to grow up under the shadow of evil, but many of whom had to bear the stigma of their mothers' part-time occupation as prostitutes. There were over twenty children in all.

In writing this book I hoped to shed light on the plight of these forgotten victims; how, in killing thirteen women and seriously injuring many others, Sutcliffe destroyed whole families and ruined the lives of countless others. To try to contact the families, I placed adverts in local newspapers in the Manchester and Leeds areas. A small number of the women's children and families responded.

Although each story was equally important, moving and often tragic, I was particularly drawn to Neil's. He was seventeen at the time of his mother's death, which gave him more of an insight and awareness than might have been the case if he'd been a younger child. Sadly, as Neil's mother was the second victim, it also meant he'd had to live through the Ripper's long reign of terror, revisiting his mother's death time and again as Sutcliffe killed another eleven women over the following four years.

I also found Neil's story compelling because of events that had led up to his mother becoming a prostitute – from Neil and the family's earlier loss, to the shock of finding out about his mother's part-time occupation.

That said, despite Neil being older when it happened and more aware of what was going on around him, he could not explain everything that had happened to him before and after his mother's death. He had been so traumatised that he had blocked it out.

It was difficult for Neil to piece everything together in a way that made sense to him. In order for me to write his story, we needed to carry out further research together. This involved us reading previously published accounts of the Ripper case, as well as undertaking hours of research in local newspaper archives and the national press – and sometimes using these as a prompt to Neil's memories or looking at them in the light of his own recollections. Slowly we were able to piece the story together.

The major undertaking in terms of research, however, was our exploration, with other members of Neil's family, friends and former neighbours, of the events that had led up to, and followed, his mother's death. To this end, Neil found himself on a painful journey of discovery, where he learned things that could not have been pleasant for him, having struggled for so long to come to terms with what Peter Sutcliffe had done to him and his family.

In telling his story, I hope to have provided some insight into the plight of the forgotten victims of violent crime, particularly in high-profile cases.

Jane Carter Woodrow, July 2009

Prologue

I followed the policeman past the marble slabs, until he stopped at a particular area which had a curtain round it. The pathologist was at the sink opposite, carefully washing his hands and then drying them on a roller towel. He saw me, nodded, and came over and introduced himself; his handshake sent a chill through my body. He said he wanted to prepare me for the horrific injuries the person under the sheet had received, stressing that, although they had done their best to clean up the body and reassemble the shattered skull, the throat, back, chest and abdomen had multiple holes in the shape of small crosses, possibly made by some kind of screwdriver. And there were other injuries too, including a boot mark where the victim had been stamped on. Then he thanked me for what I was about to do.

'Screwdriver, shattered skull, horrific injuries?' I knew this couldn't be Mum but some other poor person lying there. Then the pathologist pulled back the curtain and began to lift the sheet.

'Ready, Neil?'

I was seventeen when Mum was murdered by the Yorkshire Ripper. This is the story of my life before Mum's murder, and my life after.

Part One

I

We moved to the village of Churwell, a suburb of Leeds, in the autumn of 1968. Our new home was a bright, newly built semi on the edge of the village, bordered by scrub land to one side, woods and a railway viaduct to the other, and bound by hills on either side. Back Green, the road where we lived, was mostly just a building site with new homes still going up – in fact the only house that was finished was ours – but moving there was like a breath of fresh air after the dark, narrow Victorian streets and cramped back-to-back terraces we'd left behind in Armley in Leeds. Rolling up in the removal van that day was a moment of triumph for us Jacksons: we'd finally made it; the roofing business Mum and Dad had set up a few years earlier was at last beginning to pay off.

I was coming up to eleven at the time, and my brother Derek was almost fourteen. We'd been looking forward to the move for weeks, ever since Mum had came rushing home with the details of our new home from the estate agents. 'Our dream house!' she said, waving the picture under Dad's nose.

'*Dream* on love,' Dad said, 'people like us don't buy their own houses.'

We'd always rented before, but Mum wasn't having any of it. 'Everyone has to start somewhere,' she said. Insisting that me and Derek change back into our school uniforms, she wrapped our baby brother Chris up in his fluffy lemon blanket, planted a dummy in his mouth, and we set off for the estate agents in town to pick up the key. But by the time we'd changed buses and arrived there, it was closed.

'Come on Em'ly love, let's go home now,' Dad said, 'forget this daft idea.'

But once Mum got an idea in her head, she was like a terrier with a bone.

'You've got to see it Sid!' she said. 'And th' boys will love it,' she smiled at us.

'Well we can't look round in the dark now, can we, love?' Dad grumbled, as dusk began to fall.

Derek saw Mum was disappointed and, grinning at us both, produced a rusty torch from his pocket. 'I don't see why not,' he said. Mum smiled back at Derek; he always had an answer for everything.

'Right then, we better get down to the bus stop,' she told Dad.

Dad didn't look too pleased, but he knew better than to argue when Derek and Mum were on his case.

By the time we arrived at Churwell, it was pitch black. Derek shone the torch through the large downstairs windows and the letterbox. It was impossible to see much with such a tiny beam. All I could make out was a set of dark empty spaces, but I could tell Dad was excited. 'Nice size rooms,' he kept saying to Mum, 'very decent. But how on earth can we afford it?'

When we got back home, Mum got out her Post Office savings book. 'Through the business,' she said.

Mum had always been good at finding ways to make

money. Dad had been working for some years as a roofer, when he and Mum decided they wanted to have their own business instead of Dad always working for a weekly wage for someone else. But they needed capital for this, which, coming from modest, working-class families, they didn't have.

Mum wasn't much of a smoker, well only on social occasions, but she collected the coupons from Embassy cigarette packets to get items for the house. If you saved enough, you could exchange them for goods from the Embassy catalogue: things like saucepans, tea services, socket sets, even furniture.

Mum never managed to get more than a set of teaspoons from what she smoked herself, but she realised that if she and Dad collected as many coupons as they could lay their hands on, buying them at one price and selling them on in bundles at a higher price, they could make a tidy profit.

Mum's plan worked and within two years they were able to set up in business: 'S & E Jackson, Roofing Contractors'. Mum studied at nights to learn how to do the books and Dad did the manual work. With the money from the coupons they bought tools and equipment and set up an account at Wakefield's, the local builders' merchant.

'Told you S & E Jackson would make money!' Mum grinned, showing him the savings book where she'd stashed enough away to put a deposit on a house.

'By love,' Dad was beaming all over his face, he was that made up about it; and just a few weeks later me and Derek were helping Mum pack up the old house into tea chests.

'The new house – Churwell – it's going to be our fresh start,' Dad told Mum, who looked really happy.

It wasn't until many years later, after Mum's savage death,

that I would come to understand just what Dad meant by
their 'fresh start'.

Although Churwell was only four miles down the road
from Leeds, our new home was a million miles away from
the two up, two down – with its tin bath hanging on a peg
in the kitchen, gas lighting and toilet in the yard – we'd
left behind in Armley.

Seeing our new house in daylight for the first time was
like stepping into a different, modern era. It was light, bright
and spacious, and smelt of paint. Even now, as an adult,
if I smell freshly emulsioned walls, it takes me back to that
house in Churwell. The house was painted magnolia, and
had a tiled bathroom and inside toilet.

The tiny windows of our old back-to-back, that had
barely let in a shaft of morning light, were replaced by
ceiling to floor windows and glass-panelled doors, from
which the sun streamed through and danced off the walls.
The downstairs had a large lounge and through-diner,
and a brand new white melamine fitted kitchen with a
waist-high fridge, instead of the usual meat safe and pantry.

Mum was beaming as she looked round the new kitchen,
opening cupboards and running her hand along the top of
the work surfaces and fridge. 'By,' she murmured to herself
over and over, '. . . well I never,' as if she couldn't quite
believe all this was all hers. She'd become seduced by the
new age of consumerism; there was no question, Mum had
definitely arrived.

I was quiet, shy and small for my age, and with my freckles
and reddish-blond hair that wasn't quite ginger, it still meant

I was fair game with other kids wherever we went. My brother Derek, who was three years older than me, was everything I wasn't – a tall, strong, outgoing boy who, with his dark hair and grey eyes, looked a lot like Mum. But despite our age difference, Derek was my best friend as well as my protector.

'Hey, ginger nut, get back in t' packet!' some kids would shout, waving their fists in my face as I played footy against the wall by the ginnel. Derek would come racing out of nowhere, 'Pick on someone your own size, you toe rags!' squaring up to them and sending them flying in all directions. As Derek stood there, arms folded, watching them go, I glanced up at him and felt proud: you couldn't have wished for a better big brother.

Here, so far, there weren't any neighbours; the semi attached to ours still needed fittings, while the next pair along were still going up and had a tarpaulin over the top. But I knew, even though we were 'outsiders' in the village, I'd be OK with Derek looking out for me.

Dad lifted the estate agent's 'Sold' board out of the earth and laid it on its side by the hedge. Derek picked it up and started attacking me with it. 'On guard!' he shouted, as if he was in one of the swashbuckling adventures he'd read about in his Boys' Own Annual. Soon I'd got the broom handle off the back of the lorry and we were having a sword fight of sorts.

Before renting our back-to-back in Armley, Mum and Dad had started married life in a caravan on a windy cliff top. Now they had their own home at last.

'It's all ours,' Mum was fond of saying, until Dad

reminded her, 'Emily lass, it's only "ours" just as long as we keep up the mortgage repayments.'

Mum was jangling the keys in her hand, when Dad swept her up in his arms, opened the front door and lifted her over the threshold.

'Put me down, Sid Jackson!' Mum laughed, beating her fists into his chest in protest. Me and Derek looked at each other and cringed – your parents weren't supposed to act like this. Mum had put on a fair bit of weight lately and Dad quickly set her down, clutching his back as if he'd pulled a muscle. 'You need to go on a diet, love,' he joked.

After the removal men had taken the beds and other heavy furniture into the house, we helped unload the lighter stuff, forming a human chain from the back of the lorry to the front door. I took my eye off the chain for a moment and, as I looked around me, was struck by the hills and vast tracts of open farmland.

'Here, stop your daydreaming and give us a hand!' Dad said, throwing a standard lamp that had seen better days off the back of the van and to me. I threw it to Derek who caught it and winked at me, 'We'll go exploring later.' He threw the lamp to Mum. 'Hey, watch what you're doing with that!' she warned him. 'That was a wedding present from your Gran.' And she set it down carefully in the hall.

Next in was the battered wringer and Christopher's old carrycot that had long since served its purpose. 'What are you keeping that for, Mum?' I asked her, 'It's just old rubbish, that; you might as well take it down t' tip.'

'Hold your horses, young man,' Mum said, giving me a sideways look. 'You never know when these things might come in handy.'

At our old house, me and Derek had shared a bedroom with our little brother Chris, who was eighteen months old. His cot was pushed up against the wall by the top of my bed and every morning he'd wake me up by shaking the rails and putting his hand through and tugging my hair. 'Wake up, Neil, wake up!' he urged me; he wanted to play.

Now, in our new house, Chris had the small bedroom next door to Mum and Dad, while me and Derek had our own large room that ran at the back of the house, with a window onto the garden and another at the side of the house. The walls were papered with wood chip which me and Derek soon plastered over with our sporting heroes: Billy Bremner, Alan 'Sniffer' Clarke, Eddie Gray, Norman Hunter, Peter Lorimer, Johnny Giles, and the rest of the Leeds United team. Derek was a sportsman and had his football trophies lined up on the side, with just enough room for my football stickers album and stamp collection.

The only drawback was that we had no curtains, so we'd wake as soon as the sun came up, and go to sleep watching the stars on a clear night or the moon move across the top of the bare woodland trees on others – chatting about the game on Saturday or what it must be like to play golf on the moon like the American astronauts were doing.

'If Neil Armstrong hits the ball really hard it might travel through space, straight into our bedroom window!' I said to Derek.

'Shut up, you daft bugger!' Derek grinned, as I dived under the covers giggling.

Our room was no different to the others in the house, as none of them had curtains up at the windows to start with. Mum and Dad had stretched themselves to get here, and we'd taken most of the heavy old furniture from our previous home with us. A large utility table and a worn, green leather settee from the 1940s that the neighbour had given Mum when she'd got a new three-piece on credit, stuck out like a sore thumb here in our modern home. Mum spent each evening on her Singer, furiously turning the handle as she ran up new curtains from two or three pairs from our old house, trying to make them fit the new, large front room windows.

When we first arrived at Churwell, it was just after the half-term holidays before Christmas, so we didn't have to start our new schools until the New Year. With nothing to do all day while Mum unpacked tea chests and Dad shifted furniture around under her direction ('Try it here Sid . . . Mmm, perhaps not, what about over there?' – until she got him to shift it all back the following day) me and Derek set off exploring the village, fancying ourselves as country lads now. In reality, we'd never seen the fields and open countryside before – well, not right on our back doorstep. We'd only known the narrow cobbled streets and row upon row of back-to-back houses of Armley, all blackened by smoke that had belched out from a thousand chimneys for over a century.

'Look at the peasants everywhere!' I called to Derek. 'Pheasants, you dick!' he replied, as we watched them flying up from their nests in the fields.

We set off for the beck, looking for fish and skimming stones across it. We watched trains going over the viaduct, putting pennies on the line to flatten them, and walked across fields of purple rhubarb stubs not yet cleared on the rhubarb farms – something we didn't even know existed before. Finally, we'd play football in the park, throwing a couple of jumpers down for goal posts and practising penalties – me being Gary Sprake in goal for most of the time, and Derek being his hero Billy Bremner. Derek called over to some local boys and asked them if they wanted a game; soon we had a couple of sides going.

We didn't notice dusk had fallen and carried on playing by the dim light of the nearby street lamps, staying out until we heard Mum yelling, 'Neil! Derek! In!' at the top of her voice from the front doorstep. When we got back, Mum would still be sewing. She didn't stop until she'd got her curious patchwork curtains up at all the windows that could be seen from the road, using some material from a bedspread her sister had given her when she'd used up all the curtains from our old house.

The following week, when we'd had time to settle in, Mum's family, the Woods, came to tea. Mum came from a large, working-class family from Hemsworth, a mining town between Leeds and Wakefield. When she and her brothers and sisters were in their teens, Grandad and Grandma Woody had upped sticks and moved the family to Leeds. Then, later, as the children got married and had families of their own, they'd stayed close to Grandad and Grandma in the Armley and Bramley areas.

Mum had seven brothers and four sisters, and was close to them all; those who weren't working or who couldn't come for some other reason, trooped round with their families to visit us that Sunday afternoon. Grandad Woody also came; he'd moved in with his sister Winifred soon after Grandma had died. Winifred was in fact Mum's auntie, but we all called her Auntie Win. Auntie Win and

Grandad Woody always looked quite whimsical together. Auntie was short and portly and always bustling around, the very opposite of Grandad Woody, who was tall and wiry and more relaxed; Mum, at a willowy five foot ten, took after him.

Mum made me and Derek keep our best clothes on for the visit, clothes that we'd worn to Sunday school that morning. I felt stifled in a collar and tie, but realised Grandad Woody did too when, shortly after arriving, he took his tie off and put it in his pocket, sighing with relief as he loosened his collar. Auntie Win might have been small but she soon scolded him.

'Woody, we're in company!'

'But it's chaffing me neck,' Grandad complained.

Nonetheless, he soon put it back on under Auntie's watchful gaze, and I realised it wasn't just us, but the relatives too, who were on their best behaviour.

As soon as the aunts and uncles arrived, they were admiring our new house with all its mod cons and the large glass windows and doors that made it so bright and airy. Grandad asked if he could have a tour of the central heating system, and Dad took him and some of the uncles round to view it.

Mum set up a separate tour of her own, showing Auntie Win and her sisters the new-fangled immersion heater, airing cupboard and fancy tiled bathroom, while me and Derek and my cousins, mostly girls, sat staring at each other, bored with the whole thing.

'Ee lass, you won't want to be speaking to us now,' Grandad Woody said on his return, 'it's that posh.'

'Aye, happen you'll have to mind your p's and q's now, Grandad!' Win chimed in. 'We all will!'

Mum laughed, a little embarrassed, but there was no doubt she and Dad were proud of their new house.

Mum had spent hours baking in preparation for 'the visit' as she called it. Mostly everything she baked was apple: apple pie, apple crumble, apple turnovers, apples in their jackets – to go with the two large platefuls of ham and egg sandwiches she'd made.

'By, you shouldn't 'ave spent all that on us, Em'ly,' Auntie Win remarked. But in truth Mum had hardly spent a thing. While me and Derek had been exploring a few days before, we'd climbed over the fence of an orchard near the back of our house. We'd only intended to use it as a shortcut to the village when an old lady, bent double with arthritis and a hard look in her eye, came out of the house nearby. I recognised her as Mrs Stone, who Mum had met in the street the day we moved in.

Me and Derek looked at each other and were about to make a run for it, when she said, 'You boys can take whatever you want off the ground,' and held out a large brown paper bag to us. Derek took it. 'Thank you,' he said, glancing at me, surprised.

We started picking the apples from the ground; most of them were badly bruised or had holes in them where the maggots had burrowed. Old Mrs Stone tilted her neck and watched a moment as we began filling the bag. 'Only off the ground now!' she warned us, still keeping a beady eye on us as she went inside.

The lower branches of the trees were almost touching

the ground under the weight of the apples ready to fall when Derek's arm accidentally brushed against a branch, sending a torrent of apples thudding to the ground. We looked at each other.

'You thinking what I'm thinking?'

'Happen.'

'Go on then.'

I stood beneath a branch while Derek shook it and caught the apples in my outstretched jumper. We had quite a system going, tipping them out of my jumper into the brown paper bag and filling our pockets, when Mrs Stone suddenly reappeared.

'I saw you! I saw what you boys are doing!'

'Quick! Run!' Derek shouted.

We took the bag of apples and fled, but Mrs Stone chased after us. 'I'll crack t' pair of you! You see if I don't!'

I couldn't believe someone so old and crippled could run so fast; before we'd got back over the fence she was whacking the back of our legs with a stick. The pain was searing and Derek dropped the bag.

'You wait till your mum hears about this!' she called after us as we ran off up the road.

I felt sick.

'Stop worrying. She won't tell Mum!' Derek reassured me. 'She's just saying that.'

We hadn't been five minutes through the back door when there was a loud knock at the front. Mum opened it.

'Your boys have stolen my apples!'

Mum turned on us, and gave us a clip round the ear:

'That hurt!' I complained, rubbing my ear.

'It was supposed to.' Mum said. 'Stealing Mrs Stone's

apples like that! After all I've taught you! Now apologise.'

We mumbled an apology . . . 'Sorry.'

In fact, I really did feel sorry as it seemed to take all the energy Mrs Stone had left after chasing us, to lift her head from her chest and nod at our apology.

'Poor Mrs Stone,' Mum said, as she watched her toddling off up the road. 'Don't let me catch you boys upsetting her again.'

Me and Derek felt really ashamed as Mum closed the door. Then Mum turned to us and, looking thoughtful for a moment, asked,

'I don't suppose you two have got any apples left?'

We shook our pockets out over the draining board; dozens of apples rained down and tumbled into the sink.

'Not that you haven't done wrong; and let that be a lesson to you both . . .' she said as we rubbed our ears, 'but if you take them back it'll only upset Mrs Stone again, and there's no point in letting them go to waste.'

Mum was soon boiling up the apples and baking all afternoon. I put the pies, pastries and crumbles on the front door step to let them cool down in preparation for the family visit on the Sunday.

When Grandad Woody felt he understood all the ins and outs of the central heating system, which he'd discussed at length on his return from the tour, Mum began serving up the tea. The policy at visits was always 'family hold back', not just out of politeness but because there wasn't always enough to go round.

Me and Derek drooled at the sight of the sandwiches and the apple pastries, but when they were offered to us, we grudgingly mumbled, 'Not hungry thanks', as Mum had instructed us to do beforehand.

As soon as the others had finished, Mum gave us a discreet nod, and we grabbed what was left.

'By, you'd think those two hadn't had a bite all day,' Auntie said, as she watched us wolfing it down.

'They're growing lads,' Mum said sheepishly.

A bit later, as the family said their goodbyes and set off for the bus stop en masse, Mum said to Dad, 'I think that went well.'

That winter, me and Derek hoped for snow so that we could go out and have snowball fights, but it was to be a mild winter which suited Mum and Dad even less than us. This was because, without any storm damage, there was little roofing work around. But, as luck would have it, Dad spoke to the builders in our road and was soon working on the pair of semis next to ours, putting on the roofs as quickly as possible while the weather held up.

Dad wanted Derek to follow in the business when he left school, but Derek had set his sights on becoming a footballer and playing with Billy Bremner and the boys at Elland Road. But to keep Dad happy, Derek at least appeared to make the effort. As he climbed unsteadily up a ladder with the hod, Dad would shout at him, 'Watch out lad, you'll fall!' or 'Just keep looking up if you're nervous!', and 'That the best you can do?' as he looked in disbelief at the mere half dozen tiles he'd managed to bring up in the hod in one go.

I went to my room to read my comics; I knew it wouldn't be long before Dad had had enough and sent him packing. Then me and Derek would set off down to the village again, kicking a ball back and forth between us until we got to the rec.

'Poor old Dad, he thinks I'm worried by heights!' Derek grinned, then blasted the ball past me into the back of the net.

That Boxing Day, just a few short weeks after we'd moved in, something happened that I would never forget. As me and Derek came in from the park for our cold turkey dinner, Dad came rushing out of the house in a panic and all red in the face.

'Thank God you're here! Get down the phone box quick! It's nearly here!'

'What?' I asked, completely baffled. 'What's here?'

But Dad was too busy cursing the GPO for not having connected us up to a phone line yet when Derek said, 'The baby of course.'

'The baby? What baby?' I asked.

Derek gave me the same sideways look Mum had given me the day we moved in.

'Mum's! Who do you think?' he said. 'Come on!' and he rushed off to phone box, with me trailing behind.

Derek pushed the coins in and spoke to the midwife. Nurse Dyson arrived at the house in minutes.

'New house, new baby then, love?' I heard her say to Mum as she disappeared into the bedroom, but I still couldn't take it in. The extra weight Mum had put on was a *baby*? I just thought she'd been eating too many puddings; she'd certainly been eating a lot lately. When she was having Chris I suppose I was that bit younger and didn't take a lot of notice. Dad said she was going away for a couple of days and then she stepped out of a taxi clutching a bundle. Now it was about to happen again.

Dad started boiling up lots of water, and Granny Jackson arrived with her short, swollen legs wrapped in bandages, to help out with Chris. Not long after, Nurse Dyson appeared at the bedroom door, 'You can go in now,' she said.

Mum was sitting up in bed holding a pink blob wrapped in a shawl. 'She looks like an angel,' Mum said, smiling at the blob, before handing her carefully over to Dad.

'Perhaps we should call her Gabriel then?' said Dad.

'That's a boy's name, daft,' Mum told him, 'although Gabrielle might do.'

'Bubby!' Chris suddenly said, pointing excitedly to her, 'Bub, bub, bubs!' and from then on her nickname, Bubs, seemed to stick.

With three boys, Mum said she'd always wanted a little girl and now she'd got Bubs, the family was complete. Bubs opened her mouth and started yelling.

'She's got a fine pair of lungs on her,' the midwife said. We all looked at Bubs and burst out laughing. Derek held out his arms; Dad passed him the baby, who stopped crying the minute he held her.

'She likes me,' Derek said, cooing over her and tickling her hand.

'He's got the magic touch,' said Mum.

And I really think that's what Derek had with everyone.

2

After Christmas we began our new schools. I started the last two terms at the nearby junior school, and Derek went to Bruntcliffe Secondary School two miles away in Morley. Mum bought Derek a brand new blazer with the school crest on, and which was at least two sizes too big for him. What worried me was I knew that, before long, that very same blazer would be handed down to me when I went to the secondary school. But Derek was at least six inches taller than me and a larger build; if it was big on him now, it was going to swamp me.

'You'll grow into it!' Mum told Derek who, for a moment, looked bewildered by it. Then, with the arms of the blazer completely covering his hands, Derek crouched low and started dragging his sleeves along the floor behind him as he walked around the kitchen, doing a gorilla impression. Nothing ever worried Derek and, as usual, he had Mum in stitches; the two of them got on like a house on fire.

Mum looked over and, seeing I wasn't laughing, asked, 'Neil? What's the face for?'

I knew from all the past hand-me-downs where I'd pleaded with Mum, 'Please don't make me wear that,' that it would be useless my protesting when she finally sent me off to school in that blazer. Like a Christian thrown to the lions, I'd be a laughing stock in the playground. At my new junior school, Mum had cut down a pair of Derek's long trousers and turned them into shorts for me. She sewed some elastic into the waistband so they fitted at the top, but then they flapped out around me like a skirt. 'It's just until I get you a new pair,' Mum said, but the tormenting went on for at least two terms after I'd finished wearing them.

Derek obviously didn't care what anyone thought, and as he carried on flailing his chest, I wished I could be like him and soon found myself laughing too.

No sooner had Dad started work on the houses in our road than the builders left the site and Dad had to look for work further afield. Mum always had the roofing materials dropped off on site by the suppliers, but now Dad was working out of the area, they needed their own van to deliver them in. Dad heard of a pal in the business selling a van and he and Mum scraped enough money together to buy it. Dad's mate parked it up on the drive at the side of the house; the only problem was that neither Mum nor Dad could drive. Mum took it on herself to learn, and began driving lessons in an automatic, before realising that the van was a manual.

Mr Green, a retired Army driving instructor, pulled up outside the house every Thursday afternoon. Me and Derek waited by the kerb keeping hold of Chris while Mum put Bubs on the back seat in her carrycot. Granny would normally have looked after her; she'd stayed on after Christmas to help Mum out for a while, but wasn't feeling so well today.

Mum got in the driver's side, checked in the mirror and signalled, then started waving to us as she set off.

'Keep your eyes on the road!' the instructor yelled at her.

The car rattled and stalled for several yards down the road, before it finally got going.

Dad came walking along the road and stopped to watch. 'I know he's taught people to drive tanks,' he said, shaking his head, 'but even so . . .'

The funny thing was, Mum never lost her temper as he teased her, or said to Dad, 'Why don't you learn to drive yourself?' She just said he wasn't interested in driving, so we never asked him about it, but just accepted it. Mum never asked Dad to test her on the Highway Code either, but pestered me and Derek at every opportunity instead. The real reason behind both these things and the part it may have played in Mum's murder was something I would not come to understand for many years hence.

'What does that mean then, boys?' Mum asked, pointing to a sign by the road, as we walked along beside her, taking it in turns to push the pram, on the way to get the weekly shop.

'A man having trouble putting up his umbrella!' Derek snapped back.

'Ha, very funny,' Mum replied.

'Men at work, by the look of it,' I said.

'See, your brother knows,' Mum grinned.

'What about that one then?' I asked Mum as we passed by a narrow turning.

'A motorbike flying over a car?' Derek suggested.

'You daft 'apporth!' Mum laughed. 'It's no access for bikes or cars.'

My favourite was the car driving over the harbour wall into the sea, which I tested her on from the Highway Code when we got home.

'What's the point of asking me that one?' Mum said. 'There's no sea wall in Leeds!'

A second-hand blue Commer van, registration BNK 953K, sat on the drive at the side of our house for several months while Mum took lesson after lesson. Every so often Derek would jump in and turn the engine over, to stop the battery going flat. Finally, Mum took her test one day and jumped out of the driving instructor's car afterwards, waving a piece of paper, 'I've passed!'

Dad smiled, 'Well done, our lass! I'll frame that and put it on t' wall!'

'Said I'd do it!' she beamed back at him.

We put some kitchen chairs in the back of the empty van to sit on, helped Granny in, then lifted the pram in with the baby, and all piled in after. Granny Jackson sat jogging the handle of the pram to keep Bubs asleep as Mum crunched through the gearbox then sounded the horn as we finally got going. The neighbours, who'd just moved in, came out to look. It was our first family trip out together; we went over the moors to look at the sheep and to the garage to get some petrol. I could never have imagined the part the van would eventually play in our lives and the tragedy that was about to unfold.

A year had passed since we'd moved to Churwell and I'd now started Bruntcliffe Secondary School, catching the bus to Morley each weekday with Derek. Thankfully, Derek hadn't outgrown his blazer yet, so I wore my old one from junior school. Gran was still with us too, but she was now sleeping in the front room, unable to get up the stairs with the veins in her legs turning into ulcers. Mum spent all her days looking after Gran and the little ones, and delivering the roofing materials at this time. It was that winter, during the school Christmas holidays, that me and Derek finally got our wish.

Derek woke me up, jumping on my bed and slapping me round the face,

'Neil!' he yelled excitedly. 'Neil! Wake up! Look out there!'

I didn't move fast enough for Derek, who dragged me from my bed and shoved my face up against the window. As I looked out, I slowly grinned; the hills around the village were covered white, the tall pines were snow-capped, and the snow was still falling: thick, white flakes against the window: Churwell looked just like one of Mum's Christmas cakes. Snow at last!

Because of Dad's job, there were always odd bits of wood lying around. He brought it back and stashed it in the lock-up he'd rented in our road, rather than let it go to waste. Derek asked Mum if we could use some of Dad's wood and nails – and an hour later we were going hell for leather down the slopes, me crouched on the front of our sledge and Derek behind, steering it. Soon we were joined by other kids on their tin trays and assorted home-made sledges. Derek had made a lot of friends in the village since we'd moved here and, while I hung back, shy as ever, he was soon throwing down the gauntlet to the others,

'Bet we can beat you on those old crates!' he chortled, casting an eye over their sledges. They soon took up the challenge.

We started off slowly at the top of the hill; Derek seemed almost to be letting them pass us and get some distance ahead.

'Derek?' I looked up at him. 'What are you doing?' He just smiled and, affecting a posh accent, said something about, 'lulling them into a false sense of security, old boy!' Then he started picking up speed.

'Hold onto your hollyhocks!' he yelled at me, and suddenly we were off, rattling down the hill and whooping with joy as we caught up the others, one by one, and then overtook them on their sledges. We were uncatchable on our superior wooden model.

'We've done it!' I yelled at the bottom of the hill, as Derek turned the sledge round to watch the others still coming down. We dragged our sledge back and forth up that hill for hours that day, the unassailable champions of the Churwell fells.

As the snow continued to fall over the following days, so we spent long hours out on the hills on our sledge – little realising that these few happy days were to be the last we would ever spend together.

The only time we broke off from sledging was to go in to eat and to do Derek's newspaper round. In the first week of arriving at Churwell, Derek had gone in to the local newsagent, Mr White's on the corner, and got himself a job. I was too young to get my own round, so Derek gave me a few bob to help him out.

One day, just after Christmas, when we were due to go back in for tea, Derek looked at his watch and said, 'Time for one more go!' I jumped back on the sledge and he took the reins behind me. There were very few kids left on the snow as dusk began to fall, but a couple of boys suddenly appeared on a sledge from some trees to the side of us and cut straight across us. Derek struggled with the sledge, managing to avoid them, but then lost control of it and we hurtled headlong into a tree.

Derek was holding on to his foot, his face screwed up in pain.

'I think I've done something,' he said, while, apart from a scratch, I was completely unscathed.

I helped Mum get Derek into the van, and she drove him to the hospital. A few hours later Derek was back home wearing a large slipper on his right foot, with his toes set in plaster.

'That's an end to your shenanigans, young man,' Mum told him. But Derek still wanted to do his paper round.

'I can't let my customers down,' he insisted. Most of them had given Derek good Christmas boxes and he was keen to keep them happy for the next twelve months. That evening, I helped Derek with the paper round as usual, him pushing the bike wearing his oversized slipper, as I ran up the paths and shoved the papers through. But as soon as we got home, and without bothering about supper, Derek took himself off to the lock-up and stayed there until he'd mended the sledge.

'You can forget that, young man!' Mum told him in no uncertain terms, when he re-appeared an hour or two later with the sledge all back in one piece.

'Mum, I've only broken a couple of toes,' Derek appealed to her, 'and the doctor said I was to carry on as normal.'

'Within reason,' Mum reminded him. 'And going out on that again with those toes is not "reasonable".'

Derek always managed to talk Mum round – or maybe it was because she was so busy with Gran and the little ones she was too tired to say no for long – but the next morning, just a day or two before the New Year, we set off up the hill with the sledge.

Derek had wrapped a plastic bread wrapper over his large slipper and secured the top with one of his football boot laces; it looked like he was wearing one half of a pair of ski boots.

With the blanket of snow all around us and topping the trees, it felt like we were in a magical wonderland. I imagined this must be what it was like in Switzerland or France, with snow-capped mountains on every side. Not that I'd ever been abroad; none of us had. We usually went on holiday to Bridlington or Blackpool, and Mum and Dad could never afford more than a week at most. No, 'abroad' was just a faraway place I'd seen in pictures in my school books.

Derek promised Mum he'd keep away from the other kids sledging and he was as good as his word, when as luck would have it we skidded on a patch of ice half way down and the sledge went over, sending us sprawling into the snow. It was only the smallest of accidents that kids have every day in the snow, but it was to have the most devastating effect imaginable on Derek and all our lives.

Mum was sitting opposite Derek's bed in the Casualty Ward at Leeds Hospital, rocking Bubs in one arm and holding on to Chris with the other, as the doctor set the plaster on Derek's leg and three of his fingers. It was the second time this week she'd taken Derek to Casualty.

'That should stop t' lad getting into any more mischief!' Mum laughed with the nurses as they waited for his plaster to dry.

Mum was always laughing – I can never really remember a time when she wasn't, and though at first she blamed Derek for the accident, she couldn't stay mad at him for long.

As soon as the plaster was dry, Derek heaved himself off the bed.

'Don't expect to be able to walk straight away,' the sister told him, giving him a walking stick. But the sister didn't reckon on our Derek, who, twirling his stick like a cane, waddled off down the ward in his plaster cast, doing a Charlie Chaplin impression. Mum and the nurses burst out laughing. Then one of the nurses looked over at me and caught me smiling to myself.

'He's a quiet one.'

'And you know what they say about them!' Mum winked at me.

Chris was getting tired and started to whine.

'Right then, let's get you lot home!' Mum announced, and we all trooped out of Casualty in convoy behind her. The sister followed behind us, calling to Derek.

'And I don't want to see you here again, young man – except to have that plaster off!'

Derek saluted her, 'Yes ma'am!' then held his stick aloft, grinning cheekily at her as we left.

Back home, the kids were queuing up outside the newsagent's to sign Derek's plaster; the queue went for quite some distance down the road. By the end of the day, Derek's plaster was covered in different coloured signatures, tattoos from bubble gum wrappers and badly drawn and rude pictures.

The next day, as the snow began thawing and turning to sludge, Mum stopped worrying about Derek going out on the sledge behind her back and having another accident. She was busy helping Gran bandage her legs and shouting at Derek to keep his plaster dry in the bathroom, when she asked me, 'Pop out to the shop for me love, we're out of sugar.'

I was just coming back across the rec, opening the packet of football stickers I'd got for my album with the change Mum said I could keep, when I heard behind me, 'Hey Ginger, give us your stickers!'

I tried to ignore the boys as I fumbled inside the packet to see if I'd got Billy Bremner, who I'd been trying to get for ages.

'Oi, didn't you hear us!' They weren't giving up. I started to walk faster; they picked up the pace. I broke into a run; so did they, only they were bigger and faster than me and I could feel their breath on my neck. Or at least I imagined I could. In my mind, I was the fox and they were the hounds, and soon they were going to bring down their prey and savage it: me!

I was panting hard as I reached the top of our road and was expecting to be felled at any moment, when Derek shot out of the front door, and far from his plastered leg slowing him down, it actually appeared to give him more speed.

'Get your hands off him!' he roared at the boys and, lowering his head, charged at them making a terrifying noise. The boys took fright and screamed for help, scattering in different directions before disappearing off up the road.

Then, as if nothing had happened, he ruffled my hair.

'C'mon, let's go in and play Subbuteo. But I'm Leeds United, mind.'

I could never have imagined then, that by the afternoon, my brother, my hero, would be gone.

3

That afternoon, me and Derek helped Mum take the Christmas decorations down and pack them away. Mum had kept back a tin of Jacob's assorted biscuits from Christmas for New Year's Day tea, and put them on the top of her posh, new melamine kitchen cupboards. Mum was tall and reached up without much effort. She saw us watching her hide the biscuits and warned us.

'Hey, and don't you two get any ideas now while I'm out – else there'll be no pocket money next week!'

Mum had to pop out for a moment to give Dad a hand with pricing up a job a couple of doors down. Being typical lads, the moment she'd gone, we were after the biscuits.

'Bet you daren't get the tin down,' I said to Derek.

'How much?' said Derek.

'More than you can afford.'

'Yeah, you're just chicken,' he said.

'You are!' I said.

'Chicken, chicken!' we clucked away, as we goaded each other to get the tin.

In truth, I wasn't that bothered by the biscuits but was just enjoying the game. But if there were one single moment in my life when I could turn the clock back, then I wish with all my heart this was it. If I'd only known what would happen next, I'd have dragged a kitchen chair over and clambered up to get the biscuits myself, but I didn't. Instead, I carried on fooling around and in doing so changed the course of our family's history for ever.

'You're the biggest chicken, 'cos you're bigger than me!' I taunted Derek as I strutted around, scratching the floor with my foot and bobbing my head.

Derek was taking a breather; leaning against the corner wall, he rested his leg in the plaster cast against the open back door as I carried on clucking.

'That right?' he said, barely rousing himself.

'That's right,' I carried on goading him.

'Yeah, well I'll show you who's the chicken round here!'

Then, suddenly gripping the door handle with one hand, and using the ledge at the bottom of the door to lever himself up, he reached up to the top of the kitchen cupboard. Just at that moment I heard Mum and Dad coming back and a key turning in the front door.

'Quick Derek, they're here!' I shouted.

Derek's fingers had just touched the tin, when Mum came through from the front room with Dad following behind. The back door caught a through draft and slammed shut, taking Derek with it, straight through the plate glass panel in the middle.

Large jagged shards of glass sliced through Derek's body and under his arm; blood began gushing from him as he lay on the floor at my feet.

'Neil?' Derek's voice was weak as if he was calling me from a distance. Everything then appeared to happen in slow motion, and as if it was happening to someone else, not to me. I desperately wanted to help Derek, but I couldn't move. I was screaming, but nothing came out as, all the while, Derek's plaster cast with its drawings and signatures began to turn a deep scarlet.

Mum slumped to the floor and, cradling Derek's head, shouted for Dad to call an ambulance. Dad came through and stood there, ashen faced and staring. This seemed to bring me to and I rushed to the hall, snatched up the phone and started to dial 999. But my hands were shaking so badly, I couldn't dial the number however many times I tried. Dad came out and took the phone from me. His voice was breaking as he made the call, while in the kitchen I could hear Mum telling Derek over and over, 'You're going to be alright love; you'll be alright.'

I rushed back in the kitchen, dropped to the floor and, pushing Mum out of the way, put my arms around Derek to try to make him sit up.

'What are you doing?' Mum yelled at me.

I couldn't answer, but I think I thought if I could just get Derek upright, he'd soon be cracking jokes and back to his old self again. But Derek couldn't move; his body was lifeless and heavy. He just looked up at me a moment, gave a small smile, then his eyes flickered shut.

Gran came back at that moment with the kids from the shop, and clasped her hand to her mouth as she let out a cry.

'Quick! Get the kids out!' Mum shouted to her.

Gran backed out of the door. I heard the rusty wheels of the pushchair squeaking as Gran pushed the kids slowly back up the garden path, and thought Gran's legs must be playing her up today.

'He's still with us,' the ambulance men said to Dad as they wheeled Derek out on a stretcher. *Well, of course he's still with us*, I thought. *He was always with us. Where else would he be?*

Dad went with Derek in the ambulance, while Mum and me followed behind in the van. The blue flashing light of the ambulance lit up the inside of our van; I looked down at my clothes and saw I was covered in blood. I looked over at Mum; her jumper and skirt were soaked in blood too.

The trolley flew through the Casualty doors and past the sister who'd said to Derek only this morning, 'And I don't want to see you here again, young man!' I saw her do a double take as she recognised Mum running alongside Derek.

I waited in a small room near to the operating theatre with Mum and Dad. The surgeon came out in a blue gown and clogs and took them aside. I heard Mum give out a small cry and, feeling that my feet were wet, looked down to discover my shoes were filled with blood. The surgeon told them Derek had severed the major artery under his arm; he wouldn't be coming home this time. I began to feel angry with the surgeon; if Derek wasn't coming home tonight, then when?

When we got back, Chris and Bubs were sound asleep in their beds while Gran was on her hands and knees silently weeping as she tried to mop up the blood from the kitchen floor with a ripped up sheet. Every so often she would wring it out in a bowl of red swirling water; the task looked never-ending.

She'd already swept up the broken glass into a heap in the corner, but when the police arrived they told Mum and Dad to leave everything as it was until they had what they needed for the inquest.

Gran took no notice. Although she hadn't finished mopping up, she filled a bucket with soapy water and started scrubbing the floor. Big tears ran down her face into the bucket as she scrubbed. Mum took the bucket from her and made her sit in a chair; she said she and Dad would do it later.

I kept thinking, you never saw people washing away the blood in horror films, but someone must've done it because the next day it was all gone. Maybe it was people's grannies all over the world.

One of the police officers took me aside and asked me what happened; but I still couldn't speak. I tried but when I opened my mouth, I felt like a fish out of water, gasping for air. Mum said she saw it all and to ask her instead, and took them into the front room with her.

After the police had gone, she made me and Gran a glass of hot milk, but I couldn't control my hands and it spilled everywhere. Gran left hers and threw her apron over her face as she sobbed. I watched her milk begin to crinkle as she cried; then it formed a skin which set solid and I remember thinking how it looked like the skin on her face.

Mum closed the makeshift curtains at the front of the house that night as a 'mark of respect' and didn't open them again until several weeks later. Although Mum got into her stride as she took charge, she didn't cry, although I knew she was heartbroken.

'I wanted a little girl . . . but not this way,' I heard her saying over and over to Dad one evening. Dad said nothing; he seemed to have shrunk like a tortoise, into his shell.

That night, as I lay in bed, alone in my room for the first time without Derek, I heard Dad knocking out the rest of the glass in the back door which was below my bedroom. The bedroom still had no curtains up and, when I turned the light off, I could see Dad taking the door off its hinges and replacing it with a panel of plywood. He was knocking nails into the architrave long into the night as he boarded up the back entrance. I heard Mum begging him to come in, that he'd finished it now. But Dad just kept on knocking the nails in until Mum found him slumped against the back doorstep, his head buried in his hands, sobbing. Although I didn't realise it at the time, something changed in Dad that day; he seemed to harden and nothing would ever be the same again.

With the front room curtains closed and the back door boarded up, we lived in semi-darkness; it was New Year's Day, but a light had gone out in our lives.

A week later, I went back to school; Mum said I needed to get on with things. A special service was held in school assembly for Derek. The head teacher said that although Derek had only been there a short while, he'd made his mark in that time; he'd been a great sportsman and was a very popular boy. I realised then everyone was looking at me, and I slid down into my seat.

The coroner recorded Derek's death as a tragic accident. Derek's funeral service was held in the chapel in our road where Mum had sent us both to Sunday school when we'd first arrived in Churwell.

Me and Derek had fought bitterly against going to Sunday school and eventually she'd given in and we'd stopped going, but as I ran my fingers under the pew where we used to sit, I found his initials, 'DJ', carved into the grain. Every Sunday he'd hack out a bit more oak with his penknife, using a tiny piece of broken mirror to look at his handiwork during the sermon as the elderly preacher droned on.

Finding his initials again with my fingers, I felt as if he was with me at his own service and knew that when the sermon started, he, like me, would be bored rigid. 'Right Neil,' I heard him say, 'the minute the old boy says "Amen" we're out of here!' Then, dumping our hymn books by the door, we'd scarper off up the field to play footy. But today was different and I had to stay put.

The chapel was packed with Derek's schoolmates, friends from the village and family. So many people turned up for the service, they had difficulty fitting everyone in and some people had to stand at the back. Gran stayed at home looking after the little ones; she was too upset to come. As I glanced behind me during a hymn, I caught sight of Mrs Stone in a maroon mac and furry bonnet, bent double with her face practically resting inside her hymn book. Mrs Stone looked up beneath her bonnet for a moment and caught me watching her with her beady eyes. Then she lowered her eyes and carried on singing. I couldn't help thinking if she got any more bent, she'd end up touching her toes.

As I turned back, I noticed Dad was singing but held his hymn book upside down. Mum turned it up the other way. 'Where's your reading glasses, Sid?' she mouthed to him.

After Derek's death, we somehow became more accepted in the village. Derek had always been part of Churwell from the moment he arrived – he'd made sure of that – but now people went out of their way to say hello or put their hand up to Mum and Dad as they passed; we were

no longer 'those outsiders from Leeds'. And, once a fortnight after that, Mrs Stone brought eating apples and pears
round for Mum from her orchard.

There was a large turnout at Cottingley Crematorium
afterwards. I stood with Mum and Dad at the front and
watched as Derek slid away from us, towards the furnace.

As we came out of the crematorium chapel an icy blast
stung my face, and it had begun to snow again. When we
went back to scatter Derek's ashes a few days later, the
snow had settled on the frozen ground.

Soon after returning to school, the children in Derek's class
made a collection for him and there was another collection in the village organised by Mr White and the people
who Derek delivered papers to. With the money raised, they
commissioned a chair to be made by a local, specialist
furniture maker. The chair had a small, but intricately carved
mouse on one of the legs, and bore the plaque 'Presented
by the Leeds Brach of the National Federation of Retail
Newsagents, Booksellers and Stationers. In memory of
Derek Jackson, 1969'. It was presented to me and Mum in
a special assembly at school. The head teacher placed it in
the hall after that and I saw it every day when I went into
assembly.

When I got home from school that night, as I bent down
to untie my shoelaces, I noticed a small speck of blood on
the architrave around the back door. Despite Derek's funeral,
the chair and this, I still wouldn't let anyone touch his
things in our room in case he came home again.

4

In the long, dark days and weeks that followed, I found myself looking out for Derek everywhere I went. As I got off the bus and walked home from school, I even thought I spotted Derek in the road by the newsagent's and gave chase. Eventually, the boy stopped and turned round – a complete stranger.

'Want bother, Ginge?' he enquired, giving me the evil eye. He was at least a foot taller than me and looked pretty handy. I had to think quickly. Pointing to another boy ahead in the distance, I carried on shouting, 'Derek! Wait!' and legged it as fast as I could in that general direction. It was the first time I'd had to manage without my protector, and it made me realise I'd have to develop my own way of dealing with things if I was to survive.

But if the days were bad, the nights were worse. I'd lie awake in the bedroom, expecting the door to fly open and Derek to barge in. Then he'd sling his bag on my bed to make sure I was awake and tell me all about the winning goal he'd scored for the school team or the number of tries he'd made.

I sat there for hours staring at the door in the dark, but as hard as I tried to will him to come through it, he never did. And when I did finally manage to fall asleep, the demons would come: great shards of glass cracking and smashing to the ground like pieces of ice; Derek's blood splashing up onto my face and hands and over my shoes, and I'd wake up screaming in terror and covered in sweat.

'Neil love? Neil, you OK?'

Mum was standing over me as she snapped on the bedside lamp. Looking round at Derek's trophies on the side and the pictures of United we'd put up together on the walls, I was able to draw some comfort from them.

But I was so tired after the nightmares that I couldn't concentrate at my new school and soon got behind with my work. In truth, even though I'd seen Derek's life ebb away with my very own eyes, I still didn't believe that he'd gone and I'd never see him again. And the nightmares became even more frequent and terrifying.

Some few months on, when I'd woken up from yet another nightmare with my heart pounding in my chest, I crept downstairs to get a glass of water and heard Mum and Dad talking in the front room.

'He needs a break,' Mum was saying. I wondered who they were talking about, but could hear the concern in her voice.

'If we could afford to move, we would,' I heard Dad mumble in reply.

This was probably as much as I'd heard Dad say since Derek had died, and he'd taken to spending long hours at work, even when there wasn't much on. At other times, Dad would put his head round the bedroom door and just stare at Derek's empty bed, then nod to me and turn off the light.

While Dad went into himself, Mum did her best to carry

on as normal. Only once did I see a chink in her armour when I came home early from school a week or so after Derek's death to find her sorting through the laundry bin in the bathroom. I stayed behind the door as I saw her take Derek's school jumper from the bin, then, pressing it gently to her face, she wept, 'My boy, my baby boy.' I bit hard into my bottom lip to stop myself crying out, then felt a trickle of blood running from my lip, down my chin. As I wiped it away with my sleeve, Mum looked up and saw me. She smiled briefly and quickly folding up the jumper, put it back in the laundry basket.

It was the start of the long summer holidays when Dad's sister, Auntie Vi, and my Uncle Bob drove up in their Ford Anglia to collect me.

'Well, say hello then,' Mum said, pushing me forwards. I nodded, feeling awkward. This was the London side of the family and I'd never laid eyes on them before, nor they me: we were complete strangers to each other.

Mum packed me a small suitcase and handed it to Uncle Bob, who loaded it in the boot. Two other boys, a couple of years older than me, were already sitting in the back. The one with red hair, my cousin Jeff, nodded, while the other one spent a full minute scrutinising me, before grunting, 'Your bruv' kicked it then?' I hadn't seen him for a while but recognised him as my cousin Kevin.

I nodded. Everything about my cousin Kevin was straight to the point. I hadn't seen him or Jeff since we'd moved to Churwell. They were the sons of my dad's two brothers who lived the other side of Leeds and while Jeff hadn't changed much except to grow taller, Kevin was still short but even tubbier and his face was now plastered with large, inflamed spots the size of walnuts.

'We've been sent to keep you company,' he informed me, in case I was in any doubt. 'Poxy London! Who wants to go there?' he complained. 'I made 'em double me pocket money!' He flashed a couple of one pound notes at me from his pocket. In truth, I didn't want to go to 'poxy London' either, I wanted to stay at home and spend the holidays with Derek as I'd always done. But now I'd got Jeff, Kevin and the walnuts.

Dad wasn't there to see us off; he'd got a weekend job on.

'You'll be alright, love,' Mum said. Then, after a few hushed words with Auntie and glances in my direction, we set off in the car. Mum stood at the front path with Chris and Angie, waving us off until we turned the corner.

Auntie Vi leaned over the back seat and gave us each a paper bag with some sandwiches in. I put mine in my pocket.

'You going to eat them?' Kevin enquired, eyeing them up before he'd finished polishing off his own. I shrugged, unsure of how hungry I might be during the journey, when Kevin plucked them out of my pocket.

'Waste not, want not,' he said, and started tucking into them.

Auntie Vi lived in a semi in South Benfleet in Essex and Uncle Bob worked on the assembly line at Ford at Dagenham. I'd never been to London before, although some locals still insisted on calling it Essex. Wherever it was, it wasn't so very different to Churwell with its mixture of old and new houses bordering on open countryside, although I missed the fells. Around the area of Benfleet where Auntie lived, all the houses had been built in the 1960s, and everyone's dad worked at the Ford car plant, the largest car factory in Europe at that time, as Uncle Bob informed me.

Auntie Vi had five children of assorted ages and sizes: four boys and a girl, twelve-year-old Mary. Jeff, Kevin and me were put in a bedroom with the three oldest boys. The mattresses were taken off the divan bases and put on the floor, which we took it in turns to sleep on; the room wasn't a bad size, but as there were so many of us, it was a tight squeeze. There was barely enough room to pick your way through the bodies, beds, sports kits, smelly shoes and discarded socks, to get to the door.

'Hey, mind me leg!' Kevin said as I clambered over him in the night to get to the toilet in the dark.

'Shut up, Pimple,' one of our mutual cousins said, 'I'm trying to get to sleep!'

'Please, Lord, don't let it happen tonight,' I said over and over in my head as I lay on my divan base every night, frightened to go to sleep in case I had another nightmare, and they heard me yelling. One by one the boys went quiet as they dropped off, while I did everything I could, even pinching myself, to fight off sleep and make sure I was the last one to nod off.

Just as I was to go to sleep, so I was also the last to wake up in the morning and was constantly tired. But there was no lying in as the boys crashed across my divan base, making their way to the door, chucking shoes at each other as they rucked on their way out.

*

At first, with our accents, me, Kevin and Jeff were like aliens.

'You speak funny, you do,' one of my younger cousins said.

'Funny? You want to hear your'sen then,' said Jeff. 'Up the apples and pears and lay your lump of lead on t' weeping willow and go t' Bo Peep,' he tried to say in a Cockney accent, before lapsing into Yorkshire. This appealed to our cousins who shrieked with laughter.

'*He* don't say a lot,' said the oldest boy, John, looking in my direction.

'He's a thinker, aren't you, kid?' Jeff replied.

I smiled. Me and Jeff were different heights, and he was older than me, but because we both had vaguely similar red hair, the cousins delighted in calling us the Carrot Top Twins. With his purple spots, Kevin was known as The Scarlet Pimple-Nel, and the three of us would sometimes be called the Yorkshire Puddings. In return, we called them the Cockney Barrow Boys and the Pearly Kings; 'very original,' I couldn't help thinking.

But the ice was soon broken between us when Jeff challenged them to a game of football over the rec: Leeds United versus the Hammers. Kevin might have been chubby but he could lumber up that pitch and block anyone coming on the attack. Our games soon became a daily event, stopped only by Kevin insisting on going for his dinner on the dot at 12.30 p.m. and 5.00 p.m. for his tea, in case he missed it.

One evening, me, John, Jeff and Kevin sloped off from the younger ones to play footy on the green. Before we got started, John produced a ciggy he said he'd 'procured' from a packet of No 6 in his dad's pocket. He lit it up, then started blowing smoke rings into the air. We all stood there in awe, when Kevin boasted, 'There's nowt to it! I can do that!'

'Go on then, let's see you,' John said, passing him the cigarette.

Kevin took a long drag, pursed his lips to make a ring, then started to cough until he turned purple and his eyes bulged.

'We're still waiting,' John grinned, as Kevin carried on cagging and we all exploded with laughter. John grabbed the cigarette from him as Kevin began to get his breath back.

'Aye, well, I've not got over me cold yet,' Kevin said, 'but if it were a steak and kidney pudding-eating contest, I could beat you hands down at that!'

John smiled to himself as if he was thinking 'no doubt' then took another drag, and handed the ciggie to me. I had just turned twelve and was still small for my age but felt like I'd been invited to join an exclusive club for grown-up boys and, although I didn't really like the smell of smoke, took the ciggie and puffed on it.

'Not like that,' John said, 'you've got to take the smoke right down,' and he demonstrated, sucking in air and taking the smoke deep into his chest. After what seemed like an age, he exhaled and blew a stream of smoke out of his nostrils.

I inhaled the smoke, taking in a long, deep breath the way he showed me. *This isn't so bad*, I thought, when my head suddenly started swimming and I keeled over into a heap on the grass.

'Quick, open his collar!' I could hear Kevin's voice over me as I began to come round. 'I've seen me dad do it,' he continued, 'he used to be in t' Blue Cross!'

'Red Cross,' Jeff corrected him.

'I know that, dick! I were joking!' Kevin said, trying to save face.

'Yeah, 'course you were,' Jeff laughed, as they carried on arguing above me.

I think they'd almost forgotten I was there but, as I scrambled to my feet, I saw a look of fear cross their faces as they took a few steps back from me.

'That what happened to your bruv'?' Kevin asked nervously, keeping his distance.

'Leave it,' Jeff said.

Kevin shrugged, 'I were only asking!'

'You OK, kid?' Jeff asked.

I nodded, when curiosity suddenly got the better of John, who came closer. 'So, did you see it when it happened?' he wanted to know.

'What was it like?' Kevin asked, his eyes widening with relish.

I looked at them a moment and, not knowing what to say, did the only thing I could think of and started backing off, then turned and started running away.

I didn't stop running for about twenty minutes, until I reached a shallow wood and the creek behind it where I stood for a moment catching my breath. Then, ripping off my shoes and socks, I rushed into the creek and began flailing wildly at the water with my arms, letting out an almighty scream to the heavens.

I have no idea how long I was doing this for, but I didn't stop until I was too exhausted to go on. Then I slumped down onto the bank and, lying on my back, allowed the cool water to lap round my legs and soothe my feet.

Soon, as my eyelids dropped, I lay there listening to the sound of the birds and the wind gathering in the trees behind me. I must have been there for some time when I heard a rustling sound to one side of me.

'Neil, we've been looking everywhere for you!' Mary leaned her bike against a tree and came over. 'You better come home now before it gets dark.'

We walked back along the road to the house in silence. But as we approached the house, Mary suddenly said, 'You don't want to take any notice of that lot, they're just boys.'

I'd been so busy with the boys since I'd arrived, I'd hardly noticed Mary, but as I glanced across at her, I was filled with admiration; she'd had to learn to cope in a house full of men.

At weekends, especially Sundays, Uncle and Auntie took all us kids down to Canvey Island, walking round the mud flats near Dead Man's Point and passing dozens of pill-boxes which the youngest boys spent hours running around and exploring. Uncle said they were there to spot a German invasion, though Auntie said why they'd particularly want to take Canvey Island she wasn't sure.

Once we got to the beach, we'd have a picnic and go looking for oysters; other days, we'd go on trips to the creek where the Thames winds round, or to Southend, not leaving until we'd all had a go on the Cyclone at the Kursaal amusement park.

With so much company in the day and all six of us boys in one small room at night, giggling and cracking jokes until we went to sleep, there were times when I was truly happy again. Then a black cloud would come sweeping over me and I'd remember why I was here. And I'd break out in a cold sweat, ashamed that I'd forgotten about Derek, however briefly, and the part I'd played in his death. It was my fault, after all, if only I hadn't kept goading him on to get the biscuits.

One of the strangest sights in South Benfleet was watching Uncle Bob and his work mates driving crazily round the estate in various car chassis as they tested out the parts of the cars they'd assembled at the Dagenham Ford plant, before they put the cab on. Uncle sat bolt upright on a metal seat raised several feet from the ground, with his cap and scarf on and wearing a large pair of goggles, as he tested out the different cars' steering wheels.

For a treat Uncle Bob took me, Kevin and Jeff with him to watch him on 'the strip', a private piece of land at the back of Benfleet where they carried out more rigorous car testing. Later, he let us take it in turns to put on the goggles and sit in the welded-on metal seat. I tested it out as if I was Stirling Moss at Brands Hatch instead of stuck fast in a chassis with the ignition switched on but the gears stuck in neutral. Kevin had to go one better. Pulling on the goggles, he yelled, 'Watch this!' then, madly revving up the car, he leant to one side as if he was taking a bend at speed, and promptly fell out of the chassis onto the concrete. I looked at Jeff and tried not to grin, but soon we were bursting into fits of laughter.

'Give us a hand up then!' Kevin said, red-faced, his pride more bruised than his butt. I realised that this was the first time I'd really laughed since Derek died, and later, looking back, feel nothing but gratitude to my cousins and auntie and uncle for that happy time.

'I'm sorry,' I said, as I helped Kevin to his feet, feeling bad we'd been laughing at him again.

'Oh, it speaks then,' he scoffed.

Coming back from our day out at 'the strip', I stopped in my tracks as I saw the works van parked outside Auntie's. I couldn't believe the six weeks was up, and that the nightmares, without my even noticing, had disappeared.

'Bloody great, I'll be in me own bed tonight!' Kevin exclaimed, sitting on one of the wheel hubs in the back of the van as we travelled home to Yorkshire. 'At least I'll be able to get some sleep now without listening to you thrashing around all night and going divvy.'

I turned to Jeff, sitting on the other wheel hub, what was dick-head walnut face going on about? But Jeff nodded in agreement, 'The whole house heard you, kid.' I felt my cheeks burning and couldn't wait to get to home.

But when we finally arrived back I found things had changed. Gran hadn't been well and had gone into a home, where Mum said she'd get proper care. And Dad had taken the boarding off the back entrance and put up a new solid wooden door without any glass in it. He'd also redecorated; the walls were now all primrose yellow.

I ran upstairs to my room but, instead of feeling at home, found it had changed too. My bedroom was practically empty apart from the new curtains Mum had put up; it seemed strange to have them at the windows after all this time, and they made the room darker. Mum had cleared out all of Derek's things and Dad had redecorated here too; now my room just felt silent and odd. And I suddenly realised what our old neighbour in Armley had meant when Mum made her a cup of tea after her husband had died.

'Missing a limb, Em'ly,' she said. 'I'm missing a limb.'
And so was I.

I opened the wardrobe to put my bag away and found
Derek's oversized blazer hanging on a peg in the back.

'You don't have to wear it,' Mum said. 'We'll get you a
new one.'

I tried it on and decided to keep it. It was so big I could
slide down inside it; it felt like I was wearing a suit of
armour when I started back at school that September. And
that Derek was still protecting me.

There were other changes that had happened while I was
away that I wasn't aware of yet. But what I did realise was
that an invisible line had been drawn in the sand: there was
life before Derek, and life after. The magic of my early
childhood years with Derek had now gone, but there was
to be a new magic.

Yet I could never have imagined how this new magic and
new life would conceal yet another tragedy; how Derek's
death would lead to Mum's, and that in just a few short
years she would be savagely murdered at the hands of a
man about to become Britain's most notorious serial killer.

5

It was 1971.

'Oh Sugar, Sugar . . . Oh honey, honey!' Mum was singing along to The Archies on the car radio as we made our way across the Moors that warm spring afternoon.

While I was away she'd bought a car, a white Cortina, which was second-hand but like new, with leather bucket seats and a large steering wheel.

'It's time we travelled in style instead of going everywhere in the van!' she grinned. The car was to be the first of many.

Now the weather was nice, Mum took me, Bubs and Chris for trips out whenever she managed to get a breather from work. Now that I was the oldest, I sat in the front passenger seat next to Mum, keeping an eye on my little brother and sister in the back as Derek had done in the van.

'Come on you two, join in!' Mum called to Bubs and Chris, and pretty soon she had them singing along at the top of their voices and bobbing away to the music.

'And you, Neil! Come on!'

'Mum, I'm nearly thirteen, not two!' I scoffed.

Mum loved singing; she was always singing before our Derek died, and now, since his death, she seemed to be singing even more. It was like a switch going on and she somehow became even happier, if that was possible.

Mum had worked as a mill girl at a weaving factory in Leeds after leaving school. She and her friends were always singing as they worked the heavy mechanical looms. Because Mum was always laughing and happy, they called her 'Smiler' at work, the nickname of her brother who she'd been closest to as a girl. Like Derek, Uncle Smiler loved to play football and hoped to be a professional one day, when he'd tragically died as he had a kick around with his mates in the park. The ball had struck Uncle Smiler in the chest; he had an undiscovered heart defect and the blow had killed him. He was just twenty. Mum was heartbroken; she'd known long ago about tragedy and loss.

'In the Summertime', by Mungo Jerry came on the car radio.

'Come on, Neil, you like this one!' But I was still finding it hard to smile some days, in spite of her best efforts.

She pulled a sour face at me and carried on singing. Turning away, I hid my smile from her and began secretly tapping my foot in time to the beat.

Pretty soon the tyres were scrunching over gravel, and I realised this wasn't in fact our normal day out. The sign at the side of the driveway said 'Cottingley Cemetery' – the place made famous by the fairies, and which was near to where Mum had lived as a kid. It was also the place where Derek's ashes were scattered.

There was snow still lying on the ground when we were last here, but now all the spring flowers were out and the birds were building their nests. Mum said it was new life coming to the cemetery, but I felt numb being back here again.

*

At home, as well as redecorating while I was away, Dad had taken out the sledge he'd hidden away in the lock-up after the accident, and chopped it up, making a bonfire with it at the bottom of the garden.

With almost every trace of Derek now gone, I got up in the night and crept downstairs to look at the architrave round the back door. The speck of blood had somehow miraculously survived Dad's paintbrush and was still there which I was oddly grateful for. It gave me comfort that Derek really had existed: I hadn't just imagined it all.

At night, the terrible nightmares still returned; I'd wake up in a cold sweat in the early hours, wondering for a few moments where I was as I looked around my empty bedroom. If Mum heard me, she'd get up and make me a hot milk. But hot milk always reminded me of that fateful night and I couldn't face it again. So I'd wait till she'd gone then tip it out of the back bedroom window onto the garden, making sure I got rid of every last drop before a skin formed and made me retch.

'What are you doing in there?' Dad called out from his room one night.

'Leave him, Sid,' I heard Mum say.

'But he's going for a Jimmy out of the window!' he said to Mum. 'Anything rather than come out of his room.'

I knew I was making Mum and Dad worried and before they sent me away I had spent as much time as possible in my bedroom when I wasn't at school.

'Love, he misses his best mate,' I could hear Mum saying. I took the milk to the bathroom after that and quietly tipped it down the toilet and flushed it away.

Although they rarely spoke of it, I knew Mum and Dad

were grieving for Derek too. I could never make Mum laugh the way Derek did or make Dad so proud. Despite Derek's poor performance with the hod, Dad used to put his arm round Derek on the building site and say proudly to his work mates, 'This is my eldest; he's a chip off the old block and no mistake!'

Even though Mum and Dad never said anything to make me feel that way, in the back of my mind I kept thinking, 'The accident happened to the wrong son; they wish it was me.'

Since I'd got back from Benfleet, Mum was always asking me to come with her to price up jobs or to give her a hand with the little ones. Now that I had become the oldest child by default, I accepted it was my job to do this as Derek had done, so I didn't complain. Mum also encouraged me to take on Derek's newspaper round. As I knew it so well and I was older now, it seemed a good idea and a way to make some extra pocket money. I also got to know the other paper boys and made friends with a boy about my age, Ian, who lived in the village. What I didn't understand at the time was that Mum was deliberately trying to keep me busy to take my mind off things. Our trips out over the Moors and getting me to help her out with Chris and Bubs were part of Mum's plan to get me out of myself.

At the cemetery, Mum sat the little ones on the bench by the water tap and gave them some sandwiches and a Wagon Wheel each for lunch.

'I think they'll be alright for a moment or two,' Mum said as we walked the few short yards to the plaque marking where Derek's ashes had been scattered.

Mum rested a bunch of white chrysanths against the plaque while I stood and silently read it: 'Derek Jackson, aged 14, a dearly beloved son and brother.'

Fate is a funny thing, full of 'if onlys': if only I hadn't egged Derek on; if only I'd stretched up myself to get the biscuits, then our Derek would still be with us. If only. I couldn't get it out of my head.

Looking at the plaque again, I was overwhelmed with remorse and grief, when Mum came and stood next to me and said a remarkable thing: 'Neil lad, we mustn't mourn your brother, we've got to celebrate his life and be thankful for the short time we had with him.' Then she looked at me a moment and said, 'Life's for living son, and that's what your brother would you want you to do.'

She'd brought me here to tell me this. But it would be many years later before I would come to realise the importance of these words, and how they would eventually save my life. It would be years too before I would come to realise what they meant to Mum and Dad who, in my absence, appeared to have made a pact of sorts: life was short, best to make the most of it while you can; and all our lives were about to change again.

6

The weekend I got back from London, a brand new 24-inch television set was delivered to our house, and sat in pride of place in the front room. We'd only had radio at our old house and now we had this state-of-the-art model. Even the electrician installing it was impressed. Set in a cabinet with roll-back shutters, it was the only colour telly in Churwell, never mind our street and, as Dad said, was probably the only one this side of the West Riding.

As soon as the kids round about learned of our new colour TV, they came knocking at our door to see it. We'd still got very few neighbours to speak of as the new houses in our road hadn't as yet been finished, with rumours of further problems between the developers and the builders – although no one really knew for sure – but kids as far away as the other side of the viaduct turned up at the house on the off-chance of being allowed to watch our new TV.

Suddenly there were kids my age in the village trying to make friends with me so they could come round, dragging their mates or kid brothers and sisters behind them. The new telly was power and suddenly it was payback time!

'Clear off and get your own colour telly!' I told a couple of boys in my class from the village.

'We're not all well off like you!' one of them replied,

quite put out, I thought, for someone who'd spent the last two years tormenting me over my red hair.

'F'ing ginger snob!' the other called after me as I shut the door in their faces.

'Mum, did we get this on hire purchase then?' I asked her later, suddenly wondering how we could afford it.

'Me and your Dad saved for it – there's no point in having your own business if there aren't any perks,' she smiled.

Despite my best efforts to fend off all these unwelcome visitors, the knocks at the door continued and Mum could never say no to the little kids that arrived on our doorstep saying, 'Can we watch telly, Missus?'

'As long as you've told your mums,' she'd say, then nod towards the front room, and they'd dash inside.

Soon the front room was full of kids sitting cross-legged on the floor, with Chris, now five, and Bubs, three, at the front, watching *Banana Splits* or *How*. You could hear a pin drop – until the programme ended, then all hell broke loose as they argued over what to watch next!

At the weekend, when Dad was trying to have a nap after Sunday lunch, the kids round the house started arguing over which programme they wanted to watch. Soon Dad was banging his shoe on the floorboards for quiet.

Mum quickly rushed upstairs to take him a cup of tea. 'That should see him right,' she said. 'Better keep the kids quiet though, Neil, we don't want to upset him after he's been working all week.'

'Shut up, you lot!' I yelled at them, 'Dad's trying to sleep!'

Dad could be like a bear with a sore head at times and

I was worried he might fly into one of his tempers with all the kids there. It didn't happen very often, and was usually when he was short of sleep, but you knew about it when he did.

Dad wasn't straightforward like Mum. He had recently begun to come out of his shell since Derek's death and while he was often quiet, he also liked to be the life and soul of the party. Not only that, he liked to have his own way in how things were done, especially at work – but then, as Mum said, 'he was a perfectionist'.

Dad, like Mum, came from a large family who lived in the Holbeck area of Leeds. The family didn't have a lot and Dad had to leave school early to go to work, getting himself a job in roofing with his brothers. In the area he was from he'd also had to learn pretty quickly to stick up for himself, and he still did now, especially if he thought someone was trying to pull a fast one or short change him, but he got on with most people.

'Mum, do you think we can have a kid-free day for once?' I asked her one Wednesday evening. 'I want to watch mid-week match special tonight.'

'Course love,' she said, but that night she and Dad picked Gran up from the home and we ended up watching *Calendar*, the local news programme with Richard Whiteley, at 5p.m., followed by *Crossroads* and *Bless This House*, instead. Even our new neighbour, Gwen Henshaw, who came round to pick up her boy playing with Chris, stayed to watch it.

'By, you'll not get 'em to bed now wi' that in th' house,' she said, unable to peel her eyes off the screen.

'Well, they're only young once,' Mum laughed. Dad immediately shushed her, then signalled to me to turn the light off, and we all watched *Barlow at Large* in the dark and silence.

If, on week days, it got to six o'clock and some of the little ones still hadn't been collected, Mum would say, 'You better make sure they get home safely, Neil.'

'Mum, do I have to?' I complained.

'I'll never forgive myself if anything happened to one of them,' she said, though sometimes, if it was raining, me and Mum took them home in the van instead.

Mum'd make sure they all had their coats and gloves on, and I'd lead them off in a crocodile, with the youngest at the front, down Back Green and across the rec, to their respective houses. Sometimes Ian came too and it took us over an hour to get them all home as grateful parents made us stop for a cup of tea, then we'd get back round mine and miss an episode of *The Persuaders*. But Mum said to think ourselves lucky, tonight's episode had been boring. I eyed her suspiciously; it didn't stop her watching it the next time it was on. She had a thing about Tony Curtis who played Danny Wilde, while Ian said he saw himself more as Lord Brett Sinclair, the nobleman, played by Roger Moore. Mum said in that case he better improve his manners and take his shoes off the next time he came round so he didn't ruin her new beige carpet.

As well as the colour telly, I had my first trip on an aeroplane at this time; it was to be the first of many such trips.

I'd had a particularly bad night that night, when the following morning Mum got up early and came rushing back from town.

'We're off!' she said. 'You better get packing!'

Dad barely looked up from studying his football coupons. 'What's that, lass?'

'I've booked us a holiday!' she said, waving some tickets at us.

'Tickets? What do we need them for?' Dad asked. I nodded, thinking he had a fair point; Mum never bought the tickets in advance when we went on the train to Bridlington.

'Have you two got no sense of adventure?' she said, glaring at us. 'We're going to Tunisia!'

Dad looked bewildered.

'Tunisia?'

'You know – abroad!' Mum said.

Dad's mouth hung open. 'By . . .' was all he managed to say, but I could see he was taken with the idea, even if he wasn't exactly sure where Tunisia was.

'It's north Africa, Dad,' I told him.

'Africa? Bloody hell!'

'It looks very nice in the pictures at the travel agent's,' Mum said, 'and we're staying in a three-star hotel.'

'By . . .'

We set off in the car to get our pictures taken at Lewis's for our new passports. The photographer snapped my picture and turned to Mum.

'You're going to need a fair bit of sun cream wi' his colouring – abroad,' he said, as if to remind Dad where we were going.

With my reddish-blond hair and fair skin, I'd even managed to get burnt when the sun peeped out between cloud bursts on a day trip to Brid. Mum said she knew she'd forgotten something and rushed out to buy a few pots

of cream, packing them in her emergency first-aid kit she
got together in a Tupperware lunch box to take on holiday.

Me and Chris scrambled to get the seat by the window;
Chris got there first and then for most of the journey
complained there was nothing to see. I enjoyed the new
experience of flying; I wasn't worried about it one bit –
unlike Dad, who got out a lucky plastic rabbit's foot he'd
won at prize bingo with Mum. Clutching the rabbit's foot
in one hand, and the arm of his seat with the other, Dad
stared rigidly ahead as we took off over the grey skies of
Leeds, until we landed at the other end.

We couldn't believe Tunisia when we arrived there; the
sun, the blue sea and the silver beaches. It was, for us, as
Mum said, 'paradise', and as different from Leeds as it was
possible to be. Except for the markets which Mum tripped
off to every day, haggling with the stall-holders over some
small trinket, which she liked to do at home in Leeds before
the market there burnt down.

Dad even went swimming in the sea, which we could
never get him to do at home, not even down the local baths.
The weather and warm blue sea may have helped of course,
but Dad took to Tunisia after that like a fish to water.

When we got home we went straight round to see Auntie
Win and Grandad Woody to give them their presents – a
little blue pot from the market for Auntie and some figs
which she said in a hushed voice she was 'grateful of'; and
a fez for Grandad which Dad wore on the plane back,
doing Tommy Cooper impressions and making the other
passengers laugh. Dad was a different man on the way
back. He'd got a taste for flying and foreign holidays, and
was always on at Mum to book up the next one after that.

Soon we were going for a fortnight three times a year, to all sorts of places: Italy, Spain and Majorca, but which Dad just referred to as 'abroad'.

Grandad hung the fez on a hook by the front door.

'I'll wear that it in t' winter to keep me grey matter warm when I go to the lav,' he informed us; the lav was out in the yard.

Mum laughed, 'I thought you were going to give us a sand dance, Dad!'

'I will if you like,' he said, putting it on, then began shuffling his feet, giving us a demonstration of sorts.

'Careful, you'll hurt your back!' Win laughed, shaking her head.

Win and Grandad were tickled pink when we showed them the photos.

'By, you're getting above your station now!' Auntie laughed when she saw a picture of Mum and Dad sitting on the beach wearing straw hats and sipping cocktails.

'Well, business is good, why not go further afield?' Mum said.

While it was true, business was good and Dad spent long hours roofing, I knew it wasn't just that with Mum. Since Granny Jackson had passed on a short while ago, Mum felt freed up to do the things she felt she couldn't do before, or didn't like to, when Gran was alive. She no longer had to worry about Gran or take her to hospital appointments and get her the things she needed from town. I know she missed her, we all did, and even though she was Dad's mum, she had seemed closer to Mum than to Dad.

As well as looking after us kids and the business, Mum also took on an allotment after Gran died. Her plan was to make the family as self-sufficient for food as possible. The allotments were down a narrow lane across the road from the house. They'd been created from a square of land left over when the farmer sold off part of his field for new housing and an electricity pylon. Mum and Dad, being the first to rent a plot, had a choice of which one they wanted. Mum took the one on the end, which was almost twice the size of the others, and set to work with a spade and fork, digging the ground over and planting onions, carrots, and potatoes for next year. Later she planted fruit bushes – blackcurrant, redcurrant and gooseberries – to make jam when they were ready.

Mum spent hours digging, planting and weeding. I gave her a hand when I came back from school and Chris copied us with his little shovel. There was still a large uncultivated area to one side of the allotment and a couple of weeks later Mum took delivery of four pigs and three goats. She said that as a girl in Hemsworth she'd always dreamed of having a smallholding when she saw it in a book about Australia at school, and now her dream had come true. Except absolutely nothing she tried to grow, came up – well apart from the lettuces which went straight to seed, and an impressive crop of weeds.

'I don't know what t' opposite of green fingers is, Mum,' I told her, as she surveyed her veg patch, 'but you've definitely got it.'

Mum looked dismayed for a moment. 'Weed killer fingers?' she mumbled, and then she started to grin. 'Tell you what,' she said, 'I've always fancied some chickens.'

A week or so later we'd cleared the fruit and veg area and Mum got a hen house and a dozen or so hens running around.

It was my job to feed the animals every day with the scraps from the bin at the side of the house, and Grandad Woody and Mum's sisters came over clutching newspaper wrappings full of slops for the pig bin every so often. Chris and Bubs liked helping Mum out with the animals too and collecting the eggs, and when they were just a few years older, Mum went out and bought them another surprise.

7

The Land Rover was parked in the middle of our road. The man undid the bolt at the back of the horse-box, dropped the flap and Goldie came charging out backwards, then, kicking his back legs in the air, he bolted off up the road, as Chris and Bubs squealed with delight.

'Quick, Neil! Get him!' Mum yelled as I ran up the road after him with a sugar lump in my hand.

Thankfully, Goldie stopped to chase some pigeons on the green, and I grabbed at the rope attached to his worn bridle and managed to pull him up sharp before he charged off again. Mum and the little ones came rushing up the road behind me. Mum fed him a biscuit and stroked him until he calmed down, then had to calm down my little sister who was nearly sick with excitement.

'I don't know who's more tickled, the kids or the horse,' Mum laughed.

Goldie was a honey-coloured, scruffy horse, well past his sell-by. He was nothing like the groomed and shiny-coated ponies that went by on the bridleway from the pony club stables in the next village. I think Mum had saved him from the glue factory and he somehow knew it.

He'd been used to pulling a rag-and-bone cart in the past, slowly walking in a straight line with his blinkers on, oblivious to what happened around him. Now, with his blinkers off, which Mum insisted the man threw away before he delivered him to us, you could tell Goldie intended to kick over the traces in his old age.

We went on holiday to Spain soon after, and Mum bought Goldie a leather strap with 'Torre Del Mar' written in gold lettering along the length of it, with a cowbell attached. When we got back, I tied the strap round Goldie's neck while Mum fed him a biscuit to keep him still. You could hear Goldie coming a mile off with his bell clanking as he ran up the middle of our road, with me running alongside him holding the reins, and the little ones taking it in turns to sit on him.

Soon, Goldie's cowbell was alerting all the kids in the street who'd come running out, 'Give us a go, Neil!'

'I'm like the flaming ice-cream man, me!' I complained to Mum, 'but wi'out getting paid for it.'

'Oh, stop your moaning,' Mum said. 'You were their age once your'sen.'

Mum often stood on the front step, watching the kids have a go on the horse as she chatted to the neighbours. Liz, who lived three doors up, in the next house that had been finished in the street, came out and shouted for her Alice to come in for her tea. Mum looked at her watch.

'That time already?' she said, then yelled, 'Chris! Bubs! In! Now!'

'I'm just having my bloody go!' Chris shouted back, throwing his jumper on the floor in rage.

'Ee, I knew they'd be trouble when you got them that horse!' Liz said as her Alice turned a deaf ear to her. 'They'll not come in now if *Starsky and Hutch* is on t' box.'

Mum laughed, but Liz wasn't wrong; the kids would stay out all night if they could, taking it in turns to have rides on Goldie.

Mum scolded Chris when he came in.

'And don't let me hear you use language like that again, young man! Else they'll be no more rides on t' horse for you this week!'

Mum looked at me as Chris went inside. 'It's the second time this week,' she said. 'Something's going to have to be done about his mouth.'

I took Goldie back down to the allotment each evening and staked him to the ground with his straw and feed, next to the goats' pen. Every morning I brought him up to the house and left him in the back garden before I went to school. Goldie got so tame, he'd knock on the door for his first biscuit of the morning from Mum and wouldn't budge from the step until he'd had it. Then he'd wander around out of the garden and into the neighbour's and round the backs of the unfinished houses, waiting for us kids to get back from school.

While the hens had been laying enough eggs for the family, Mum had so many left over she had started giving them away to the neighbours and people she knew through the roofing business. Dad wasn't too happy about it. 'You should charge for them,' he said, 'we're not a charity.'

'Sid, it's just a few eggs,' Mum laughed.

But as it happened, people soon began offering Mum money if she would deliver them a dozen or so every week. They wanted a reliable source and Mum soon rose to the challenge.

'Demand's outstripping supply, Neil,' she said. 'We're going to have to do summat.'

So Mum bought some more hens and set up a little egg round from the boot of her Capri to make some extra cash. Soon, customers started asking her if she had any fruit and veg for sale and Mum went down to the wholesalers and picked up what they needed and, as word got round, so her fruit and veg business grew into a proper round.

I was coming up to fifteen by this time and started helping Mum out at weekends and sometimes after school to deliver the veg in the car.

'It'll take half a dozen trips to deliver this lot in t'car,' she said. 'We're going t' have t' come up with summat better than this.'

The only idea we could come up with and which didn't cost anything, was to use the van. The van had been looking a bit worse for wear lately with the bad weather, so me and Mum spent the weekend cleaning it up. I washed the outside while Mum scrubbed the interior, sectioning one part off for the site materials, and the other for the fruit and veg round.

Me and Mum set off at five in the morning to the wholesalers and picked up sacks of spuds, onions and anything else her customers wanted. Soon, Mum had made enough to buy some new furniture for the house, and replaced the last of the old curtains with modern ones covered in tango, beige and brown blocks of colour.

We dropped off a sack of spuds or a bag of veg for Grandad Woody every fortnight or so where he lived with Auntie Win across the road from Armley Jail. Grandad and Auntie always gave Mum peelings for the pigs parcelled up in old newspaper, and at Christmas Mum would give Auntie a large joint of pork. As Mum went out the back to pick up the parcel, I heard Auntie say, 'I see you got your little helper wi' you again, Em'ly.'

'Aye, he's a good "little helper" an' all,' Mum said.

'Ay, not so much of the little, if you don't mind you two,' I said. 'I'm taller than Grandad now!'

I pulled myself up to my full height, but Grandad was a tall man and even though I was in my teens and he was in his sixties, he still had the edge on me.

'You? Get out of here lad! You've a way to go yet!' Grandad wheezed as he laughed.

Auntie looked at me with a puzzled expression. 'By, what's happened to you then?' Then turning to Mum she said, 'Lad's come right out of his shell.'

'Shell?' I scoffed. 'What are you on about Auntie? They're for tortoises!'

'Ay, you keep that up an' you can go right back in yours an' all!' Mum retorted.

'I was only making a statement of fact, that's all!'

'Ay, watch your step, clever clogs,' Mum said. 'I better have a word with your Head, if cheek's on the school curriculum these days.'

'Fair dos,' Grandad said. 'Lad's only telling truth! Tortoises do have shells,' and he wheezed as he laughed.

'Right, I've had quite enough of you pair! We're going!' Mum said, pushing me out of the door, as Auntie stood there grinning, taking it all in good part.

As we set off in the van, I started to think about what Auntie had said. Maybe I had come out of my shell, and I realised that, without even noticing it, I was happy again.

*

There'd been another change since Derek had passed away and I'd returned from London – Mum and Dad had started going out for a drink. They'd always gone out to the local in Armley on the odd occasion, but now they went out at least two or three evenings a week. Sometimes they went to New Star Inn in Churwell or to the Gaiety in Leeds while I babysat. Mum also liked to go to bingo, and would leave Dad at the pub and set off in her new pink Corsair to play at the Mecca off Roundhay Road. If Dad was in the mood for it, he'd sometimes go with her too.

On a weekend, we'd all go out. Mum and Dad took us over to Wortley Working Men's Club near Armley. I had a few games of pool with Dad while Mum chatted to her friends and with Chris and Bubs, as they tucked into their bags of crisps and Vimto. Other couples used to take their children as well and my sister and brother would play with them. Mum loved to put songs on the jukebox and sing along to them. She played 'Old Shep' by Elvis every Sunday at the club and I crooned alongside her sometimes, making a joke of how the man in the song had shot his faithful old dog that saved his life.

'It's corny Mum,' I complained, as she put it on again.

'I know, but he was putting his best pal out of misery,' she laughed through her tears.

I shook my head at her, 'You're a hopeless case, Mum.'

She chuckled and leaned her head against my shoulder.

'Mum!' I moved away; I felt really embarrassed when she did that.

*

As families gradually moved in to the newly completed houses in our street, so it became full of small business people; people like Mum and Dad, who came from humble origins but who were trying to do well for themselves and their families. There was no doubt about it that Back Green, at that time, had an aspirational air about it; people felt proud to be living there, even if, as we'd been, they were struggling at times.

Mum and Dad were stalwarts of the community by this time. People called on Dad for building advice and always knocked on the back door for Mum when they ran out of veg.

Dad had recently had a garage-cum-lean-to built on the side of the house with a concrete drive up to it, so that Mum could put the car away at night. But because Mum's fruit and veg round was doing well, she mostly used it to store her King Edwards, apples and other fruit and veg in. She also kept the weighing scales and cash till in it when she wasn't out on the round, so the garage began to look more like a greengrocer's than anything else.

By now, Mum was good friends with the neighbour Gwen and they took it in turns to pick up the children from school. Gwen would also look after the horse when we went on holiday every three or four months, and Mum would help out when Gwen got a bit short.

Mum put the kettle on in the garage when Gwen came round one Saturday.

'Thanks love,' Gwen said as she sank down in one of the old easy chairs Mum kept in the garage, and started rubbing her legs. 'I could do wi' a brew. I've been on me legs for hours.'

'Ay, we noticed you were burning the midnight oil, Mrs H,' I said, weighing up the carrots.

'Me and lad saw you on our way to wholesalers this morning,' Mum explained.

We'd got up early this morning to get to the market by five, and passed Gwen in her garage conversion turning out another order on her knitting machine.

'Aye, and no doubt you'll see me there tomorrow morning an' all – I've got the leccy bill to pay and the mortgage is due.'

Gwen looked tired and Mum could see it.

'Here, love,' Mum slipped some extra veg in her bag.

'Nay, Emily, I don't want credit.'

'And you're not getting it. Wholesalers gave us a bit extra this morning.'

She looked at me to confirm her story.

'That's right, Mrs H. If you don't take it, it'll only go to waste.'

'Well, if you're sure.' She put away her purse. 'Thanks, love.'

'Why don't you go to bingo with Mum tonight?' I suggested. 'You never know, you might get a win. Mum usually does.'

Gwen shook her head. 'Not wi' my luck at moment, love,' she sighed, then, rounding up her Colin half an hour later, she set off across the back garden to her house, Mum giving her a hand with her bag.

Dad put his head round the garage door.

'Your Mum weren't giving away any more produce, were she?' He'd just woken up from his afternoon nap, and was sounding grumpy.

'Course not, Dad,' I said, 'you worry too much.'

*

Mum changed into her shirt and jumper, put on her lipstick in the front room mirror, and blotted it on a tissue.

'Make sure they don't stay up late,' she called to me in the kitchen, as Chris and Bubs sat quietly in front of the television watching a kids' programme.

'OK, Mum,' I sighed. I'd heard it all before.

'And don't forget your homework, miladdo!' she said as she went out of the back door with Dad.

'I won't!'

I watched from the door as Mum slid behind the wheel of her Corsair and Dad got in beside her. Then, lighting a cigarette, Mum put the car into gear and they set off for a night out. Mum usually dropped Dad off for a pint or two at the pub while she went on to bingo. Dad would sometimes go with her too, especially if there were prizes or a big jackpot that week; he also liked to play the slot machines in the Mecca bingo hall. They usually brought a few bob back and gave it to me for babysitting and brought home some crisps on occasions as a treat for the little ones, who weren't quite so little now – Chris had just had his eighth birthday and Bubs was now six.

I went back in the house and opened my maths home-work book lying on the kitchen table, then heard the *Looney Tunes* cartoon theme playing on the television so I wandered into the front room instead.

'Budge up,' I said to Chris and Bubs, who shuffled along the settee so I could sit on the end. I couldn't wait to leave school.

8

It was 1975; I was seventeen and life was good. I'd left school some eighteen months earlier to join Dad in the family business, after helping him out in the school holidays and at weekends on the last new house going up at the end of our road.

Dad had always expected Derek to join him in the business and I sometimes wondered if he was disappointed that he'd got me instead.

This also struck me as odd as I knew Derek had no interest in roofing and even less in joining Dad in the business, had he lived. I never mentioned this to Dad, as I knew how disappointed he'd be.

On the other hand, roofing suited me. Working away from the noise and hubbub of the streets; being high up on the rooftop in the fresh air, watching people coming and going about their business below, I felt as if I was on the top of the world! And if it was the summer, with the sun beating on my back and shoulders, as long as I was coated in the sun cream Mum bought for our holidays I was in my element.

Dad was tall, at six foot three, although he'd developed a stoop after Derek died. With his height, he'd sometimes had to struggle to get up the scaffolding, but now it was even more difficult for him. Since that fateful day, Dad had lost interest in eating and his trousers had started hanging on him; he now had to tighten his belt to keep them up. In spite of this, Dad was still strong, and could carry a full load of tiles in the hod at any one time. Dad had learnt about roofing from his older brothers before he'd even left school; he knew just about everything there was to know about it which he then passed on to me and later to Chris.

Dad had become well-respected locally over the years because he was a reliable and good worker; and with Mum at the helm, the business had built up a good reputation. Because of this, 'S & E Jackson' was always in demand, and not just in Churwell as work had now started to come in from all over the country.

Me and Dad began spending a lot of time away from home, travelling the length and breadth of the country, from Cornwall to Newcastle and even Scotland, staying in B&Bs and guest houses then going home at weekends. Dad took on Keith, who was one of Mum's in-laws; he turned his hand to most jobs and could drive, so he drove the works van when we were away.

We knew we had to work as hard as possible during the good weather, particularly the spring and summer, as we could be out of work in the winter. There was also talk of a downturn in the building trade, but so far we'd seen no sign of it on the horizon, so we didn't worry.

Roofing paid pretty well too, and with my very first pay packet, which Mum handed to me at the tea table on Friday night, I rushed into town the next morning and bought a pair of South Sea Bubble loons and a cheesecloth shirt.

'You off to San Francisco then?' Dad asked me in the

working men's club that night. 'Or is it a night out in Batley?' Dad liked his jokes.

'Very droll,' I grimaced. 'This is the seventies, Dad, not the sixties.'

Dad had a dry sense of humour, which I think I took after him in, although not much else. But the more we worked together, the more we got used to each other's ways and rubbed along well together. All in all we made a good team. I knew Dad still missed Derek, but I also knew he accepted me and seemed pleased to be working with me. His approval meant a lot to me.

While Dad saw himself as the head of the family – although I'd always thought it was Mum – Mum was the backbone and the glue, holding us all together. She booked the work in, looked after the firm's books and did the wages, deciding after a year that I could have a pay rise.

'What are you going to do with it?' Mum asked.

'Stash it away so I can set up my own firm one day and put you and Dad out of business.'

'Hey! You're not too old for a clip round the ear'ole, miladdo!'

Mum also drove the works van, dropping us off and picking us up again at night from wherever we were working in the locality, as well as collecting the building materials from the suppliers and bringing them to the site. People used to remark on how strong Mum was. Even though she was very slim and feminine, she'd developed a knack of picking up the heavy rolls of building materials at the builders' merchants, and throwing them onto the van as well, if not better, than any labourer.

Mum was very much for women making their way in a

man's world, and for not letting men get the better of her. I came home one day to find Mum giving her younger sister, Auntie Tess, a lesson in self-defence in the kitchen,

'Just because you're a girl, don't mean you can't stand up to a man,' she told her. 'You're as good as any of them.' Then she showed her how to disable a man in just two moves that didn't involve her 'kicking him in the family jewels' as she put it. I never knew where Mum learnt this from, but it certainly worked when she tried it on me and I yelped in pain. 'Bloody hell, Mum!'

'Aye, pack that language in before I give you another one!' she laughed.

For all this, I still hated to see her arrive at the building site and lift heavy blocks of bitumen from the van.

'Mum, stop! I'll do that!' I shouted to her as I rushed down the scaffolding.

'Stop fretting lad, I can manage!' she said, as I took the materials from her. 'Nothing's going to happen to your old mum.'

If only that had been true.

At half past three each weekday, Mum picked up my sister and brother and the rest of the kids in the street from junior school in the van. The van was jammed full of the kids and as it turned the corner of Back Green at 3.45p.m., Mum honked the horn to let the other mums know they were back. When me and Dad were working on the last house in our road to be finished, I'd run alongside the van as Mum pulled up outside the different houses.

'One for number nine!' and 'Three for number eleven, prepare for landing!' Mum yelled as I pulled back the door on its runner and the kids tumbled out onto their respective grass verges, giggling and screaming with laughter.

On the weekends, Mum made sure Chris and Bubs went to Sunday school every Sunday morning just as she'd made me and Derek. As a special treat I sometimes brought them home on Goldie, running alongside him and holding the reins as he trotted down the middle of our road with his cowbell clattering away. Sure enough when the kids in the street heard Goldie coming, they all ran out.

'Hey, Neil! Give us a go!,

'Go on, pl . . . ease!' they begged.

'Get in line and wait your turn!' I told them, as I knew from past experience they wouldn't give up until they'd all had a go.

I ran up and down that road with the kids on the back of Goldie so many times since we had him, I'd lost count. It usually took until Sunday lunch time to get Chris and Bubs home.

This Sunday, when we got back, there was a gent's bike with a crossbar leant against the kerb on its pedal outside our house.

Chris burst through the house into the kitchen where Mum was baking, and ran straight into a stern-looking policeman. Mum wiped the flour off her hands down the front of her pinny and, for once, looked serious.

'There's a boy round here I've heard's been swearing,' the policeman said, folding his arms and looking down at Chris.

Chris looked sheepishly at him then blurted out, 'Well it's not bloody me, it's that bloody bugger at number twenty-three!'

The policeman's face started to twitch, as if he was about to break into a grin, but then he said in a sombre tone, 'Well, it's just as well it's not you young man, because if I find out who that boy is, I shall have to run him in t' police station.'

Chris went pale.

'I'll let you know if I see him,' Chris said timidly.

'Aye, you do that.'

I'd never known my little brother go so quiet. As the local bobby put on his hat and went out to the hall, he turned and gave me a sly wink, then, lowering his voice he said to Mum, 'I hope that does the trick, Em'ly. My regards to Sid.' PC Palmer was one of Dad's friends from the local police station, and Dad had done some work on his house. Mum handed him a bag of cakes she'd made, 'For the family,' which he slipped inside his coat, then touched the brim of his hat and left.

As soon as Mum closed the door, Chris raced past us upstairs to the safety of his bedroom, slamming the door shut behind him. Me and Mum couldn't contain ourselves any longer and exploded into fits of laughter!

Just a few short weeks later, I was to see PC Palmer again, but this time he didn't wink . . .

9

It was near Bonfire Night. As I brought a sack of onions in from the van, I found Mum in the shop having a cup of tea with Gwen. Although it was a bitterly cold evening, that didn't stop Chris and Bubs and a bunch of kids running in behind me on their way to raid the freezer for Mum's home-made ice-lollies.

'Careful! You nearly had Neil over!' Gwen scolded her Colin, when there was a strange tapping sound at the door.

'Get it will you, luv.'

'It'll only be a penny for the guy,' I said, as I opened the door – but instead I was confronted by a huge pair of teeth, glowing yellow in the dark. The kids leapt back, screaming.

'It's a ghost!'

Even Mum went pale. Then the creature tossed its head in the air and snorted; Goldie had got loose from his peg at the allotment, found his way home, and was now tapping his nose on the back door for a biscuit.

As we all fell about laughing, I caught sight of a news report on our new portable TV in the kitchen. The police were making an appeal for information about the brutal murder of a twenty-eight-year-old single mum in Chapeltown, the red-light district of Leeds, the night before.

The detective, who was Detective Chief Superintendent Dennis Hoban, the Head of Leeds CID, as the caption said, warned the public that a psychopath was on the loose who must be caught before he killed again. As he spoke, behind me, I could hear Goldie snuffling with pleasure as Chris fed him a custard cream at the door.

Quite often there were reports of murders in Leeds, but this was the first time I'd heard the police say publicly that a 'psychopath was on the loose'. It sent a chill through me and I couldn't take my eyes off the set, when Goldie decided to walk into the garage, stick his nose in a box of Golden Delicious and start munching on them.

'Pack it in, Goldie!' Mum yelled at him, smacking him on the rump, but he carried on munching as the kids and even Gwen shrieked with laughter.

'Neil, stop him!' Mum shouted. 'Before he eats all me profits away!'

Then even Mum began to see the funny side of it.

'Will you just look at this horse!' she laughed, then, glancing in my direction, suddenly stopped as she caught sight of the news report on television, and the photo of murder victim, Wilma McCann, filling the screen. Mum went white as a sheet.

'You alright, love?' Gwen asked Mum. 'You look like you've seen a real ghost.'

'Mum?' I asked, not used to seeing her like this.

The news report went on to say Mrs McCann had four young children under nine.

'You didn't know her, did you, love?' asked Gwen.

'What? No, course not,' Mum said.

'No, well, how could you wi' what she were doing?' Gwen said sniffily. 'She weren't in a red-light district by accident.'

'. . . It's just those poor little mites,' Mum replied, quietly. 'Left all on their own like that. I wonder what will happen to them.'

It was so typical of Mum to worry about other people. No one could have guessed that this was the work of the man who was to become known as the Yorkshire Ripper, or that on the day Wilma was buried, my mum was to be his next victim.

A week or so later I was cleaning the van when Mum came out and attached the pink fluffy dice she'd had in the Corsair to the rear-view mirror. Mum had recently sold her car as she said it was 'a waste, just sitting on the drive all the time'. These days she had started using the van for everything, even when she went to bingo or took the kids to school.

I went in the kitchen to change the water in the bucket. Mum was back at the table doing the books and she and Dad were having a bit of a set-to. It didn't happen often but like all couples they bickered, then it was soon over and forgotten.

Dad was looking at the invoices that Mum was going through on the table.

'I told you, just leave 'em love, else you'll get them out of order.' Mum was irritated by him interfering with her paperwork and was having difficulty concentrating. 'Go and watch your programme – I'll bring you a cup of tea when I'm done.'

'But these are all red!' Dad said, picking up some of the bills from the table.

'Sid, you wanted to go on holiday,' Mum was getting snippy with him. 'It was your idea, just remember that.'

'Well I didn't hear you complaining!' Dad snapped back.

Mum rolled her eyes. 'I haven't got time for this. Now, are you going to let me get on with the books, or not?' Dad went quiet and after a moment Mum went back to the books, but Dad was still hovering. Mum looked up from her reading glasses and had another go at him. 'Anyway, I don't know what all the fuss is about, we always pay the bills on the red, all businesses do; you get a bit more interest on your savings that way. Surely you know that by now?'

Dad thought about it a moment, but let it go. Then he noticed the time on the kitchen clock. 'Never?' He quickly turned the radio on and got out his football coupons, waiting for the results to come on. No one could speak when *Sports Report* started: 'It's Saturday, it's five o'clock . . . and here are the classified football results.' Dad always turned the volume up high while he carefully followed every result as they were read out; he was starting early today.

'Sid, for goodness sake! I can't concentrate!' Mum yelled at him.

Dad snapped off the radio and stormed off into the front room, turning on the television to catch the results on there instead.

'One more bucket should do it,' I told Mum, as I wrung out the sponge under the tap.

'Ta, love!' she said. 'I've been meaning to clean it for ages.'

Then, looking back at the accounts, she asked, 'Babysit for us tonight, love?'

'Mum, can't you play bingo another night? I've got a pool match up the club tonight.'

I'd arranged to play Ian; we had an unofficial mini

tournament going on between us for a while now and tonight was to be the decider.

Mum sighed. 'Well if you can't, you can't,' she said, when Dad came back into the kitchen looking for a pen, and caught the tail end of our conversation.

'It's a big jackpot tonight, isn't that right, love?' Dad turned to Mum, in a better frame of mind now.

Mum nodded.

'And she'll give you some of her winnings.'

'If I get any tonight,' Mum said, looking over the top of her reading glasses at him.

'You usually do,' he replied, as he scribbled on some paper to see if the pen Mum had shoved at him had any ink in it.

I could see Mum look worried.

'Oh, go on then,' I caved in. 'I can play Ian tomorrow night – I presume you won't want to go out then an' all.'

'He's not a bad lad!' Dad said, clapping me on the back.

'Steady, Dad,' I choked, 'you nearly done me an injury!'

'Thanks, love,' Mum said. "I shall feel like a night out after I finish these flaming accounts!' she joked, though I could tell she was forcing a smile.

'You OK, Mum?' I asked her.

'Book-keeping!' she laughed. 'It's enough to give anyone a headache.'

'Mind they're in bed by seven thirty,' Mum gave me my instructions, as she blotted her lips. 'And don't play your brother up!' she turned to Chris and Bubs who were watching TV.

'That'll be a first!' I scoffed.

Now that everyone had colour televisions, we no longer had all the kids round to watch ours. Chris had recently moved into my bedroom so that our little sister could have a room of her own. I thought seven-thirty was a bit soon and gave him an extension till eight, or nine at weekends, with strict instructions not to tell Mum as I knew what she'd say.

As soon as Chris moved in, he'd covered the walls with posters of his sporting heroes, just as me and Derek had done. Chris was now ten and tall for his age, and with dark hair and features, looked a lot like Derek. There were times when I'd catch a glimpse of him asleep and, just for a moment, think it was Derek.

In the three or four years since we'd had Goldie, he'd become a part of our family. Dad wanted to change his name when we first got him. 'Goldie sounds like a girl,' he complained. 'Like that American actress, Goldie Hawn.' But whatever name we tried – macho ones like Butch and Rex and horse-type names such as Igor and Prince – he only came when you called him Goldie, so we gave up and stuck with that.

The school Christmas holidays had only just started when the kids got up early before anyone else, and disappeared down the allotments to feed the animals. Soon they came running back in the house, out of breath and red in the face,

'Mum! Mum! Goldie's slipped his peg again!'

I exchanged a look with Mum, who'd been worried sick about telling them since the night before.

'He was old, love, and what with winter coming he needed stabling.'

'And there's none round here,' I told them.

'They've got stables up t' road at t' Pony Club,' Chris said.

'They won't take an old horse like Goldie,' Mum told him. 'And it's not fair to keep him out in the cold.'

'Well, where's he gone then?' Chris wanted to know.

'To live in a retirement home for old nags,' I said, but Chris was a bright boy and wasn't convinced.

'So what's it called then, this "retirement home"?'

'Animal sanctuary.'

'Animal sanctuary?' Chris still wasn't so sure.

'Well at least it's better than "knackers' yard"!' I said.

'And he'll be happy with all the other old horses,' Mum told him. 'It's like when Granny Jackson were in the care home; they'll be good company for him.'

I felt sick seeing Goldie go off in the horse-box that day, and Mum was in tears; neither of us daring to think about what his fate might be now. Mum said, 'I feel like I've let him down; like he only had a temporary stay of execution.'

'At least he'd spent out his last days happy with us,' I tried to console her, although the sound of his cowbell clattering as he disappeared up the road in the horse-box is something I will never forget.

Mum promised to buy the kids a watch each with the little bit of cash the horse trader had paid for Goldie. The next day she got them off the market and took them home.

'Cor, ta!' Chris said, looking at his watch, then ran off out to show his mates.

Mum was too tired to cook tea that evening; she was busy getting her fruit and veg orders ready and seemed preoccupied, so I took Chris and Bubs up the chippie, where they sat on the wall outside and ate their chips. Bubs stopped to show anyone who went by and would stop and look, her new timepiece.

By the time I got her home, her mouth was smeared in tomato ketchup.

'Well fancy letting her get in that mess!' Mum had a right go at me. 'Come here, love!' she said, getting out her hanky and wiping at Bub's mouth as she struggled against her and shrieked.

If Mum had money worries, I had no idea about it. It seemed no different to any other time, and besides, everyone complained about the bills coming in, even Gwen next door with her knitting business. Yet if only I'd looked more closely, I might have seen the signs. But the phone never stopped ringing and that autumn we'd taken on Keith on a permanent basis.

10

Every Boxing Day evening, apart from the year when Mum had our Bubs, we'd have a get-together at Auntie Win's. Most of Mum's sisters and their families came to the 'do'; it was the one time of the year we'd all get to see each other. We had no idea then that Christmas 1975 was to be our last together.

Mum drove me, Dad and the little ones over to Wortley Working Men's Club after Boxing Day lunch. Me and Dad had our usual few games of pool, while Mum entertained the kids and chatted away with the regulars, her usual friendly self.

As I went to get a round in at the bar Dad called over, 'And if your Mum asks you for any change for the juke box, for goodness sake don't tell her you've got any. Else I'll put Old Shep down meself!'

'Ay, I heard that, Sidney Jackson!' Mum said, scowling at him as the regulars laughed.

'Now fair dos,' the landlord said, 'if your good lady wife wants to hear Elvis at Christmas, then I reckon she ought to be able to.'

'Thank you, Harry,' Mum said.

'It's not just Christmas I'm worried about,' said Dad. 'When she's not got it on here, she's playing it at home for best part of th' year. And then she *sings* to it!' And he did an impression of a cat being strangled.

'Ay, I don't sound that bad!' she said, as Dad had the club in stitches.

Bubs began tugging at Mum's sleeve.

'Can we go now, Mummy?' she asked. It was her birthday and as always she was chomping at the bit to get to Auntie's to pick up the rest of her presents.

'Give us a minute, love,' Mum said, as she tried to drain her half a shandy in one go, but couldn't manage it.

Mum had never been much of a drinker at the best of times; maybe she never got into the habit because she always had to do the driving. She might have a snowball or Babycham on a special occasion, but half a shandy was usually her limit. Dad, on the other hand, liked a pint, and particularly enjoyed his post-Boxing Day tipple at the club, which set him up for the rest of the evening.

As soon as Dad put his glass on the bar, we all climbed into the van and set off to join Auntie Win and the family in Armley for the traditional Boxing Day get-together.

I must have been to Auntie Win's a thousand times since I was born. Her tiny back-to-back was directly across the road from Armley Jail. The jail, which is still there today, is a black and foreboding Victorian castle, standing on a hill. Every day, when the sun begins to set low to the west, the prison casts a dark, gloomy shadow across the street and Auntie's house. As a boy, when I came with Mum on her veg round to drop a sack of spuds off to Auntie, the jail would always make me shudder. These days I barely noticed it – although a few short years later, the chill it once gave me would return with a vengeance.

Grandad Woody met us at the door in his cap, on which

he'd stuck a sprig of mistletoe. He was a little unsteady on his feet and, these days, walked with a stick.

'Come on, love,' he said to Mum, pointing to the mistletoe before planting a kiss on her cheek, as we all filed in behind her.

'Here you go, Grandad.' I handed him a brown-paper parcel as I passed him on the doorstep. Inside was a joint of pork Mum had saved for him from one of the pigs that had been slaughtered before Christmas.

Auntie Win greeted us all with a hug, then took the parcel from Grandad to put in the meat safe.

Grandad grabbed hold of my elephant-ear collar and laughed. 'What on earth are thee wearing lad! Some kind of fancy bow?'

'Hey, watch the shirt, Grandad! I've only just bought it.'

'Ee, you look like a reet lassie an' all,' Grandad's eyes twinkled as he grinned.

The rest of the family, including Auntie Win, Tess, Uncle Paul and our cousins Jackie, Val, Muriel, and the others were sitting around the old gas mantle in the parlour wearing party hats and singing along to 'White Christmas' on Auntie's old radiogram as we went in. Keith, who was working for us, was also there as he was going out with my cousin.

Win came back and took our coats while everyone hugged us. Of course, me, Chris and Bubs had to endure the usual comments on how we'd grown, then everyone squeezed up to make room for us all. I sat on the floor by Auntie's armchair. Even though I was seventeen and had grown in confidence, I was still shy – but felt safe and comfortable with Mum's family and could be myself.

When Slade came on the radiogram, I burst into 'It's Christmas!' along with Noddy Holder at the top of my voice. Auntie Win laughed.

'Lad's got a fine set of lungs on him!' Then the radiogram crackled and died.

'It's knackered, that, Auntie. You want to get a modern one,' I told her.

'Here, Cheeky! It'll do me! It just needs mending!' she laughed, then, looking in Mum's direction said, 'We're not all comfortable off like some I could mention.'

'Comfortable?' Mum laughed. 'That 'ud be nice!'

'Aye, well, I wouldn't mind your posh house, all t' same,' Auntie said.

'Ay, me an' all!' Tess piped up.

'Yeah, well, suppose we are slumming it a bit round here,' I grinned, although, in truth, the house was always neat as a pin.

'Ay, you're still not too old for a clip round t' ear, miladdo!' Auntie made a playful swipe at me.

'You'll have to catch me first!' I grinned, dodging her hand.

All the family were laughing now; then someone suggested a game of charades. Dad loved games and was soon on his feet. Donning Mum's headscarf and hooking Win's wicker basket over his arm, he began walking up and down the room, snaking his hips.

'Who am I then?' he asked.

'I see now where you get it from, son!' Grandad said. 'Your fether's a lassie!' And he laughed so hard at Dad he began to wheeze.

After some wild guesses including a 'lady of the night' and Danny La Rue, Dad gave up.

'You're all hopeless!' he rolled his eyes.

'Give us a clue then!' Mum said.

'I just have! What do you think this get-up is?' Then Dad relented, 'Oh, go on, but if you don't get it this time, someone else can have a go!'

Dad composed himself then started singing, 'Cockles and Muscles Alive- Alive-o . . .' Soon the whole family were joining in. Dad closed his eyes as he sang and swayed along with his basket; with all our voices in harmony, I suddenly felt the back of my hair stand on end.

As the last strains died away, I looked over at Mum, who was smiling as she straightened Bubs' skirt. Perhaps if I'd looked a bit harder, I might have noticed Mum was worried about something – but then I'd just have thought she was concerned about our Bubs who wouldn't sit still until she'd got her birthday presents which, so far, the family had kept quiet about.

Auntie started banging a teaspoon on the side of the glass to get everyone's attention.

'If you can all quieten down, I've got summat to say – '

'Happy Christmas!' someone shouted.

'Well yes, but before I get to that –' Auntie said, but soon everyone was raising their glasses,

'Happy Christmas!' they all chimed in.

Auntie gave in and raised her glass, 'Happy Christmas!', had a sip of her sherry, then said, 'Right, now that's out of the way, perhaps I can get on with my announcement – our Jackie is getting wed.'

'Wed? Who's th' poor fella?' I piped up.

'Neil!' Mum gave me a look.

'Fair do's, I think lad's got a point!' Keith grinned.

'Hey you!' Jackie glared playfully at him.

'As you all know, Keith is the "lucky groom",' said Auntie. 'Let's raise a toast to Jackie and Keith.'

'Jackie and Keith!' everyone raised their glass again.

'I shall be plastered at this rate,' Mum joked, then put her glass down without taking a sip.

'Now then,' Auntie said, 'we're coming to our Bubby's birthday present.'

Bubs sat up at this.

'We're hoping Bubs will be one of the bridesmaids.'

'If that's alright with you, Auntie?' Jackie asked.

Bubs squealed with delight. 'Can I Mum? Can I?'

For a moment, I thought Mum looked worried.

'Well, I don't know. Do you think you can sit still long enough in church?'

Bubs' face dropped; Mum saw this and said, 'Aye, love, 'course you can! I were only joking!'

Bubs was on her feet, bouncing around the front room,

'I'm going to be a bridesmaid!' she cheered.

'Well that's just as well,' Jackie said, 'as we've got you a little summat for your birthday to wear on the day.'

Bubs unwrapped a little gold necklace with a St Christopher on it.

'That's to guide you through life,' Auntie said, as she put the necklace on Bubs and fastened the clasp at the back.

'The bridesmaid dresses are going to be lilac taffeta,' Jackie said. 'Mum's going to make them.'

My mum was a good dressmaker and quite often ran up her own clothes when she had time. But if Mum was good, Auntie Win was a professional, and made all the clothes for her family, including the men. She made them for the neighbours too when they asked her and gave her a few bob.

I lifted Bubs up to admire her necklace in the mirror.

'I like it,' she smiled.

Auntie set a date for Mum to bring Bubs for the fitting: Wednesday, 21 January. At the time, this date meant nothing to me, but it would soon be forever etched on my mind as the day when my life, and my family's, changed for ever.

'Looks like you'll be having morning off school young lady!' Mum smiled at Bubs as she carried on cheering.

A little later, we got our coats on, thanked Auntie and said our goodbyes. Grandad gave Mum a big hug on her way out.

'You take care of my little girl now, Sid,' he said to Dad, 'she's a good lass.'

'Dad, will you stop fretting?' Mum grinned, a little embarrassed, as she pulled away from him.

It was funny seeing Grandad treat Mum like a child, but Auntie Win said he'd always doted on her. 'Even before she'd cut her first teeth,' she said, 'as she were always cooing and smiling at him.'

'You can rely on me, Woody,' Dad said, before turning to the little ones and clapping his hands. 'OK, let's be having you then!'

As Dad ushered the little ones out to the van, he called out 'Happy New Year!' to the family.

'Happy New Year!' they chorused back.

As I followed Dad and the little ones out, I realised Mum wasn't behind us and waited. Mum was hanging back by the doorstep, trying to have a word with Auntie Win out of earshot of the family in the front room.

'Auntie,' I heard her ask, 'will it cost much, our lass's dress?

'No, luv, if you're worried about it, we can get t' material from t' market. Or I could cut up one of our Jackie's posh evening gowns. She's got one in mauve, and there's plenty enough material.'

'No, no, Auntie, we'll get her new, I was just wondering, that's all.'

Mum was still hovering, and I could tell from her voice she were embarrassed.

'. . . Actually, Auntie, I hate to ask but you couldn't see your way clear to lending us a few bob? Just to tide us over; I'll pay you back at the end of the week.'

I could tell Win was puzzled. '. . . Everything alright, Em'ly love?'

'Oh aye, it's just wi' it being Christmas with kiddies an' all. You know what it's like.'

Auntie disappeared into the house, returning a moment later with her purse.

'Here love,' she said, 'take it.'

In the dark I could just make out her handing Mum a five-pound note.

'Thanks, Auntie,' Mum said sheepishly. 'Happy New Year.'

'Aye love,' Auntie said. 'Happy New Year, love.'

But it wasn't to be.

11

January 1976. The New Year storms had been good for business. Me, Dad and Keith had been working on a job in Ripon when Mum got a phone call from Mr Rawlinson; some slates had fallen off his roof and water was leaking into the shop.

On the way back from Ripon, the tyre blew on the front passenger side. Dad didn't have enough cash to buy a new one, so he and Keith went down to the scrap yard to find a replacement. Dad was always talking about getting a new van but so far it hadn't materialised. The only thing new about it was Mum's fluffy dice.

Mum was waiting for us to come back with the van so that she could pick up the materials we needed for Mr Rawlinson's. She wanted to have them ready so that we could fit him in with the new job we were starting the following week – but by the time we got back, the supplier was shut.

Mum and Dad went out at the weekend as usual while I babysat and watched the match highlights on television with Ian. Leeds drew one-one away at Wolves, but we weren't too despondent as even Mike Bailey, the Wolves skipper, said we looked a class act and tipped us for the title. Me and Ian celebrated with some cans of cider from the off-licence.

On Monday 19 January we began working on a newly built, detached house in the country. The house stood right in the middle of the field and was finished, except that it had no roof on it. It was a big job, so Dad was relieved we still had Keith to help us. Mum dropped us off at the gate by the roadside.

'See you later!' she waved from the van as we made our way across the field with the ladders and materials. The ground was still damp from the rain we'd had last week, and the long grass was making the bottom of my jeans wet. Behind me I could hear the van refusing to spark up. It took a couple of goes before the engine spluttered into life.

'You better get that seen to,' Dad called to her. 'Reckon it's due for a service!'

Mum smiled and set off to pick up the blocks of bitumen for the newsagent's that she hadn't been able to get on Saturday. Earlier that morning I'd asked Mum if I could come with her to give her a hand.

'You're such an old fusspot!' she laughed. 'I'll be fine!' But even though she was so sure of her own strength, and wouldn't let any man get the better of her, I couldn't help worrying about her and always had, ever since our Derek had gone.

I scrambled up the ladders between the scaffolding with the hod, while Dad, stooping a little, took his time. I started at one end of the roof while he started at the other. In a couple of weeks, weather permitting, we would meet in the middle. Keith was busy on the ground below sorting the materials in preparation for tarmac-ing the drive.

Two or three hours later, when the sun managed to peek through, I sat on a ledge and took a break. Dad came over.

'Shift up!' he said.

I shuffled along and he sat beside me. Then Keith came up the scaffolding and joined us, and we shared a flask of tea and the sardine and tomato fish paste sandwiches Mum had made us. Looking across the fields and the village in the distance, from our vantage point, high up on the roof, it looked like a miniature landscape beneath us. I scrambled to my feet.

'I'm king of the world!' I shouted at the top of my voice, as I swung from a side strut.

'Sit down, you bloody fool!' Dad said. 'Before you do your'sen some damage!'

He and Keith exchanged a glance, and I saw Keith smile.

'Bloody young fool,' Dad mumbled again.

Soon we were back at work, when an hour or so later the wind began to get up and, in the distance, storm clouds gathered.

'Dad!' I called across to him, but my voice was drowned out by a gust of wind. 'Dad!'

Dad rested his hod on scaffolding at the gable end and looked over at the dark skies now heading our way.

'You better call your mum,' he said.

The nearest public phone box was a mile down the road in the village. I was about to set off for it when Mum, realising a storm was brewing, came back for us in the van.

Me and Dad battled against the wind that was now whipping round the building as we dragged the heavy tarpaulin sheets over the gable ends to cover the gaping hole in the middle. Dad and Keith then carried the ladders back to the van, strapping them onto the roof-rack in case the weather had changed by the morning and was good enough for us to mend Mr Rawlinson's roof.

Mum put on her lipstick in front of the mirror. She and Dad were taking advantage of the early finish and heading off for the pub a bit sooner than normal. Mum blotted her lips; they formed a red bow on the tissue that she left on the mantelpiece. She'd changed out of her work clothes as soon as she got in, and put on a skirt and a couple of jumpers to 'keep out the cold'.

Mum was fixing her earrings when the phone rang,

'Get that will you, love?'

It was Mrs Stone, who owned the orchard me and Derek had stolen the apples from all those years ago. She must've been well into her eighties by now. In her shaky voice, I could just make out that the roof on her lean-to, where she stored the apples, had collapsed.

'Hang on, Mrs Stone. Mum?' I passed her the phone and workbook to write down the details.

'I'll come and look first thing, love,' she told her, 'and send th' lads round as soon as I can.'

'Thank you, love,' I heard Mrs Stone say before Mum hung up.

'You're going to have to work this weekend, Neil, and probably th' next one an' all,' Mum said, as she scrabbled around in her handbag. 'The water's ruining Mrs Stone's produce.'

'Oh great, thanks, Mum,' I said sarcastically, but in truth I didn't mind as I was saving up to the buy the new Supertramp album and a back copy of an old Shadows LP.

Mum glanced up from her bag.

'You should think yourself lucky to have a job, miladdo!' she said, producing another tissue from her bag with half a toffee stuck to it.

It was true, there was talk of a recession in the building trade but it hadn't hit us yet, if it was even coming at all. Mum pulled the toffee off the tissue, dropped it in her bag, and went back over to the mirror to check her teeth for lipstick. She seemed to be taking an age to get ready tonight, although it was probably only a matter of minutes, but I was in a hurry for her to go.

'Neil, can you see any lippy?' she flashed her teeth at me.

'No, Mum,' I said, without looking up, as I scoured the television pages of the *Post*.

'Kids?' she turned to Chris and Bubs for a second opinion as they sat in front of the TV absorbed by the Bugs Bunny show.

'Mum, don't bother them! You've already checked your teeth; I saw you.'

'Don't see how,' she said, 'unless you can see through that newspaper.' I slammed the paper down. This was hopeless; she was never going to go. Mum gave me an old-fashioned look, then, taking a small bottle of Coty L'Aimant from her bag, she patted a few drops of the perfume behind her ears and on each wrist.

'I hope I get a win tonight,' she said, as she rubbed her wrists together to spread the perfume around; it was like a ritual with Mum before she went to bingo.

'You won't get anything if you don't get a move on; they'll have started without you at this rate!' I replied. *Columbo* was on after the news and then *International Pro Golf*, and I didn't want to miss either of them.

Mum fumbled in her bag and, producing her lighter, flipped up the lid and struck it, producing a flame. Putting her cigarette to the flame, she drew on it, blowing out a stream of smoke which wafted over in my direction, making me cough.

'Oops, sorry, love,' she said, dropping the lighter back in her bag and flapping away at the smoke.

'Never mind sorry, just *go* will you!'

'You are in a hurry to get rid of me tonight.'

I was beginning to think she was going deliberately slow to annoy me. Dad came down the stairs dressed casually for his night in the pub.

'Ready, our lass?'

'Don't you start now!' Mum retorted.

Dad looked puzzled and went out and waited in the van; the ladders were on top ready for tomorrow's job first thing.

Mum slipped on her sling-backs, swept up her coat and, turning to the little ones, gave them her usual words of warning: 'Bed by seven thirty, you two, and don't play your brother up or else I won't bring you any crisps home!'

They nodded without taking their eyes off the cartoon.

'That's it, you're done now,' I said, slapping her bag on the top of the coat she was clutching.

'OK, OK! I know when I'm not wanted!'

I practically shoved Mum out of the door that night, not realising it would be the last time I would ever see her.

'OK, you two, SCRAM!' I yelled at the kids as, through the net curtains, I saw the van pull off the drive into the road.

'But that's not fair! Mum said we could watch what we want till we go to bed!' Chris complained.

'And you can,' I said, 'in there!' pointing to the portable in the kitchen.

'I want to watch the big telly!' Bubs whined.

'Never heard of square eyes?' I asked her. 'Now if I was you two I'd forget about telly and go upstairs, and read a book.'

Then I settled back on the settee in preparation for a good night's viewing.

I finally had to bribe them with sweets and pocket money to get them to bed that night. Ian came round later that evening to watch the golf tournament and brought some cans of cider. Just as we opened them, Bubs came downstairs.

'I can stay up late 'cos I don't have to go to school tomorrow,' she told me, as she stood at the bottom of the stairs.

She was excited about her bridesmaid dress fitting at Auntie's in the morning, and couldn't sleep.

'That's what you think, young lady,' I said, taking her back up. 'The sooner you go to sleep, the sooner it'll be time to get up and go round Auntie's!'

Bubs saw the sense in this and screwed her eyes up tightly to try to sleep, but I was up and down the stairs all night trying to settle her.

Just as Bubs dropped off, the phone rang and I rushed out to the hall to answer it.

'Can you ask Em'ly t' pick me up at half seven outside Bramley station?' It was Keith on the other end; his car had had a prang, and he needed a lift to work in the morning.

'OK, Keith.' I hung up and looked in on Bubs again. Fortunately she was still asleep, and so was Chris next door.

As soon as the golf finished, Ian went home and I got off to bed myself, trying not to wake Chris. I was beginning to doze off just before midnight, when I heard a car pull up at the side of the house on the drive. I thought it was Mum and Dad back from their night out, but realised it was a taxi when I heard its engine running. Dad was talking to the taxi driver as he paid him, then the back door shut.

I was puzzled at first, then remembered the van had been playing up, so thought it must've broken down and Mum and Dad had had to get a taxi home. I didn't realise it was just Dad on his own, and turned over and dozed off again. I slept well that night. It was one of the few proper nights' sleep I'd had since Derek died, and I didn't wake up in the grip of a terrible nightmare. That only began when I woke up the next morning.

12

The alarm went off at seven; Chris's bed was empty. He was already up and downstairs. I looked out of the window but the van wasn't on the drive below as usual; then I remembered the taxi.

I got washed and dressed and, running downstairs, found Chris sitting in the kitchen, but there was no sign of Mum. Dad came in from the front room.

'Dad,' I asked, 'is Mum getting the van picked up for a service, only Keith needs a lift?'

I hadn't finished speaking when I saw Dad had two police officers with him and another man I took to be a detective from the way they stood together. One of the policemen in uniform was Dad's friend, PC Palmer.

'I didn't swear, honest!' Chris said to the policeman, as he came through from the kitchen.

'It's alright, son,' PC Palmer replied, as the other officer ushered Chris back in the kitchen.

Dad's face was ashen, and PC Palmer didn't wink at me this time as he'd done before, but just looked grave as he nodded to me.

'Dad? What's wrong?'

'Take t' kids round t' neighbours,' Dad mumbled. 'Ask Gwen to take 'em to school.'

'But Mummy's taking me to Auntie's to try on my bridesmaid's dress!' Bubs protested as she came downstairs. 'I'm not going to school today!'

I knew something was seriously wrong and just said, 'Get your school things together; we'll go to Auntie's later.'

In the end Dad took them round to Gwen's himself while I sat in silence with the three policemen in the front room, waiting for him to come back.

'It's best if you sit down, Sid,' PC Palmer said, when Dad returned. Dad sat in his favourite armchair by the TV.

'We found a body, Mr Jackson,' the detective said, 'this morning, on some waste ground. We believe it's your wife. I'm afraid she's been murdered.'

Dad gazed at the detective, then looked away. I could see he was confused, while I suddenly began to feel as if I was on stage in a play that we used to do in drama at school.

'No, Mum's not dead!' I said, jumping to my feet as if I was saying my lines to an audience. 'The van's been playing up! Mum's took it in to be looked at this morning!'

How stupid were they? I thought to myself as they stared back at me. *They shouldn't be in the police if they couldn't do their job properly*, I thought.

PC Palmer cleared his throat, and mumbled, '. . . I'm sorry, son.'

Sorry? Now even Dad's friend had lost the plot.

The other uniformed policeman asked me to sit down and after a moment I did. Then the detective turned to Dad.

'We need you to identify t' body, Mr Jackson, but I'm afraid the injuries . . . well,' he struggled for words, 'it's best you know to prepare your'sen – they're horrific.'

Horrific? I shuddered.

'She was the victim of a frenzied attack – there's dozens of stab wounds to the back, stomach and chest and two severe blows to the back of the head. Her skull's been caved in –'

Suddenly I wanted to jump up again and say what the hell did they think they were doing, coming round here telling us this rubbish when we were about to go to work? I looked at Dad; surely he was going to tell them where to get off, but he didn't say a word.

The other policeman carried on; there was no easy way to say it but the pathologist had found over fifty stab wounds – at last count – on the body and most looked like they'd been done with some kind of a screwdriver or a similar instrument. He was saying Mum was peppered with holes like a colander that Granny Jackson washed the lettuces in. I felt sick.

'Sid, if it's any consolation, it would've been quick,' PC Palmer said, touching Dad's arm.

The police let themselves out, after arranging for another car to come and take Dad to the mortuary.

'. . . Murdered? They're daft!' I said to Dad the minute they'd gone. 'Why didn't you tell them they've made a mistake?' I was furious with him.

But he didn't reply.

'Dad? I'm talking to you!'

'I can't go,' Dad said. 'I can't do it.'

'What?' I asked him.

'I'm not going to the mortuary!' Dad tried to get to his feet but was shaking so badly he had to grip the side of the chair to stand up.

'Look, don't get up,' I told him. 'Sit there, stop worrying and I'll make you a drink. It'll all be a mistake, you'll see.'

I went to the kitchen and made Dad a glass of hot milk to steady his nerves like Mum had done for me when our Derek had died. Dad just stared at it. Then I realised Dad didn't like hot milk either, and made him his usual cup of tea without any milk.

In the end Dad couldn't face going to the mortuary on his own so the police asked me to go with him. We sat in silence in the back of the police car as we were driven into Leeds; those four short miles seemed to take a lifetime and something inside me made me hope we'd never arrive. We passed the allotments where Goldie had been tethered, and stopped in traffic by Mr Rawlinson's where Mum had dropped the materials off only yesterday, then went under the viaduct where me and Derek had put pennies on the line as kids. Finally, going down the hill into the centre of Leeds, we pulled up outside the city mortuary. I shuddered when I saw the sign.

The policeman took us into an ante-room at the morgue, where another police officer met us. He offered us a seat but Dad just stood staring at the floor, not speaking.

All I could think was they've got it wrong, it's not my mum they've got in there behind those dark, heavy swing doors. If they'd just hurry up and sort it out we could go home.

Every so often, as we waited, I caught a glimpse of the white-coated pathologist through the porthole window in the centre of the doors, as he chatted to a colleague or wrote something on his clipboard, casually going about his everyday work.

One of the policemen came back over and tried again.

'Mr Jackson . . . Sid,' he appealed to Dad. 'I know it's difficult for you, but we *do* need you to identify the body.'

Without taking his eyes from the floor, Dad nodded but he still didn't move.

The policeman waited in the hope of some further response but, realising it wasn't coming, turned to me and lowered his voice.

'Could you have a word with him, son, only we must get identification soon. There's some maniac killer on the loose.'

I turned back to Dad.

'Look Dad, it's obvious they've made a mistake. Just do it, eh? Then we can get off home and make a brew for Mum when she comes back from Auntie's or wherever she's been.'

Dad looked at me a moment with his dull, heavy eyes, then shook his head. 'They've got her handbag,' he mumbled.

My heart was racing and my mouth went dry. *It can't be Mum's bag*, I said to myself, *it just can't be*. And then it struck me: 'Dad,' I grabbed his arm, 'that doesn't prove anything! If it is Mum's bag, then someone must've stolen it!'

But Dad just slumped down on the long wooden bench and dropped his head in his hands. The two policemen, who had been in quiet conversation on the other side of the room, saw the state Dad was in and looked over at me. My stomach lurched as I realised what was coming when one of them approached me.

'Son, if your dad won't do it, I'm afraid we're going t' have t' ask you. As next of kin.'

I looked down at Dad for assistance but, just like when our Derek had died, I could see he'd retreated into his shell. I swallowed hard, then began to move forward towards the swing doors that looked, at that moment, like they guarded the entrance to hell.

'I should warn you, it's not going t' look like your mum,' the policeman said. 'You'll have to look for an identifying feature – her wedding ring or a birthmark.'

Then he pushed open the heavy swing doors, and at once the smell of death and disinfectant hit me in the back of my throat. I put my hanky to my mouth to stop myself gagging, pretending I had to wipe my nose. It was only the icy cold air of the mortuary that stopped me from being sick. I followed the policeman past the marble slabs, until he stopped at a particular area which had a curtain round it. The pathologist was at the sink opposite, carefully washing his hands and then drying them on a roller towel. He saw me, nodded and came over and introduced himself; his hand-shake sent a chill through my body. He said he wanted to prepare me for the horrific injuries the person under the sheet had received, stressing that, although they had done their best to clean up the body and reassemble the shattered skull, the throat, back, chest and abdomen had multiple holes in the shape of small crosses, possibly made by some kind of screwdriver. And there were other injuries too, including a boot mark where the victim had been stamped on. Then he thanked me for what I was about to do.

'Screwdriver, shattered skull, horrific injuries?' I knew this couldn't be Mum but some other poor person lying there. Then the pathologist pulled back the curtain and began to lift the sheet.

'Ready, Neil?'

I nodded, but my heart was now pumping so hard I thought it was about to explode in my chest, while all I could think of was Derek lying there in a pool of blood, asking for help and I couldn't give any.

The policeman stepped forward to support my arm as the pathologist began to lift the sheet, when suddenly Dad appeared at my side and mumbled, 'I'll do it.'

I stepped back, my head swimming, and concentrated on looking at Dad and only Dad as the sheet was lifted.

Dad's face went grey, then, after what seemed like several minutes but was probably no more than thirty seconds, the pathologist said, 'Don't worry, take your time, Mr Jackson.'

Then Dad slowly nodded. The policeman turned to him, 'Are you quite sure?'

Dad nodded again. Without yet realising it, my youth was over at this point.

I rushed out into the ante-room and threw myself on a bench. Dad came out soon after, with the policeman supporting his arm.

'Why did you do that for?' I turned on Dad. 'Why did you say it was her!' I was furious with him. We'd lost Derek; I wasn't about to lose Mum as well.

Later I realised I had gone into shock, but as the police took us back to Millgarth police station, there were yet more shocks awaiting.

13

As soon as we arrived at the main police station in Leeds, we were separated. I was taken into one room and Dad into another; we were kept apart for the rest of the day.

At first I couldn't understand why they wouldn't let me speak to Dad or why we were there at all, and as police officers and clerks bustled past the room or peered in and disappeared again, I felt too dazed and numb to care. It was like everything was in the distance, people and voices were far away, and I was watching this happen to someone else, not to me.

Eventually, three plain-clothed police came in and introduced themselves as detectives. I could tell by the way they spoke that they were top brass, but couldn't take in their names or much else they said at that point. One of them, a smartly dressed, middle-aged man in a well-cut suit and polished leather shoes, said he was sorry about Mum, but if they were going to catch her killer, he and his officers had to ask me some difficult questions. He appeared to be the most senior of the three and I later realised he was Detective Chief Superintendent Dennis Hoban, who I'd seen being interviewed on television after the murder of Wilma McCann. Mr Hoban flitted between interview rooms as the questioning began.

'What time did your dad come home last night? Was

your mum with him?' the one in a dark shiny suit with a moustache asked me. I could see him tapping his foot under the desk.

I told them Mum and Dad had come home no later than usual in a taxi. The van had been playing up lately and, obviously, it must have broken down last night.

The two detectives glanced at each other. Had I seen Mum or heard her getting out of the taxi last night? Had I seen her this morning? I shook my head, beginning to take in my immediate surroundings. Millgarth police station hadn't been open long; it was built near the site of the outdoor market that had burnt down, close to the bus station. The police station was large and the rooms and corridors were bright and clean and smelt of paint. I hadn't smelt that smell since we'd moved to Churwell, before our Bubs was born. What had Dad said about her not being there?

'Nothing,' I told them, 'because we both knew Mum had gone back to have the van towed to the garage this morning.'

Then the overweight detective with greasy hair, who was sweating a bit, told me they'd recovered the van this morning, from a pub car park in Leeds. It had stood there all night.

Before I'd had chance to take this in, he suddenly asked me, 'Do you know what your mum did for a living?'

'Know what she *did* for a living?' I suddenly realised they were talking about Mum in the past – when we couldn't even be sure if the body in the morgue was even hers. Not with all the injuries they'd been talking about.

'Son? What she did for a living?' The detective asked me again.

'Course I know! She runs th' business, looks after the family and does a fruit and veg round,' I said. 'She works all the time.'

The detectives looked at each other, then one of them turned to me.

'Did she do anything else you were aware of? Anything at all?' He seemed slightly embarrassed.

Isn't that enough? I wanted to say, and had no jot of an idea what they were getting at until much later that day, when it would shock me to the core.

'She had an allotment,' I told them, 'a small-holding,' remembering Mum's words when she got it. 'She looked after t' goats and pigs and collected the hens' eggs.'

Now *I* was talking about Mum in the past and felt like I was betraying her.

'What about social stuff? She liked a drink?'

I told them Mum wasn't bothered about drinking but she went to the pub with Dad two or three times a week while I babysat.

'Do you know where they went?'

'The New Inn nearby, or t' Gaiety by Roundhay Road in Leeds. On Sunday afternoons we all go to the working men's club in Wortley.' Then I suddenly realised if what they were saying was true, we wouldn't be going again, at least not as a family, or anywhere else with Mum there. I turned on the detectives. 'Look, why are you asking me all this?'

'I'm sorry, son, but like Mr Hoban said, we need t' catch th' nutter who done it before he strikes again.'

'You say she went to the Gaiety with your dad? Did she go out on her own often?' the detective asked, now tapping his foot wildly under the table.

'No. She never went out on her own. She were always with Dad. Except when she went off to play bingo for an hour or two.'

'Bingo?' The detectives exchanged another look.

I nodded.

'Tell us more about bingo.'

'There's nothing much to tell – Mum and Dad had a drink in the pub, then Mum went off in the van to play bingo up the road at the Mecca; she picked Dad up again after; or sometimes they'd both go together. Dad won a lucky rabbit's foot once. Ask him, he'll tell you.'

They went on to ask me other things, but I saw one of the detectives write down BINGO in capital letters.

The questioning went on into the afternoon. *Did Mum have friends? What kind? How many?*

She had lots of friends. She was friends with everyone in our street.

Men friends?

She had a joke with the men on the counter at the suppliers in Wakefield Stores who she saw most days, and passed the time of day when she passed old George, the former newsagent in the street, if that counted.

Had she been unhappy lately? Was anything worrying her?

No, she were always smiling, always! I thought about her last night as I'd hurried her out of the door. She'd even made a joke of that. I felt sick.

One of them fetched me a drink of water. 'You OK?' I nodded, they carried on.

'Had she gone out more lately? What about since Christmas?'

'No, just th' same.'

Had she been treating herself recently? Bought new clothes? Short skirts? Sexy clothes? Make-up?

I shook my head, bewildered. Sexy? Mum? Mum wore a bit of lipstick sometimes, but she never bothered with anything else, and she didn't wear the kind of clothes they were suggesting. She wore shift dresses in the summer and cable-knit cardies and jumpers, Auntie's old cast-offs, in the winter, when it was cold. She was wearing one last night. Mum hardly ever spent money on herself; and when I thought about it, I realised it nearly all went on us kids.

Then the overweight detective, who'd been quiet for a while, leaned across the table and asked, 'How did your mum and dad get on?'

'What?'

'Did they row?'

'No. They got on very well,' I told him.

'They didn't row then?'

'Well they bickered occasionally.'

'Bickered?'

I nodded. 'But not often,' I told him, 'like everyone does.'

He paused, then leaned forward again. 'Did your dad ever hit her?'

'What?' I couldn't believe I'd heard him right.

'You know – slap your mum? Threaten her? Push her around?'

'No! Never!'

'No? Why not? I think I would if my missus were doing what she were!'

'What? Doing what?' I was about to ask, when the other detective cut him off.

'Look, son, put it this way, do you think your dad did it?'

'Dad? No! Course not!' I nearly fell out of my chair. They thought Dad was a murderer? Now I knew they were mad.

'Can I speak to him now?'

'Not yet.'

'Soon —' was all they'd say.

My mouth felt dry; I took another sip of water. I just couldn't take it in. How could they think my Dad had done this terrible thing? He had friends in the local police force; one of them even worked at Millgarth and had popped his head round the door this morning to say how sorry he was to hear about Mum. They couldn't suspect Dad. Why would they? It would be many years later before I would find the answer to that.

I was left alone in the room for some time when the one with the twitchy foot came in with a cup of tea and some biscuits for me.

'Sorry, lad,' he said, 'but we have to ask.'

As he spoke, through the window behind him I saw a blue Commer van going past, registration, BNK 953K: it was Mum's! My heart leapt as, for a moment, I thought I'd see her at the wheel, then it plummeted just as quickly as I realised the van was being towed into the compound on the back of a police vehicle.

The detective left me alone again, and I watched in silence as, outside, three men in overalls and gloves unloaded the van. As they lowered it from the tow truck, it bumped on the ground and I noticed Mum still hadn't got the offside passenger wheel fixed. One of the men in overalls got in the van, while the other two pushed it into a parking bay. The man at the wheel seemed irritated by Mum's pink fluffy dice hanging from the rear view mirror and pushed it aside; it fell off and tumbled from the cab, onto the muddy ground. Mum wouldn't be too happy about that, I thought. She liked her things to look nice. Then he hopped out of the van, picked it up and dropped it into a clear cellophane bag.

Another panda car came into the yard; I watched as a policeman got out of the back and let a man out of the other side, and I saw it was Keith. What was he doing here? The two detectives came back and restarted the interview.

After more questions they took me to the fingerprint room. Keith was ahead of me, but we weren't allowed to speak until we'd had our prints taken. They told us both it was for elimination purposes; they needed to rule out the fingerprints they'd found on the van. Keith nodded to me in passing; he was white as a sheet.

'I knew summat were up when Em'ly didn't pick me up this morning,' he said. 'She were never late, your mum, never.' He was released later, when Dad told them he worked for us.

'Can I see Dad now?' I asked again.

One of them nodded and took me to a waiting area outside the interview rooms. Through a glass panel, I could see Dad inside one of them. He didn't normally say a lot unless he'd had a drink, then he was the life and soul, like at Christmas when he'd started singing, but now I could see him talking ten-to-the-dozen to the detectives who listened intently. He'd already been in there six hours; what could there be left to ask him that he hadn't already told them? Then he started crying. I'd only seen Dad cry once before: that night when Derek had died and he'd sat on the doorstep, sobbing his heart out after he'd boarded up the back door. This wasn't that same outpouring of grief and, as Dad wiped his eyes, I could see he was worried.

Eventually, Mr Hoban gathered his papers together and left the room, nodding to me as he hurried down the corridor. The other detective still in the interview room with Dad opened the door to let him out. As Dad shuffled over, the detective nodded to a uniformed officer, who moved in close enough to keep an eye on Dad and to hear what we were saying.

Dad shook his head. 'They think it's me,' he said, fixing his gaze on the floor.

'They'll soon realise they've made a mistake,' I told him.

I couldn't believe they suspected Dad. Yes, he was fiery at times, like if he thought someone was trying to take advantage of Mum, or if he couldn't find his football pools coupon when she'd had a clear-up but, as I told the police, he wasn't a violent man. He'd never so much as lifted a finger to us kids, never mind Mum. Even when I'd opened my present hidden in Mum and Dad's wardrobe before Christmas and tried out my new reel-to-reel tape recorder, Dad just told me off. It was Mum who threatened to clip me round the ear, although, apart from when me and Derek took the apples, she rarely did. 'No, I am quite certain,' I told the police, 'Dad wouldn't hurt anyone.' Or so I thought.

'They just need to eliminate you from their enquiries,' I told Dad, 'like they did with me and Keith.'

But Dad wasn't listening. 'What are t' neighbours going to think?'

'Th' neighbours? They know you, Dad; they're not going to believe a word of it,' I said. All the same, I couldn't understand why he was worrying about the neighbours when we'd just supposedly lost Mum. But I didn't know then what Dad was hiding, and that another, bigger, shock was awaiting me when I got home.

14

That afternoon, as soon as I got out of the police station, I rushed home to get back before Chris and Bubs came out of school. For the first time I could remember since Derek had died, the house had fallen into silence. I saw Mum's pinny still hanging by the cupboard door and started having conversations in my head: if only Mum would come home now, throw on her pinny, fasten it and start baking, I promised God I'd do anything he asked me after that.

To stop myself thinking, I put the TV on. As soon as the set warmed up, a man's face filled the screen – the man I now recognised as Detective Chief Superintendent Dennis Hoban, who I later discovered had been awarded the Queen's Medal for Bravery for defusing a bomb single-handedly in Woolworths.

My heart lurched as I saw an old black and white photo of Mum projected onto the wall behind him at the press conference he was giving. It was enlarged from the photo Dad had given them of her that morning. Although it was a recent picture, I couldn't remember where she'd had it taken and didn't like it; it made Mum look weak and sad and she was never that. She was strong and kind and pretty. Mum hated having her picture taken but we had many nice colour photos of Mum on holiday, and I wondered why Dad thought this was a good likeness of her, when even the passport photo she felt embarrassed about would've been better than this.

Mr Hoban was saying how Mum liked to go to pubs and bingo but he didn't say she went with Dad. I noticed he had changed since this morning and was wearing a different suit with a colourful, floral tie and white pocket handkerchief. Mr Hoban was making an appeal for Mum's friends, 'women or men to come forward'. Then he said, 'she lived her own life really'.

She lived her own life really? What did *that* mean? Mum lived with us, her family, like she'd always done. I glanced across at the mantelpiece and caught sight of the tissue that she'd left under the mirror only yesterday imprinted red with Mum's lips.

In the background I heard the detective say that apart from the wounds to the head and body, 'Mrs Jackson had other injuries' he didn't wish to talk about at this time.

At that moment, Chris and Bubs came rushing in the back door with Gwen.

'There's Mummy!' Chris yelled.

I lunged towards the TV and turned it off.

'It's not Mum, it's just someone who looks like her,' I found myself saying, exchanging a glance with Gwen.

'Where *is* Mummy?' Bubs whined.

It was the question I'd been dreading and although I'd been thinking about it since I left the police station that morning, I still had no idea how to answer it. I mean, how do you tell your little brother and sister that their mum's been battered to death by a 'sexual pervert, bordering on the maniacal' as Mr Hoban had put it. So I said the only thing I could think of. 'Summat's happened – now get up the table and I'll get your tea.'

Gwen looked at me. 'I'm sorry, lad,' then she lowered her voice so the little ones didn't hear, 'we'll all miss her.' I knew Gwen meant the neighbours in Back Green. As she turned away I caught sight of the tears beginning to stream down her face and it reminded me of Granny Jackson when she scrubbed the floor after Derek's accident. Then I suddenly realised I hadn't cried, not once, even when our Derek had died, and I couldn't cry now, and wouldn't be able to for many years hence.

Tea was difficult; Bubs was full of questions and Chris bolted his food down so that he could leave the table as soon as possible to watch *Magpie* on ITV. I knew there was bound to be another news bulletin on soon and sent him to his room to fetch down his Subbuteo. We played it on the front room floor for what seemed like ages; I daren't move from the room in case he put on the TV as soon as I'd gone.

Some time later, the phone went. Dad was ringing from the police station where he was still being questioned. He told me to pack the little ones' things; his sister and her husband had agreed to take them in for the time being.

'When are you coming home?' I asked him.

'I don't know,' he said, then hung up.

As soon as I got back in the room, Chris had got the TV on. Luckily the news had now finished and *Crossroads* was on, so I went upstairs and packed the kids' things.

*

Uncle arrived a little after eight in a taxi; I loaded the two small suitcases into the boot while Uncle put Chris and Bubs' box of toys on the back seat.

'Where are we going?'they chorused as they waited on the pavement.

'On holiday,' was all I could think to say.

'Holiday?'

'Correct,' I said, swallowing hard, 'round Uncle and Auntie's, in Farnley, for a few days.'

'Is that near the sea?' Bubs asked.

'No, but if you behave, they might take you at the weekend,' I said.

Bubs clapped her hands excitedly. 'Tell Mummy I'll send her a postcard!'

I exchanged a look with Uncle, then nodded to Bubs.

'I'll tell her.'

Bubs and Chris clambered into the back of the taxi, and waved all the way down the street from the back window. As I stood on the pavement, waving back till they turned the corner and disappeared from sight, I had no idea then that we'd never be a family again.

I was about to go back into the house, when I heard a voice behind me.

'Neil Jackson?' I turned round – and was blinded by a flashbulb going off.

The press had arrived and would be part of my life for many months and even years to come.

'This is a respectable neighbourhood, Mr Jackson,' the journalist said. 'How long had your mother been working as a prostitute?'

I pushed my way past the journalists and photographers

who were beginning to gather outside the house and quickly closed the door in their faces.

A prostitute? No, I'd heard that wrong. The whole world seemed to have gone mad.

Suddenly they were thumping on the front door and calling through the letterbox, 'Mr Jackson, Neil, just a few words!'

'Do the neighbours know?'

Flashbulbs started going off through the large front room windows, as outside the press began gathering in numbers. The floor-to-ceiling windows that Mum had loved so much because of all the light they let in, were now being used to spy on us. I stood behind one of the curtains and pulled it across to the middle, then used the fullness of the material to cover myself as I pulled the other curtain across. I went round all the windows in the house, finding ways to close the curtains without being seen; then I took the phone off the hook. The press had got our number from the business, and the phone had never stopped ringing since I'd got back in the house.

I curled up in the darkness on the bedroom floor, listening to the chaos going on all around me. To try to make sense of it all, I began turning over in my head what the press had called out to me. I thought they said 'prostitute' but it obviously couldn't be that. So I started thinking of all the words that sounded like prostitute, even making some up: crosstitute, postitute, lostitude, attitude, destitute, constitute, substitute . . .' Substitute; maybe that was it. Maybe there *had* been a mix-up after all; maybe they'd somehow substituted Mum's name for the dead body in the morgue. But why would they ask me if I knew she 'worked as a substitute'? And what did that have to do with 'a respectable neighbourhood'?

I looked at the clock and found it was almost midnight. I realised I had been lying there for hours and not even noticed that it had gone quiet outside. When I peered out from behind the curtain, the press had gone. Then a police car drew up and I saw Dad getting out of the front. I breathed a sigh of relief, as I knew they wouldn't let him come home if they still thought it was him. I rushed down the stairs and let him in; Dad didn't look at me but just kept staring at the floor.

'The kids got off OK?' he mumbled. I said they had. He nodded, relieved, then he looked up at me a moment, his eyes red and swollen from crying:

'What are the neighbours going to think of me?' he said again, looking weak and pathetic.

'I told you, Dad, they won't think anything bad about you,' I said.

He seemed reassured by this and began shuffling off towards the stairs to bed. But there were questions I still needed answers to myself; I couldn't let him just go to bed now.

'Dad?' I called after him. But he didn't seem to hear me.

'Dad!' I shouted. Dad stopped and turned to face me, shocked that I'd raised my voice at him – as I was myself. I'd never shouted at Dad before and even with all that had happened, I felt embarrassed.

I wanted to ask him, *if* he had come home on his own last night like the police were saying, *why* hadn't he waited for Mum? Or gone looking for her? And what was she doing in an area like Chapeltown on her own? And was he even sure it was Mum he'd identified in the morgue? And when would Mum be coming home? But at that moment, Dad began fumbling in his coat pocket as if he'd remembered something important. Then, from between a pile of loose change, he pulled out a hanky with an 'S' embroidered on it in one corner, that Mum had got him for Christmas. Carefully unfolding the hanky, he produced a plain gold band, which he put on the mantelpiece by the tissue with Mum's lipstick imprint on. I recognised it immediately as Mum's wedding ring and realised, at that moment, that Mum had gone.

Dad looked at me as he waited for me to speak. I shook my head; there was nothing more to say.

Dad slowly made his way up the stairs to bed.

15

I lay awake that night, trying not to sleep so that the morning wouldn't come and I wouldn't have to face up to what had happened: that someone had done these terrible things to Mum and she wasn't coming home anymore.

I looked around the room in the dark, making out Chris's posters of the Leeds team with Jimmy Armfield at the helm. The team was different now to when me and Derek had put our posters up: Revie had gone to England, Clough had been there only slightly more than a month; just Bremner and Sniffer remained of the original team. I wondered what Derek would make of all this, but Derek had somehow been left in the past and I knew that, soon enough, this was going to happen with Mum.

Mum had done everything she could to help me get over losing Derek and, in doing so, she'd become my best mate in his place. But Chris and Bubs, who were only ten and eight, had lost the chance to have her care and support as they grew up, and would miss out on all the years of fun that I'd had with her. I felt an overwhelming sense of injustice for them but not, as yet, hatred for the person who had done this terrible thing – I think I was just too numb.

Early next morning I heard Dad getting up and I got up myself and opened the curtains. Even though I knew the van wouldn't be there I was still shocked to see the bare space on the drive where it normally stood. But, although it was barely dawn, the press were already parked outside on the doorstep and I quickly closed the curtains again.

A little later, a police car arrived with two uniformed officers in it, followed by a brand new shiny, navy blue Daimler with a blue flashing light on the top. Chief Superintendent Dennis Hoban, in a smart suit, trilby and trench coat, got out. Me and Dad watched from a gap in the curtain as the press swarmed around him and he took his hat off to talk to them. He seemed very at ease with the press, and I remembered thinking he looked just liked a detective off an American TV show.

'You'll get your story later today, at the press conference,' he told the pack as he made his way through to the front door. 'Now I'm sure these good folks would appreciate it if you left them alone.' The press started to back off, at least for a while, but we kept the curtains closed for several weeks after to stop them prying at all hours.

Mr Hoban said he felt parched and asked if I would make him and his officers a cup of tea. I could hear them talking in low voices in the front room as I put on the kettle. I could just make out Mr Hoban giving Dad a warning about something that he would be saying at the press conference that afternoon, when the kettle whistled, drowning them out. As I lifted the kettle from the ring and poured the water in the pot, I heard Mr Hoban say he was certain they had a 'serial killer' on their hands. Through the crack in the door I could see Dad sitting there with his head bowed, like a child sitting in the headmaster's study, in trouble at school.

As I took the tea in to them, with fruit cake that Mum

had made two days before, Mr Hoban stopped mid-sentence, and asked for the workbooks that Mum wrote down the customers' names and addresses in.

'It could be someone who knows her, some pervert you've done work for in t' past,' he told Dad, as he stirred several sugars in his tea. I went out to the hall and fetched the workbooks from the drawer in the phone table. The entries went back to 1965, and were all in Mum's neat and tidy handwriting.

'Thanks, lad,' Mr Hoban said as he handed them over to his uniformed officer for safekeeping. He looked at me a moment, then he said to Dad, 'My youngest isn't much older than your boy; we'll get the nutter who's done it, if it's the last thing I do.'

I remembered thinking at the time that this detective was straight talking. I didn't always agree with what he said, but you knew where you stood with him and I really believed he would catch Mum's killer.

That afternoon I put the TV on to watch the press conference Mr Hoban had been talking to Dad about. Dad didn't stay but went up to the bedroom.

Mr Hoban came on in a diagonal striped kipper tie, with a blue handkerchief sticking out of his jacket pocket. He said that he believed the brutal and savage murders of Mrs McCann and Mrs Emily Jackson were the work of the same man. He told how Mum was now known to have been soliciting in a red-light area, and used her husband's van for this purpose. He appealed to anyone who might have information to come forward in confidence.

Then, as the same picture of Mum appeared on screen

behind Mr Hoban, he said something like, 'In this case and Mrs McCann's, the killer's deep-seated hatred of prostitutes has manifested itself in the multiple stab wounds he inflicted on them.'

I looked at Mum's picture again and kept thinking if she was here now we would've laughed at her sudden fame. Mum had always shied away from the limelight, and now here she was, as large as life on television for the whole of Yorkshire to see. And they definitely weren't showing her best side.

Then what Mr Hoban was saying began to sink in, as all the questions the other two detectives had asked me at the police station yesterday about Mum – her clothes, her make-up and going to bingo – and what the press asked me, fell into place. I sank back into the armchair; there'd been some terrible mistake. It wasn't even Dad's van like they were saying in the press report, it was Mum's. And as for the rest of it, well they'd got it all wrong. I'd heard Mrs McCann called a 'good time girl' after her murder last year, but I had no idea what this meant; I just thought it was a girl who liked to enjoy herself, like going to the pictures or laughing with her mates, not something akin to a prostitute. Now I understood what it meant, I didn't care for it, and my mum certainly wasn't one of those women. It was disgusting and I felt sick.

As I tried to take it all in, I heard Mr Hoban warning women who worked on the streets to stay at home. He said he believed the killer was a maniac and they needed to catch him before he struck again. I stared at the screen; the world really had gone crazy. All the words and nasty accusations being made spun round in my head – none of it making any sense.

I turned the TV over; Mum was on the other side. I sat there watching the television late into the afternoon; every news bulletin ran the same lies about Mum. I peered through a gap in the curtains; the press were now back in numbers. I knocked on Dad's door. 'I'm going out,' I told him. He didn't reply.

As soon as it got dark, I went through the kitchen door into the garage, taking care not to stumble over Mum's sacks of onions and potatoes she'd left ready to load up the van. The press were watching the side of the house too, which was open, without any fencing, but I managed to climb through the garage window at the back unnoticed. I slipped down to the bottom of the garden and, clambering between some loose panels in the fence, set off down the back road.

I had just one thought in my mind; I had to get to Auntie Win's. The last time I'd seen Auntie, she was cutting off a length of shiny lilac material spread across the table with her pinking shears. Taking a pin at a time from her mouth, she'd carefully worked them into the fabric of Bubs' bridesmaid dress; Auntie would soon tell me they'd got it all wrong.

I sometimes took the bus to Auntie's when I popped over to collect her peelings for the pigs, to take her and Grandad a bag of veg when Mum was busy with the little ones, or to take them to the school dentist or after-school clubs.

Auntie, like Mum, was always baking. 'Have some pie, love,' she'd say, slipping a piece in a wrapper in my pocket, 'but whatever you do, don't tell your mum!' She knew Mum would say I was ruining my tea, even though I'd remind her I was seventeen now.

It was a good four miles to Auntie's from our house, but now I ran all the way. I had the money for the bus fare in my pocket, but I just wanted to run. When I turned the corner at the top of the road, I saw a police car outside her house and stood there for several moments catching my breath.

Keith let me in to the front room where the policeman was apologising to my Auntie Win and Jackie.

'Ee, lad, lad,' Auntie said throwing her arms round me and shaking with sobs.

None of Mum's family had been officially informed of Mum's death; they'd only found out from the local papers and news reports. Not even Mum's dad, Grandad Woody, had been told.

Keith, who'd been taken in that morning by the police, couldn't then let the family know until they'd eliminated him. Eventually my cousin Muriel rang the *Yorkshire Post* where she'd learnt of Mum's death. The *Post* contacted the police, who had only now turned up. I felt bad that I hadn't thought to say anything when the police interviewed me, but nothing made any sense then – and still didn't.

The policeman shifted uncomfortably as he tried to explain his version of how they believed Mum had died in a red-light area. 'It appears she was picking up a client,' he began.

In a flash, Win was on her feet.

'How dare you! You want to check your facts before you start telling your lies about our Emily!' she told him. 'Blackening our lass's good name to all and sundry when she's not yet cold!'

'But she were up at Chapeltown when it happened,' the policeman mumbled, avoiding Win's eyes.

'Aye, and so were a lot of others no doubt. Don't mean she were doing what you're suggesting!' she snapped back at him.

I stared at the dummy in the corner; Bubs' lilac bridesmaid dress had begun to take shape.

'Some of the lasses knew her up there,' the policeman said, then coughed nervously. 'Lasses on th' game, like Em'ly.'

'No!' Auntie Tess turned red with anger. 'Not our Em'ly! She were respectable; you didn't know her! She wouldn't do such a thing!'

Keith looked baffled.

'You're trying to tell us she were up there soliciting as bold as brass, wi' ladders on top of works van. It don't make any sense.'

'I'm only telling you what we know.'

'Aye, and I'm telling you what we know,' Auntie Win said; she was seething. 'Yes, she were short of cash at times. Like we all are! But happen she'd sell summat, or borrow a few bob if she had to, but she'd never do what you're suggesting! Never!' Auntie collapsed into Grandad's armchair by the gas mantle and started sobbing.

Auntie Tess had heard enough and ushered the policeman to the front door.

'You lot should be ashamed of yourselves, going around saying things like that about my poor sister!' she told him. 'If our Em'ly were up at Chapeltown, then happen she were doing her fruit and veg round! Good day to you!' And she slammed the door in his face.

I looked at the dress again. Our Bubs had grown since

Auntie had measured her for it; she wasn't going to get into it now.

Auntie Tess wiped a tear away herself. 'I'm sorry lad,' she said, 'we should be thinking of you and the little 'uns, not ourselves.'

Grandad heard all the commotion and appeared at the bottom of the stairs.

'Ee, whatever is the matter, lass?' he asked Auntie Win.

Auntie Win quickly dabbed her eyes and composed herself.

'Tek no notice of me, Dad, it's just wi' our Jackie getting wed; you know what I get like when there's another 'un leaving the nest,' she managed to smile.

As Grandad picked up one of the wedding invites from the pile on the side, Auntie Win shot a glance at me and Keith, putting her finger to her lips.

'Come on, Dad, you have a lie down and I'll bring you a brew up,' Auntie Tess said, leading Grandad back upstairs by his arm.

'Hey, I'm not an invalid just yet!' he joked.

'I'm only trying to help, you silly old beggar,' Auntie said, as if nothing in the world was wrong.

'But I want to watch me news programme, it's on soon.'

Grandad Woody always watched the tea-time news on Yorkshire's *Calendar* programme.

'I'll give you a call when it's on,' Auntie told him, glancing back over her shoulder at me and Win.

'What on earth are we going t' say him?' Auntie Tess said to Win when she came back down.

Win just sat there in an old kitchen chair, burying her head in her hands. 'She were the apple of his eye; it'll kill him when he finds out.'

Five o'clock came and went. When Grandad finally wandered back downstairs, Auntie Win told him she didn't like to wake him as he was sleeping like a baby. Grandad said he'd have to watch the news on the other side a bit later instead, but Keith had taken the fuse out of the plug while he slept and told Grandad the TV had gone on the blink.

'We can't keep it from him forever,' Keith said. 'Sooner or later, he's got to be told – before he finds out for himself.'

As I left to go home, Auntie tucked a piece of pie in my pocket; both of us painfully aware that this time she had no need to say, 'And you better not tell your Mum!'

Walking away from the house, I turned and saw the press arriving outside Auntie's. I remembered thinking Auntie only had a front door in her back-to-back house; she wasn't going to be able to avoid them – let alone Grandad.

16

It was freezing out as I walked the four miles back home, eating the pie. It was so cold I was getting a headache, but at least it stopped me thinking for a while, and I was grateful for that.

After a short while I began to feel strangely elated and, without meaning to, started laughing out loud. A woman passing by with a dog crossed the street to avoid me. I didn't mean to scare her but I just couldn't help bursting into fits of laughter as I suddenly thought how none of this made any sense; it was all just some sick joke.

As I was walked along laughing, a police Land Rover crawled past me with a poster-size picture of Mum on the side and a caption below it appealing for information, with a phone number to ring. The officer in the passenger seat leant out of the vehicle and asked through a loudhailer, 'Look closely, do you know this woman?' The police vehicle was followed by officers on foot as it slowly made its way down the street. Further along on the other side, another group of officers were placing cones in the road as they set up road blocks, staggered on either side, and began flagging down motorists.

One of the policemen accompanying the Land Rover came over. 'Son?' he asked, pointing to the photo of Mum on the side of the vehicle, 'Do you know anything about this murder?' Although it was freezing cold, I burst into a hot sweat.

'Nothing,' I said, grinning inanely. 'Not a bloody thing!' I have no idea why I swore. The officer's face hardened as he eyed me suspiciously. 'Perhaps we need to have a little chat.'

'It's a fair cop,' I laughed, almost hysterically, as I held my hands up. 'You're right, I do know something about it; that woman is my mum.'

The officer gave me the once over. 'You trying to be funny?' he said, as he blocked my path. I wished I was, and I felt the smile falling off my face in an instant as I took out my wallet and showed him my name and address.

'Neil Jackson?' the policeman read from my snooker hall membership card. 'Stay there,' he said, going over to the police vehicle now stopped a few yards ahead of us at the corner of the street.

He took my membership card and got on the police radio in the car, reading off my address to them. After a moment, he came back over.

'Go on lad,' he said, 'you better get off home before the street lights go off.'

As I set off up the road, I glanced back and saw the policeman speaking to the other officers by the Land Rover. They stopped what they were doing and turned to watch me; I felt uncomfortable at being the object of their pity.

The following day, Auntie Tess and Keith came round to see Dad. The family had talked and decided he was the best person to explain to Grandad Woody what had actually happened to Mum, as he was with her that night.

'That way,' Auntie Tess said, 'Grandad will be able to understand it, and not have to listen to all the rumours and lies flying round about her bingo sessions.'

There were things I still wanted to ask Dad myself — those same questions, like why was Mum out on her own on Tuesday night and why wasn't he telling the police it was mistaken identity — that Mum wasn't on the game? And shouldn't he ring up the press to put them right about it too? But Dad seemed to have put up an invisible barrier and I was unable to speak to him or ask him anything now.

Auntie Tess had more success with Dad, who promised he'd go round to speak to Grandad Woody that night. Keith said he'd keep the fuse out of the television plug until Dad's visit, but as the evening came and went, and several more after that until a week had passed, Dad never made that journey.

During that time, the whole of Leeds had been taken over in the hunt for the new Jack the Ripper. As well as road blocks and the police going from door to door asking questions, appeals for information were made at Leeds United and the rugby grounds in the area, on cinema screens and at the local theatres. Mum had gone, but everywhere I went, there she was staring out at me from poster-sized pictures on the sides of buses, at railway stations, on bus shelters and in shop windows.

In the end, Auntie Tess was forced to tell Grandad the truth before he found out himself. As she said, 'We can't keep telling him the TV's broken forever.' And he could see for himself the ice had melted and it was safe for him to go out to collect his paper from the newsagent to play 'Spot the Ball'.

Keith picked Grandad up in his car and took him round to Tess's house in Bramley. They thought getting him out of his own house might make it a bit easier to tell him.

'Sit down, Grandad,' Auntie told him, 'I need to talk to you.'

But Grandad seemed to think all the serious faces and secrecy meant it was a going to be a surprise party or special tea for someone, and he insisted on standing. He was wearing the battered old fez Mum had bought him on holiday in Tunisia several years ago now. Grinning from ear to ear, he produced what looked like a shortened raspberry cane from his back pocket. Then he took off the fez and, placing it the palm of his large, bony hand, addressed us like an audience,

'Now I'm going to show you a little trick I learnt as a lad,' he said, waving the stick over the hat as if it was a magic wand, while he tried to remember it.

We were all too dumbstruck to speak, when Auntie Win suddenly blurted out, 'Not now, Woody – we've got summat to tell you . . . Our Em'ly's been killed.'

Grandad looked up from his trick.

'Aye, an' happen I'll kill her an' all when I get me hands on her,' he said. 'She promised to bring me some bananas last week, and she's not set foot near me since.' He looked over at me. 'Tell your mum to pack in working for once and come up and see me tomorrow, lad,' he said. 'Now if I can have a bit of hush everyone . . . Abracadabra!' he grinned, as he waved the wand over the hat again and produced a string of coloured hankies from it.

Auntie Win snatched the stick from him and snapped it in two.

'Will you just listen to me, you silly old duffer!' she said, grabbing hold of his long, lean frame with her plump little arms and shaking him. 'This isn't a joke!' she told him, as the tears streamed down her cheeks.

The colour drained from Grandad's face in an instant, and he slumped back into a chair with the hankies strung around his neck. Auntie Win went out into the kitchen and held onto the sink as she sobbed. Auntie Tess crouched beside Grandad's chair and, putting her face close to his ear, quietly told him, "Dad, our Emily's been murdered. We don't know who did it, except it must have been a madman . . . But that's not all. They're saying things about her, Dad . . .'

I couldn't listen to any more and walked out into the garden. I'd not got as far as the shed, when I heard the long, low plaintive wail of an animal in distress, as if its calf had been taken from it. That sound would haunt me forever.

I sat on the low wall staring at the grass long after the wailing had ceased. By the time I went back in, Keith had taken Grandad home. Grandad's hat was lying upturned on the floor beside his coloured hankies; Auntie Tess caught my eye as she picked them up and buried them in the bottom of the bin.

Grandad stopped going out after this; he cancelled his papers and took to his bed.

At home, Mr Hoban turned up in a new suit and his posh car almost every day to see Dad to tell him what he could of the 'progress of the case' as he put it. He hinted to Dad that he believed the man responsible for Mum's murder was local and worked in engineering or the building trade, as the injuries were inflicted with workman's tools and there was a wellington boot mark on Mum. He was possibly a lorry driver carrying the tools with him in his cab; he also thought this because the area near where Mum was killed, and where Wilma had hitched a lift, was a through route often taken by lorry drivers. But he hadn't, as yet, got any new leads.

I wanted to say to him, 'You're wrong about Mum, just ask my mum's family – Auntie Tess, Woody, Win, Keith and my cousins, they'll tell you.' But he seemed so convinced by his mistake, I knew it was pointless.

After Mr Hoban went, Dad disappeared back upstairs, where he now spent most of his time avoiding the neighbours and retreating from life as he'd done when Derek had died. I didn't wait for darkness today and slipped out in broad daylight. There was fewer press in the street today, so I was able to slip out of the garage window and through the back fence to see Grandad, as I'd told Auntie I would.

As I climbed the dark, narrow stairs in Auntie's house, I realised it was many years since I'd been up to Grandad's bedroom. The last time I must've been about ten and had come up to sneak a look at the presents Mum and Dad had bought me and hidden in his room until Christmas. One of them was called 'Operation' and featured a man with his front removed, exposing a set of removable organs. When I got to the top of the stairs, I discovered Grandad with the box on the bed and a pair of plastic tweezers in his hand, jumping out of his skin every time the buzzer went off, and laughing to himself. With his shaky hands, he didn't get one piece out without setting off the buzzer, and laughed till the tears streamed down his face. I never told him I was watching him and waited till he'd finished and put my present back under the bed.

Now he was lying in the dark under a pile of blankets, his eyes tired and sunken, and his food untouched on the side.

'Come on Grandad, you've got to eat,' I coaxed him as I tried to spoon-feed him some jelly, but he clamped his lips tightly together and blinked. Grandad was no stranger to tragedy; he'd already lost Uncle Smiler, and now Mum. It was like he'd had enough.

I glanced over at Auntie Win and Tess behind me and tried again.

'Grandad, she weren't doing what they say she were,' I told him. 'It's all lies, you know it is.'

But Grandad was already shrinking beneath the covers, and turned his face to the wall.

'Look,' I leaned over the bed, trying a different tactic, 'if you try and eat summat, I'll take you up t' Elland Road to see the football when you're better.

Grandad turned back for a moment and looked at me in surprise.

'Nay, lad,' he said, 'don't grieve for me – when your own child goes before you like that, then happen it's time to go your'sen.'

Then I remembered I couldn't have taken Grandad to a match even if he did get up: they were playing appeals for information about Mum's murder at every sports ground in Leeds.

17

On the Friday after it had happened, I'd returned from Auntie's and, turning the corner into Back Green, saw the press knocking on Gwen's door and stopping Liz and other neighbours in the street, trying to get a quote or a story from them. Gwen had always been prim and proper, and took it very seriously when her son Colin had been caught swearing with Chris. Even though it was all lies what was being said about Mum, I was dreading what the neighbours would think, and just as I'd started using the back way to avoid the press, it had become a good way of avoiding the neighbours too.

I doubled back down the road and was about to cut through the fence at the back, when I bumped straight into the press coming the other way. Suddenly, one of them saw me.

'Neil Jackson!' he called out, and then they all started running in my direction. I backed off and turned and ran off up the road. I had never been a sprinter, and had only got as far as the newsagent at the top road, when they began closing in on me. 'That's it, it's all over now,' I thought, when Mr Rawlinson appeared at the door.

'Quick, lad, in here!'

I ran into the shop. Mr Rawlinson quickly bolted the door after me, and turned the sign to 'closed'.

I was doubled up and out of breath as I thanked Mr Rawlinson.

'They've been round us all like wasps round a jam pot, it's a disgrace!' a voice behind me said. I turned and saw Gwen getting a pint of milk from the fridge.

'Hold your head up, is my advice to you, Neil; happen they don't know your mum like we do,' she told me as she put her change on the counter. 'Now you'd better let me out, Mr Rawlinson.'

Mr Rawlinson unbolted the door and Gwen steamed out like a battleship, forging a path straight through the middle of the press, who peeled off either side of her.

'All I know is, Emily Jackson were a good woman,' she told them, as they ran alongside her trying to keep up. 'She'd give you her right arm if she thought it would help. And if she were doing what you're saying, then happen she had her reasons! Good day!' And sweeping past them, she left a trail of journalists and photographers in her wake.

Mrs Rawlinson came through from the back and looked through the glass front at the press still waiting.

'I should give it a while, son,' she said, 'they'll soon get fed up and go.'

As Mr Rawlinson rang up the till, I saw he had a copy of the *Sun* open on the counter in front of him that he must've been reading before I came in. He leaned forward to try to cover up the article with his arms and upper body, but I'd already seen the heading and first line or two: 'Ripper Hunted in Call-girl Murders: A Jack the Ripper killer is being hunted by police after the carbon-copy murders of two prostitutes . . .'

Jack the Ripper? They were now calling my Mum's

killer Jack the Ripper. A chill went through my body and I shivered.

Mrs Rawlinson patted my arm. 'Just ignore it, lovey, like Gwen said.' Then, exchanging a look with her husband, she asked, 'Why don't you come and sit down in the back, and I'll make you a nice cup of tea?'

'I'm alright, Mrs Rawlinson," I said, forcing a cheery smile at her, 'thanks all t' same!'

But I was far from alright and I certainly couldn't ignore it, nor get it out of my head. My mum had been murdered by someone named after the maniac who'd killed prostitutes in the East End of London in the nineteenth century. It was bad enough they were calling Mum a prostitute and everyone, even Mr Rawlinson, was reading about it. But now, as I thought about all the drawings I'd seen of the Ripper victims in books I'd read as a kid, it brought home the terrible savagery of Mum's murder. This was worse still than the police description of her injuries or the smell of death just two days ago in the mortuary.

Up until this point it felt as if I'd been watching events through a blanket of snow, just as we'd done when we got our new TV and me and Dad tried to work out which one was *Arthur of the Britons* as distinct from his horse. That is, until he discovered the contrast knob on the side, twiddling it until the picture came into sharp focus. Now, everything had become clear and focussed in my mind. Mum had been savagely murdered, and someone – another human being, if you could call them that – had actually done it. Suddenly I was filled with contempt and anger for this person; he was less than an animal and I hated him. And the anger and bitterness inside me grew to be part of my life for many years to come.

I picked up one of each of the different papers on display and put them by the till. The newsagent looked at his wife in disbelief.

'You sure you want to buy those, lad?' he asked me.

I nodded, and left with an armful.

The press were still waiting outside when Mr Rawlinson turned the sign back to 'open', but I thought, *If Gwen can do it, so can I*, as I walked out into the waiting pack.

The questions came thick and fast about what they saw as Mum's part-time occupation. I didn't reply, but kept my head up high; I wasn't going to hide anymore.

The back door opened that evening. I looked up and expected to see my mum but it was Gwen calling round to bring me and Dad a shepherd's pie. I couldn't eat it, but as soon as she'd gone, started scanning the papers I'd bought to see what they said about Mum. As I remember, most didn't even carry the story, but what I didn't realise then was that this was to be the start of what was to become almost an obsession.

It was Granddad's sixty-fifth birthday a few weeks later and Auntie Tess and Win threw a birthday party for him in the back room of the Albion in Armley. They knew that if he didn't get up for this, the chances were he would never get up again.

I put on the suit I'd brought from a tailor's in the Headrow for Mum's funeral, except there still hadn't been one. While Mr Hoban still came round in his Daimler to update us on the inquiry, he was now coming less often. He brought the workbook back on one occasion and said they'd drawn a blank on it. He explained they still couldn't release Mum's body until after the inquest, but hoped it wouldn't be much longer. But as the days slipped by without finding the killer, even Mr Hoban began to worry – it was less likely that they would find him unless the animal struck again.

Auntie Tess helped Grandad Woody into the pinstripe suit he'd kept since his demob days. These last few weeks had changed Grandad; he now looked hunched and shrivelled, like a little pixie in oversized clothing.

A big spread was laid on at the club, which did Grandad proud, and all the family turned out in force to support him. All, that is, except Dad, who hadn't been invited.

'Of course they've sent you an invitation,' I told him. 'It must have got lost in the post.' But when I dropped hints to Auntie Tess and Auntie Win, they didn't really say anything.

Ever since Dad hadn't shown up to talk to Grandad Woody as he'd promised, the family were angry with him and, rather than sympathising with him and trying to support him, as they'd done at the start, they now seemed to be blaming him for something. It was hard to tell, because as soon as I went into a room, they stopped talking or lowered their voices. 'What's going on, Auntie?' I asked Win one day, but she just patted my hand and went out and put the kettle on. 'I'll make us a brew.'

When Grandad arrived at the club he was so surprised to see everyone, he actually managed a smile. Not his usual ear-to-ear grin, which made his face crinkle up, but it was a relief to see him smile all the same, or to even see him there at all, after the weeks he'd spent in bed refusing to eat after Auntie had finally told him about Mum.

As the evening went on, there were times when he seemed almost like his old self again. Then, Auntie Tess tapped a spoon against a glass to get everyone's attention.

'It's time for Woody to cut the cake!' she announced, and helped to steady his hand with the knife.

He'd not cut the first slice, when Dad appeared in the doorway.

'Happy birthday, Woody,' Dad said, holding out a gift-wrapped present to Grandad.

You could've heard a pin drop at that moment. Then Auntie Win shattered the silence.

'Get out!' she shrieked. 'Get out! You're not welcome here!'

Suddenly there were screams from all directions as a scuffle broke out. Dad was a big man, but the men in Mum's family had him by the scruff of the neck, frog-marched him to the door and threw him out into the street.

I rushed out after him.

'Dad! Wait!'

Dad stopped a moment and turned back.

'Forget it, son,' he said, then, slinging the present as far as he could into the distance, he disappeared into the night.

I went back inside where someone put a beer in my hand, then I overheard one of Mum's relatives saying, 'If he was on fire, I'd cross the road to pour petrol on him.'

Although Mum wasn't on the game, I suddenly realised some of her family now actually thought she was, and they seemed to be blaming Dad. I was stunned. How could they believe such a thing about Mum? Or that Dad had a hand in it? Just because he hadn't turned up to explain things to Grandad didn't mean he had a guilty conscience, as they were taking it. He just probably found it difficult to talk about, and I was about to say this to Auntie when someone started to sing 'Happy Birthday' to Grandad and we all joined in.

18

The police finally released Mum's body for burial in May of that year, four months after her murder. She was buried near to Derek; she was just forty-two.

During the weeks and months beforehand, I cooked and cleaned for Dad and kept the house spick and span the way Mum would want it. The days passed in silence between us, and the house felt desolate and empty.

Two weeks after Mum's death, Dad had gone back to work; he needed the money and the bills were starting to come in. Only now, without Mum, Dad had to walk to work and had suddenly become dependent on others, like Keith or other workmates on the site, if he wanted to work further afield.

Mum's funeral took place on a warm spring day at Cottingley Cemetery. It reminded me of the last time I'd been here, when Mum brought me in the car when I got back from London after Derek had died.

Dad and me went together in the car behind Mum; Dad wasn't very comfortable with church services and asked me to help him pick the hymns that Mum liked.

The chapel spilled over with people paying their last respects: family, friends, customers, neighbours and dozens of little children from our street bringing flowers for her. The local police and senior CID, including Mr Hoban, who'd been in charge of Mum's case, attended. The press also turned out in force, photographing everything – from the messages on the wreaths and floral sprays, to Derek's plaque next to Mum's grave.

Grandad Woody didn't go; he was just too upset. However hard I try I cannot remember if Chris or Bubs were there either, and in all these past months there was still no talk of them coming home. But as I looked behind me in the chapel, I saw Mrs Stone in her furry bonnet and maroon winter coat, even though you could feel summer was well on its way. Mrs Stone could now barely lift her head from her waist, but just as she'd made the effort to come for Derek, she was there for Mum.

There seemed to be an unspoken truce between Mum's family and Dad at the funeral that day – although it didn't last long. As soon as the mourners at the cemetery began to drift away, Dad agreed to pose for photographers by Mum's open grave.

'Look at him, playing the grieving widower!' Auntie Tess was incensed. 'He's obviously being paid by the press.'

'No Auntie,' I said. 'You've got it all wrong about Dad; he wouldn't do that.'

But as I stood by Dad, as Mum's coffin was lowered, I realised I was beginning to have doubts of my own.

Mum's funeral tea was held at the house, but we couldn't fit everyone in. Some of the relatives had to stand in the kitchen or sit on the stairs.

As I helped Dad serve food to the mourners, I saw my cousins Jeff and Kevin standing a little way off with my uncles. Kevin's spots had cleared up and he'd slimmed down;

he even refused a sausage roll when I held out the plate to him. Jeff had grown even taller and was wearing a suit. I hadn't seen either of them since we all went to London, but realised they must be in their twenties by now.

'Sorry, kid,' Jeff said, as if the last five years had simply disappeared.

By six o'clock, people had started to drift off. I gave Dad a hand to help people with their coats and to say our good-byes, when I overheard my cousin and Auntie Win talking.

'Happen she'd only been on the streets doing it for a short while,' my cousin was saying, 'although I still find it hard to believe Em'ly would do it all.'

'Whether it were three weeks, three months or three years, I reckon someone must've known about it!' Auntie Win scoffed. 'If it were Em'ly's idea in t' first place – which I very much doubt!'she said, looking over at Dad.

I felt myself going red.

'It's not Dad's fault, it can't be,' I blustered, ''cos Mum weren't doing it anyway!'

Auntie spun round.

'Neil, lad, I didn't see you there,' she faltered.

But no one else stepped in to contradict Auntie Win, until Tess said, 'That's right, Neil, my sister would never do such a thing.'

But later, when Dad came over to say his goodbyes, Auntie Tess snapped at him, 'I'll see me'sen out, thank you very much! I'm here out of respect for my niece, not for you!'

'Sorry, Neil,' she said as she slammed out, with the rest of the family following behind.

Later that night, as I helped Dad clear up, I thought about what Win had said and all the questions I'd wanted to ask Dad before kept coming back. Why wasn't Dad with Mum that night up at Chapeltown when she was doing her fruit and veg round? And why did he come home in a taxi on his own instead of going looking for her? And so many other questions; but as I looked at Dad's face, searching for answers, I could see that after the funeral, he'd retreated inside himself again. If he was able to explain away my doubts, which I was sure he could, I couldn't ask him now.

I hadn't slept much for weeks and felt constantly tired. But that night I must have fallen asleep because the nightmares returned; huge pieces of glass shaped like giant stalactites came crashing down, slicing through Derek's body. The life was draining from him on the kitchen floor – except it wasn't Derek now, but Mum lying there as I stood by watching, helpless to do anything.

I woke up in a cold sweat and, barely able to get my breath, rushed to the window and flung it open. As I took in a deep breath, I saw some of the press were still there and felt I was suffocating.

The next day I went down Wellington Street in Leeds to the Army Recruitment Office, where I went in and signed up.

19

Two weeks later, I packed my belongings and left Churwell.
That morning, from my bedroom window, I'd watched
Dad as he trudged off for work with his tools in his bag.
Since I had told him I was going, he still hadn't said much;
there wasn't much building work around so he knew it
made sense. But I just needed to get away from home, the
press on the doorstep and everything that had happened.

I had one or two old black and white photos of Mum
and some colour ones I'd taken in recent years when we
were on holiday. I hadn't been able to look at them since
Mum had died and kept them in a shoebox at the back of
the wardrobe ever since. I slipped these into a large envelope without looking at them, and packed them in the
bottom of my bag with the newspapers that had covered
the story over the weeks. I knew this was a contradiction:
trying to escape the press and refuting the lies they printed
about Mum, and here I was buying their papers, but
somehow I just couldn't help it.

I picked up my kitbag and turned to look back once
more before closing the door behind me. Some of Chris's
things were still in the room; his posters of Leeds United
were on the wall and his games were left untouched on
the side, ready for Uncle to come and collect them. It
seemed strange that while I'd had the room ever since we

came to Churwell, both Derek and Chris had gone, leaving their posters and things behind them. And, I suppose, leaving me.

The house was still and quiet as I left, so different to the day we'd arrived: Mum sewing the curtains, Derek throwing me the carrycot as we formed a human chain from the lorry; then, later, Granny Jackson taking Bubs out in the pram. I looked for the bloodstains on the architrave; like Granny, Derek and Mum, and now the little ones, they'd all gone.

The last of the goats and the hens had gone from the allotment several weeks since, and I watched as the farmer from the next village loaded up the pigs on a trailer and took them away. Dad had found it difficult to look after the animals after Mum passed away. That was six months ago now, and the disused animal pens were already becoming overgrown. The vegetable round had also gone; Dad didn't need to tell Mum's customers, as the phone stopped ringing for her almost straight away. Dad eventually threw out the vegetables lying rotting in the garage, and sold the scales on to a man he met in the pub when he started going out again some weeks later.

A few days before I left home, some letters arrived in the post addressed to me. I didn't normally get letters and when I opened them, to my surprise I found they were birthday cards. It was my eighteenth but I'd forgotten all about it. I'd come of age, as they say, but my youth had ended that day in the mortuary, and now I just felt what it must be like to be old.

I put my cards in a drawer where Dad had put Mum's condolence cards and left them there.

Gwen saw me walking down Back Green and came to the front gate.

'Your mum would've been so proud of you,' she said. Then, 'You'll come back and see us when you're on leave?'

I nodded, grateful for her kind words, but as I looked back at the house again, I knew I would never be returning.

I caught the bus to the railway station in Leeds, not realising that it passed right by the house in the middle of the field where me and Dad had last worked together before Mum's death. Another roofing firm had taken over the job – Dad couldn't carry on with it without Mum and the van, or maybe, like the allotment, he just didn't have the heart for it anymore. Because of all the rain we'd had recently, the new firm was only just restarting work on it. Me and Dad had taken an end of the roof each, working inwards, towards each other. As I looked across at the house from the top of the bus, there was still a great gaping divide in the middle, which at that moment struck me as being like my relationship with Dad had become, though I didn't really understand why. Just as I didn't understand why he hadn't been out there defending Mum's name or why he didn't seem to be grieving for Mum. But then I wasn't grieving either.

I saw a poster of Mum by the entrance to the railway station and said goodbye to her as I boarded the train for Wiltshire that day.

I had no idea then that it would take another five years, eleven more murders, and many thousands of police hours before they'd finally catch one of the world's most notorious serial killers. I also had little idea how my life would change in that time, and how it would tear my family apart forever.

Part Two

20

Army barracks, outside York, February 1977

I sat on the side of the bed tugging at my bootlaces, then levering off my boots and peeling off my socks, I sunk back on the mattress. Propping my head against the pillow, I closed my eyes and listened to the sounds of other recruits laughing and letting off steam around me after a hard day on the parade ground. Some of them were stripping off and racing each other to the showers at the end of the barrack room; others were flicking wet towels and chucking old bits of soap at each other as they waited their turn for a hot shower.

Thinking about it now, the Duke of Wellington's Regiment saved me. I had gone straight down to Corsham in Wiltshire to do my training with a group of new recruits from Yorkshire and further afield. After Corsham we were sent to our home barracks at York. Although York was just a stone's throw from Leeds, it felt miles away and I was able to breathe again – at least for a while. The hours spent square bashing, out on exercises and applying elbow-grease to my boots and the buttons on my uniform meant that, for the best part of the day, I didn't have time to think; I could block out everything, even Mum.

In the evenings I stayed in the gym working out for as long as possible, making myself so exhausted that as soon as I got to bed I'd fall fast asleep until the next morning. Then I'd be back on the parade ground and the punishing daily regime I'd set myself would start all over again.

In truth, I was still numb with shock and there were times when I couldn't believe any of it had happened. But there was also another reason why I was able to block it out: since Mum's murder, the 'Ripper' had gone quiet – there'd been neither sight nor sound of him in over a year. The police had ruled out a horrific attack in Roundhay Park around the time of Mum's funeral in May last year. The poor lass, Marcella Claxton, was in her twenties. She only just survived the vicious hammer attack and was left in a terrible state. My stomach lurched when I heard the news. What kind of animal could do such a thing? Apart from the Ripper?

At the time of this attack, Dad was no longer getting updates on the inquiry, such as they were – actually more like social calls Mr Hoban paid us every so often to see how we were getting along. Mr Hoban had recently been put in charge of a new CID area and now worked from an office in Bradford, no longer being on the Ripper case. His former assistant, Detective Superintendent Jim Hobson, one of the detectives I'd met at Millgarth the year before, had been put in charge of Marcella's case. Auntie Win had been sending me Monday night's *Yorkshire Evening Post* each week so that I could keep tabs on United while I was away training in Corsham. I read in one of these papers that because Marcella's injuries, brutal as they were, did not involve stab wounds like Mum and Mrs McCann, the police decided this wasn't the work of the Ripper, but another maniac. Two crazed attackers running around Leeds was a terrifying prospect and if this was the case, then the police had their work cut out with a possible copy-cat attacker – although it didn't seem very likely to me.

Mr Hoban had promised Dad he would find Mum's killer and if anyone could, I believed it was him, so I was disappointed to hear he'd been moved on. However, although after Mum's murder it had been impossible to go anywhere in Leeds without seeing at first hand the inquiry that Mr Hoban had instigated, there'd still been no real progress on Mum's case in all these months – not even to say the police realised they'd made a mistake about Mum being on the game. All me and Dad knew now was what Mr Hoban had suspected some time back: the Ripper was probably local, in engineering or building, and a lorry driver.

From the moment that Mr Hoban announced they had a serial killer on their hands, I'd tried to prepare myself for seeing a news flash or report of another savage murder like Mum's. When I heard Marcella Claxton's attack wasn't linked to the Ripper, it made me dread even more the thought of hearing news of another attack that was indeed the Ripper's. But as time went on and there was no such news bulletin, I hoped the animal had done the decent thing and topped himself. And, as a year had passed since Mum's murder, I felt certain that he had, and breathed a huge sigh of relief. In fact, I was so convinced that he was dead, I'd even given up going to the gym on the odd evening, bowing to pressure to go out with the mates I was beginning to make in the barracks instead.

'Come on, Jackson! Wakey! Wakey!' A wet flannel stung

my face as I caught it full on. Eddie stood at the foot of the bed, grinning.

'Move your arse, we're on a late pass tonight!'

'I don't know,' I hesitated –

'Not that bloody gym again? Come on out with the lads for a change! It's Dave's birthday!'

Feeling lighthearted for once, I picked up the sodden flannel and flung it back at Eddie. Eddie ducked; the flannel splattered on the wall behind him, then dropped to the floor.

'Missed!' he grinned.

Eddie was a year older than me and because we both came from Leeds, we soon became mates.

'Race you down to th' block!' I said.

'You lose, you're on for tonight!'

I grabbed my towel and hared off down to the showers, trading good-natured insults with Eddie as we went, but Eddie lunged past me and got there first.

Changing into my civvies, I sat on my bed and hastily wrote a postcard to Dad and Chris in Bramley, and another to Bubs who was now living with Auntie in Farnsley on a more permanent footing.

'Come on, mate!' Eddie was getting impatient.

'Alright, give us a chance!' I replied, shoving the post-card in my pocket with my late pass.

Soon we were all scrambling into the back of a covered lorry, making jokes at each other's expense. 'Just look at the state of you,' Eddie laughed at my purple loons. 'You're never going to cop off in them!'

'I'll have you know Marc Bolan wears a pair similar to

these, and he don't do so bad,' I scoffed, to hoots of derision.

'Yeah, but he's not a ginger like you!' Dave, the birthday boy, quipped, then added, 'Oh sorry, "reddish-blond hair",' imitating my voice and patting his hair in an affected manner as if he was a girl.

The lad's were in stitches.

'Ay, I'll have you know there's a lot of successful people out there with red hair – singers and actors and that,' I countered.

'Come on then, who?' one of them asked me, but then of course I couldn't think of a single one.

They started jeering and stamping their feet on the floor of the lorry.

'Hang on, I'm thinking,' I blustered.

And then I remembered, 'Ginger Baker!'

'Who?' Dave asked.

'You know, the drummer with Cream and Blind Faith – Eric Clapton and them.'

'Blind what?' he appealed to the others in the back of the lorry who looked back vacantly or shook their heads. 'Sorry, mate, never heard of them.'

'You must know,' I said. 'Eric Clapton, he's bloody legend – Ginger Baker and Steve Winwood from Traffic!'

Then they exploded into laughter, and I realised they were pulling my leg.

'Ha, very funny, you lot,' I said, breaking into a grin, as we flew over another bump in the road.

The banter continued all the way into town, and I was, by now, looking forward to a night out – but as we pulled up outside a bar in York, some gruesome news awaited us there.

*

I posted my card in a post box in the centre and joined Eddie and the others in the bar of the Ox as they celebrated Dave's birthday. I was just getting change for the pool table when, on the portable telly behind the bar, I caught sight of a kids' playground with swings on it, a roundabout and a climbing frame, all sealed off by police tape. I recognised it at once as Roundhay Park in Leeds where me and Derek had played as kids, before we'd moved to Churwell. It was also where Marcella Claxton had been attacked last year. I couldn't hear what was being said for all the noise going on behind me, as they were about to give Dave the bumps which he was doing his best to resist, but I knew instantly what had happened when one of the detectives who'd interviewed me, Detective Superintendent Jim Hobson, came on and spoke: the Ripper bastard had struck again.

'Neil, cummon, give us a hand!' Eddie called, as they threw the birthday boy up in the air. But I couldn't move; I was frozen to the spot. Far from being prepared for this moment, all I could think about was that Mum's injuries had been so terrible her murderer had been called a modern day Jack the Ripper. I couldn't stop shaking and spilt my pint everywhere.

'Oi, watch it mate!' a soldier complained as the beer caught him, soaking his clothes. It brought me to, and, pushing past him, I rushed outside, throwing up on the side of the road.

I splashed my face with rain water from the old stone horse trough by the market square, then hitched a lift back to camp with a farmer towing a trailer with bales of straw on the back. The farmer wasn't interested in exchanging pleasantries and I was glad of that as it was taking all my energy to stop my teeth chattering and to control my tremors. As I'd clambered in beside him in his battered estate car, he'd mumbled something about having done National Service twenty years ago, and that was it. We'd gone for about fifteen minutes up the road when I noticed he had a car radio and, to this day, I don't know what got into me, but I leaned over and switched it on, whether the farmer liked the idea or not.

'Ay, ay! What are you doing?' the farmer yelled at me.

'I want to hear th' news!' I said. But I was shaking so badly I couldn't control the tuner dial and shot through the stations playing anything from light music and sports through to news programmes in foreign languages, in rapid succession. The high frequency noise was deafening and, for a moment, I wasn't sure whether it was the radio or inside my brain.

'Get your hands off that!' the farmer roared at me, and pulled up so sharply in the road that the tyres squealed.

'I don't know what they teach you in the Army these days, but it's certainly not what they taught us in mine!'

He looked at me with indignant outrage, then, after a moment and to my surprise, he began turning the knob himself until he found the news in English.

'That suit you?' he asked.

I nodded sheepishly and we set off again. Sure enough, the first item was about the murder in Roundhay Park. The announcer said it had been 'a most savage and brutal attack', and that the police were keeping an open mind as to whether this was the work of the man now known as the Ripper, who had killed two other women, both call-girls, in Leeds. I knew they meant Mum.

The latest victim had been identified as Mrs Irene Richardson, a mother of two. The police said she had severe head injuries and multiple stab wounds to the stomach. They were also keeping an open mind on whether Irene was a prostitute or not, but were going to look into it to see if she lived 'this kind of lifestyle'. I hoped they got it right this time and turned the radio off.

'Finished now, have we then?' the farmer asked.

I nodded, then began violently retching and opened the door and flung myself out of the car, not realising how fast we were travelling. I spun onto a grass verge where I rolled over several times before stopping just short of a ditch. As I rolled, I was aware of the car pulling up to a screeching halt a few yards ahead.

'You bloody fool!' the farmer shouted after me, as I lay spread-eagled on the grass, vomiting into the ditch.

I vomited until the insides of my stomach began to feel raw and I could taste the bitterness of bile in my mouth. Then, grabbing a handful of long grass from the verge, I wiped it over my mouth to try to clean myself up as best I could. I was surprised when I turned back a few minutes later, to find that the farmer was still waiting for me.

'Quite a night then?' he asked, as I got carefully back in beside him, feeling every bruise on my ribs.

'Can we go?' I said.

The farmer gave me a sidelong glance as if weighing up whether I could have had something to do with the murder we'd just heard about, then grunted and started up the car engine. We travelled on in silence for the next three miles or so, until we arrived at the camp.

'Sorry,' I mumbled as I pushed open the door and climbed out.

He stared straight ahead for a moment, and then he turned to me and said, 'War does funny things to people. Ireland?'

I realised the farmer had seen active service and thought that I had too and, not wanting to disappoint him, I nodded. In fact, Wiltshire was as far as I'd been as yet, and the only action I'd seen was chipping my tooth on the assault course going over a fence.

The farmer obviously had a story to tell but as I didn't offer him any details of 'mine', he respected my privacy but couldn't then share his with me. It was like we had an unspoken bond – that we'd both seen action and suffered. If I'd been feeling more myself, I'd have felt a fraud, but as I stood by the side of the road watching until the tail lights on his trailer disappeared over the other side of the hill as my brother-in-arms drove away, all I could think of was that the Ripper had struck again.

As I made my way back to my barrack room, I kept repeating the words over in my head: *Mrs Irene Richardson, Ripper, mother of two; Mrs Irene Richardson, Ripper, mother of two; Mrs Irene Richardson* . . .

The moment I got back, I picked up my kit and went straight to the gym, thankful it was still open. I worked out until the sweat poured off me and I was barely able to stand, let alone think. Then I went to bed, creeping quietly into the barrack room so as not to awaken the lads who were by now back and asleep in their beds.

That night, as I eventually fell asleep myself, glass began to break again, great sheets of it, crashing to the floor, and I stood there frozen, unable to help as Derek called out to me as he had done on that fateful afternoon. But when I looked again, it was Mum lying in a pool of blood on the floor, and the blood was seeping into my shoes.

I screamed and woke up with a start as something whacked me hard on the side of the face. Panting and covered in sweat, my eyes darted around in the darkness, trying to work out where I was – until somebody shouted, 'Cut it out, can't ya! There's people trying to get some sleep round here!'

As I came to, I felt my face stinging where the plimsoll had hit me. Then a black cloud swept over me as I remembered Mum and the other poor lass that the Ripper had just butchered. The day before yesterday Irene still had a life and a future, but now that life had been cruelly taken from her and her baby no longer had a mum. All these months I'd let myself believe the Ripper was dead, he'd just been toying with us, resting up before his next killing. Now he was back and I was fuelled with anger. The Ripper was pure evil and I hoped once they got him, he'd rot in hell.

I picked up the plimsoll from my bed and hurled it with force across the room in the direction it had come.

'Hey, watch it!' a voice cried.

I made my way in the dark down the barracks, stumbling past beds and shoes and boots lying around, to the washroom. Yanking the cord on the overhead light by the washbasin, I turned the cold tap on and let it run for a minute. As soon as the water began to feel icy, I put the left side of my face beneath the stream, keeping it there until it numbed my burning cheek. Then, splashing water in my eyes and on my face, I began to cool down.

With the trail for Mum's killer having gone cold, I thought if nothing else good came of Irene's death, the police would at least now have some fresh clues to lead them to the Ripper and put an end to his callous slaughter of women. Or so I thought.

But the Ripper had other plans and just a few weeks later he struck again, as 1977 was to become the year he went on a bloody rampage, and murdering four more women and viciously attacking another two – with both sides of the Pennines becoming his killing fields.

21

When Irene Richardson was murdered, and even before her murder was linked to the Ripper, Auntie stopped sending me the whole newspaper but just sent me the green sports section instead. But now that I was back in camp near York, I could buy my own local papers as well as the few nationals that carried the story, and continued to stash them in my locker in the barracks. I bought a small torch from Woolworths so that I could go through them under the bed covers at night when everyone else was asleep. It was the only time to get any privacy.

I read that Mrs Richardson, who was twenty-eight years old, had not been well after having her second child. She'd had two others already, both fostered out. She'd been suffering from severe post-natal depression when she disappeared from the family home, eventually turning up in Leeds with no money and desperately trying to find work. She'd applied for a job as a nanny and had been waiting to hear if she'd got it, but in the meantime was believed to have been working as a prostitute in the red-light area of Chapeltown, where she'd hung around, homeless and destitute. Around the park where she'd died, there were many posh flats where the police carried out their house-to-house enquiries, and I'd heard that Jimmy Saville lived there. It seemed strange to think that Irene had died penniless while all around her people were living their comfortable lives.

Like Mum's, Irene's family denied she'd ever been a prostitute. But the police weren't taking any chances and they put out warnings to women who worked on the streets to stay at home for their own safety.

As well as the many holes the beast had bored into Mum with a long-handled, cross-headed screwdriver, there'd been other vile injuries of a sexual nature, or at least contempt, that he'd inflicted on her too, but which thankfully Mr Hoban kept from the press. I realised the police probably weren't giving too much away to the public about Irene's injuries either, so that, as Mr Hoban had said, when they got a suspect in, only they and the real murderer would know certain details of the case. Nonetheless, the injuries reported in the press were horrific and word soon got round that Irene had been slashed and sliced through the stomach until the intestines spilled out, and her throat had been cut. What a hero; the Ripper was certainly living up to his name now. And, just two months later, he struck again.

Tina Atkinson was in her early thirties and separated from her husband and kids. She was a known call-girl in Manningham Lane, Bradford, and was said to take men back to her flat for those purposes. She had taken the killer back with her that fateful night when she'd been subjected to heavy blows around the head that had almost completely smashed her skull in and to a frenzied attack with a knife. And an impression of a size seven Dunlop boot mark had been found on her body. My stomach lurched when I read this. There was no doubt about this case; it was the same person who had killed Mum, including the boot mark found on her, where the animal had stamped on her thigh.

The Yorkshire Ripper was obviously a small, but giant coward of a man who'd probably taken advantage of Tina like he had of Mum's friendly and helpful nature. I always remembered what Keith had said when the police eventually told the family about Mum: 'she was a strong woman who could handle herself against any man,' he'd said. Keith believed she must either have known the killer and trusted him, or been trying to help him and was caught off guard. It was just a few years later, and now I was to find out how close this was to the truth.

I folded up the papers, crept over to my locker and put them away. Every day, I'd train as hard as I could and every evening after dinner, I'd be back to my old routine in the gym.

'You're no fun anymore, Jacko,' one of the lads complained.

'Why don't you come out tonight, have a laugh instead of getting yourself muscle bound like that?' Eddie said.

I shook my head; nothing could stop me. I was taking my gym stuff out of my locker when another soldier, seeing my pile of papers, casually helped himself to one right under my nose.

'Hey! What are you doing?' I yelled, going after him.

'What?' he looked surprised as I grabbed his sleeve. 'It's only a bit of old newspaper, mate!' Then, breaking free, he dropped the paper on the floor, and began blacking his boots on it. I felt my blood boil.

'Give us it back!' I shouted, as I made a grab for the newspaper and missed.

'Alright, mate, keep your hair on,' he said, shocked by my reaction. 'Here, it's all yours.' But as he handed it to me, he caught sight of the picture on the front, and snatched it back grinning. 'Hang about, isn't that you?'

It was a photo of me with Mum, Chris and Bubs one Christmas, that Dad or someone in the family must've given the press. The caption underneath read something like, 'murdered call-girl and family in happier times'.

I didn't want him to see it, but it was too late now.

'It is you!' he said. 'Your mum's one of them –'

Here it comes, I thought, *now they'll all know*, as the barrack room fell silent.

'– women killed by the Ripper,' he carried on. 'Soz, mate.' Then folding the paper up neatly, he handed it back.

It wasn't the reaction I'd been expecting and I was ready to take on anyone to defend Mum.

'You wanna make summat of it?' I squared up to him.

'Fight! Fight!' I could hear the others gathering round.

The soldier shook his head. 'No, I just wanna get me shoes polished,' he said, pushing past me.

I went after him, shoving him in the back, hoping he'd go for me so that I could let rip. 'She's not a prossie, OK?'

I'd never in my life had a fight, not even in the playground, and knew I'd get a real pasting but, even in the state I was in, I realised this was exactly what I was looking for. The soldier shrugged and ignored me and by now the others had lost interest and were walking away.

'Call yourself a soldier?' I yelled at him. 'You're yellow!' and pushed him again.

'Here, that do ya?' he said, punching me straight on the nose.

My nose exploded; blood spurted everywhere. I bathed my nose over the washbasin in the shower block and knew I'd have a couple of shiners in the morning. I went back to my locker, grabbed my kit and rushed out to the gym. My muscles were beginning to look over-sized for my frame.

Eddie was waiting for me when I came back to the barrack room that night.

'You look like you've gone ten rounds with Cassius Clay,' he said.

My eyes had already begun to close up.

'You better get some ice on them so it doesn't look so bad in the morning.'

I knew he was right. Sarge wasn't going to be too happy when he saw the state of me on parade. Eddie went down to the canteen and got a couple of bags of frozen peas from a mate working there; I put them across my eyes, and after a while, they began to look a little less swollen.

'That's going to have to do,' Eddie said, studying my face, 'but if we hurry, there's still time to get one in before last orders.'

We went down to the Pig and Duck in the next village; it was always quiet there as us squaddies were barred because of fights breaking out in the past. I turned up my collar as I went in behind Eddie, and sat at a table in a corner, hiding my face. I knew if the landlord saw the state of me, he'd realise we were from the barracks and we'd never get served here again.

Eddie came back from the bar with the Tetley's.

'Look, mate,' he said, 'everyone's got something they want to hide round here. Let's face it, most of 'em didn't join up because they wanted a career in th' Army!'

'I wasn't trying to keep it quiet, and I'm not ashamed,' I told him.

'Good, I'm glad to hear it,' Eddie said.

'Mum's not a dirty prossie like they're saying!'

'No one's saying it round here, mate; it's nowt out of the ordinary for some of these lads to have a mum on t' game, if they've got mothers at all.'

He took the wind out of my sails.

'Yeah, well I'm sick of hearing it everywhere – t' papers, on TV – it's all lies.'

'Don't read the papers and don't watch telly then,' he said, which seems obvious advice now but with the Ripper still at large, I just couldn't do it.

'Why do you keep all those old newspapers for anyway?' he asked.

I took a deep breath.

'I just need to know why.'

'Why?' Eddie looked at me.

That was the one question I'd kept asking myself over and again since it happened; *why* did he kill my mum of all people?

'She wouldn't hurt a fly,' I told him.

'There is no why,' Eddie said. 'It's like t' police said, he's just some nutter – a psycho – who needs putting down if you want my opinion!'

'I didn't even recognise it were me mum from what they said about her in the news. It's like each time they show a picture of her, they're talking about a complete stranger.'

'Look, mate, I should have a word with the welfare officer, take some time off, Army 'ud understand,' he suggested.

'Time?' Having time on my hands was the one thing I dreaded; time meant space and space meant thinking. And that's the last thing I wanted.

'What would I do wi' time?' I asked him.

'I think they call it grieving, mate.'

But I couldn't grieve and I knew I wouldn't be able to, not until they'd found the monster who'd killed Mum, and locked the bastard away forever. Until then my life was on hold.

22

By the summer of 1977, the unit had been sent back down to the West Country again, near Bristol, and we were busy putting up buntings in our new barracks for the Queen's Silver Jubilee.

On the one hand, I hoped that, being out of the West Yorkshire area, I could get away from the Ripper inquiry for a while, which, although it had reached some of the nationals, still obviously featured more frequently and in more detail in the local media. On the other, I didn't want to be away and miss any new development. It was a no-win situation.

No sooner had we settled in and I was on guard's duty at the barrier, when behind me on my transistor radio in the sentry box, I caught the tail end of a news report saying something about how 'the latest victim to die at the killer's hands was an innocent young woman this time . . .'

The checkpoint was noisy, with vehicles coming through and going out, and it was hard to hear what was being said, but I was certain I heard mention of Chapeltown in Leeds. And what other serial killers were there on the loose? But surely the animal couldn't have struck again, not so soon after the last murder? This was three in four months. If this was another Ripper killing, and God knows I hoped it wasn't, was he now trying to make up for lost time? And what did it mean an 'innocent victim this time'? Was Mum a guilty victim then? And the other ladies who'd died at his hands? Were they guilty too?

I knew some of the lads must have heard about the murder too, as when I went over to the canteen later, I could feel them glancing over at me from the bench tables as I collected my food from the servery. Suddenly I didn't feel hungry and went back to the barrack room and changed into my gym kit, but the gym was locked so I went for a run instead.

It was starting to rain and I had no idea where I was, but I carried on running. I ran for what must have been miles over muddy fields and fences and along paths and roadways. I'd been going for at least an hour when a car passed me, its headlights on full beam; then it dipped them and stopped a little way ahead of me. The rain was teeming down now and the driver, a middle-aged man with his wife sitting next to him, called back, 'Hop in, we'll drop you off somewhere!' I shook my head, and ran past the car. I was by now completely drenched and my clothes and hair were sticking to me. The driver looked at his wife, and drove on until they caught up with me, then crawled alongside me. The man's wife wound down the window. 'Are you sure you don't want a lift? You'll get pneumonia like that.'

I didn't feel able to speak to anyone and, putting on a spurt, ran ahead of them and diverted off across a track by a field. As I watched the car drive off and disappear into the night, I slumped down under an oak. I must have run for miles but was so fit by now with all my work-outs, I didn't need to catch my breath. I just needed to take in the news: the Ripper had struck again. Would there never be an end to it? I wanted to sob but I couldn't. I shivered instead.

I got up before dawn and slipped down to the newsagent's at the railway station, waiting by the vans that had come to collect the papers off the first train in. I bought all the nationals but when I looked at them, only a few of them, as I remember, were carrying the story. Yet here was this terrible murderer on the loose in the north of England.

The poor lass, Jayne MacDonald, was just sixteen and from Leeds. She lived just a few doors down from Mrs McCann, the Ripper's first victim, and I later learnt that Jayne had even given the police a description of the clothes Wilma was wearing the night she was killed as she had seen her going out. Now the poor lass was herself that animal's victim: murder victim number five.

Jayne was a shoe sales assistant in a supermarket in Leeds and had been for a night out at the Hofbrauhaus, a modern Bierkeller in the Merion Centre, in Leeds. I'd walked past there on occasion with Ian on our way to the Templar pub when they'd had an Oompah band on; people were spilling out of the Bierkeller onto the pavement laughing and singing; me and Ian had slapped our thighs and joined in.

Jayne had apparently met a young lad there that night who'd walked her home part of the way, but then had to go home himself. Jayne said she'd be alright as she made the rest of the journey on foot alone, passing by the shop where she worked on Roundhay Road, through Chapeltown. Her battered and mutilated body was found by three little children on a playground only yards from her home and her sleeping parents.

I remember thinking how sad and cruel it was that Jayne had ended up here, on the very same adventure playground she'd not long since been playing on herself. I had just turned nineteen two weeks before, while Jayne wasn't now going to get the chance to grow up.

When I got back, the lads were busy scrambling around getting ready for parade. I took my papers from under my jacket and put them beneath my bedcovers for further scrutiny later.

Eddie looked over at me, 'You OK?'

I nodded, 'Course – why wouldn't I be?'

'Yeah, well you better move it; we're on the parade ground in five.'

In truth, the only sleep I'd had that night was when I dropped off in the bath I ran myself when I got back from the run. I woke up some time later in freezing cold water, and was now exhausted, but at times like this I think I mostly got by on adrenaline.

That evening, in the mess, I saw Jayne's dad, Wilf MacDonald, a railway worker, giving an interview on television. He said he'd had to identify his daughter's mutilated body at the mortuary and he looked as grey and bewildered as Dad had done when Professor Gee had lifted the sheet. Mr MacDonald said he couldn't understand 'why anyone would do this to my daughter'. I pitied him and knew how this same question 'why' that I kept asking myself about Mum was going to haunt him too; but I also knew there was nothing anyone could do or say that would help him.

Because of what the police and the pathologist had told

us about the nature of Mum's injuries, most of which the police didn't release to the public, I also realised what other dreadful things might have happened to Jayne from what the police *weren't* now saying. At least I thought I did, but I later learnt he'd come up with some new and terrible trick. Although, as with Mum, he'd used a hammer and this hadn't been a sexual attack, he'd thrust a knife multiple times through the two deep stab wounds he had made on the body, among other vile things. However hard I trained, and however tough the cross-country runs I went on were, I couldn't get this out of my head and everything that had happened to Mum came flooding back in 'glorious Technicolor' as the man introducing the film on Sunday afternoon TV would sometimes say. I kept repeating *glorious Technicolor* over to myself in my head in an American accent for days after, just as I'd kept repeating *Mrs Irene Richardson, Ripper, mother of two*, before, as a wave of hysteria swept over me again.

Jayne was the first victim who was definitely not a 'good-time girl' or a prostitute, although the police believed she may have been mistaken as such as she took a short-cut home through a red-light area of Chapeltown. I realised then what the police meant by describing Jayne as an 'innocent' victim. Of course, Jayne was an innocent victim, poor lass, but weren't all the women? Even those who, unlike my Mum, *were* actually on the game.

The Assistant Chief Constable (ACC) (Crime) George Oldfield, who was now head of the Ripper inquiry, personally took over the inquiry into Jayne's death and, as with all the murders there'd been since Mum's, I just hoped and prayed he'd do something soon.

But there was a brutal attack on a woman in Bradford

the following month which was also believed to be the work of the Ripper. Fortunately, Maureen Long managed to escape with her life. Then, in October, there was another gruesome murder when he struck for the first time across the Pennines, in Manchester, where the body of twenty-year-old Jean Jordan was found in allotments by Southern Cemetery. By then, Mr Oldfield had issued a statement saying something like, 'we still have little evidence to go on' and 'it's not *if* the killer strikes again, but when and where'. I was bewildered. This was murder victim number six and there'd been other attacks: how many more victims before the police had enough to find this animal and nail him?

As well as trying to find out what was going on with the inquiry in the press and on TV, I think I started reading anything I could lay my hands on about the victims, to make them real people with real lives and families, like Mum was, rather than women who were just on the game, or lying dead in the morgue, or staring out from a tiny photo in the press or on TV – a photo that probably didn't look anything like them anyway. This was something I was to do for many years to come. I found out, for example, that Jean, like Wilma and Irene, was originally from Scotland, and was affectionately known to her mates as 'Scotch Jean'. Jean, who was said by friends to be quiet and shy, was a young single mum with two small children to care for, when she'd had the misfortune to stumble across the path of the Ripper – who really lived up to his name that night.

Jean's body had lain hidden in undergrowth on an allotment for a week until the Ripper came back and moved it to open ground so that his handiwork would be discovered in all its full glory. And not content with killing and mutilating the poor lass th' first time around, on his second visit he then defiled her again, taking a hacksaw to her in an attempt to decapitate her.

Detective Chief Superintendent Jack Ridgeway from Greater Manchester Police was assigned to the case. I later read that he was so sickened when he saw the body he said that in all his years in the force he'd never seen anything like it. The Ripper had torn out half the intestines, which he'd wrapped around her trunk, her head was part way cut off, and her body was so badly decomposed it was full of maggots. Poor Jean had to be identified by dental records in the end.

What a hero that animal the Ripper was – and what a tragic ending for a young woman described by her neighbours as a lovely lass who had only gone on the game after her marriage had broken down to try to get her home together and buy things for her kiddies. She'd recently told friends she was going to give up earning money this way as soon as she got on her feet, but sadly for Jean and her children, she never got that opportunity.

It started me thinking about Mum selling the car and sending Goldie away, and how she'd borrowed money from Auntie that last Christmas we'd been together – although she'd always made sure me, Chris and Bubs never went without. But Mum wouldn't go on the game, would she? The whole idea was ridiculous and I pushed it to the back of my mind.

23

On the few occasions I came home on leave, me and Grandad Woody would get the bus at the bottom of the Headrow and go to a rugby match in Hemsworth or make a trip to Morley to get his boiled sweets from a special stall on the market and some tripe for his Sunday night tea. More importantly, it gave Grandad the chance to get out, which he hardly ever did these days, since Mum had gone.

'Catch the fifty-one shall we, Grandad?' I asked him, as always. And, as always, he replied, 'Aye, that'll do 'eet,' while he shuffled uncomfortably, trying to avoid my eye, and I his, both wanting to get that bus for the same reason but neither of us wanting to talk about it.

There were other routes we could've taken but the fifty-one passed along the top road through Churwell, where, on a good day, you could just make out our old house at Back Green from the upper deck.

The bus pulled up and I helped Grandad on. Although he was frail now and the spark had gone from his eyes, he still never missed an opportunity to pull my leg.

'Ee, lad, you look like an escaped convict wi' that crew cut – you'll frighten all the lasses away,' he chortled as he made his way slowly up the stairs and sat himself by the window.

As soon as the bus set off, Grandad pulled a battered bag of aniseed twists from his pocket and offered me one. When he'd finished his sweet, he fell asleep for most of the journey. But the minute the bus passed the viaduct and headed up the hill towards Churwell, he'd suddenly stir and peer across in the direction of our old house. I'd lean back and look from behind him, both of us barely able to make out more than the hedge at the front, and neither of us saying a word as we struggled to take in all that had happened.

On the way back from Morley, we picked up some white chrysanths for Mum and stopped off at Cottingley to lay them on her grave. Mum hadn't yet got a head-stone and Auntie Tess had been round to ask Dad when he was going to get her one. Dad had sold the house in Churwell at a low price to get away from 'all the bad memories' as he called them, as soon as he could, and said he didn't have the money to buy one yet. He'd had to scrap the van when the police finally handed it back to him, and had used the little money he got for it to manage until he went back to work a few weeks later. The council had since given him a house in Bramley, where he was trying to get on his feet and had got Chris living back with him from Auntie's. Grandad was upset that Dad wouldn't let him pay for a headstone for his daughter, but Dad was a proud man and insisted he'd get one as soon as he could.

Wild flowers were growing among the tufts of grass on the grave; I remember thinking Mum would've liked that. When her plan to grow the vegetables had ended so disastrously, she'd left a patch on the allotment for the wild flowers to grow.

'Some weeds are better than real flowers and they're good for the butterflies,' she told me.

'Since when did you know about butterflies?' I eyed her suspiciously.

She broke into a grin. 'Well I've got to say summat haven't I, as weeds seem to be the only thing I can grow!'

Grandad stooped over Mum's grave and tugged at a patch of dandelions with his old gnarled hands; the root came away at once and I could smell the warm earth beneath it, as I had on the day of the funeral. A robin came over looking for worms in the dirt that Grandad had just disturbed. He hopped around us, coyly at first while getting our measure, then throwing back his head, let out a shrill call as if he was chastising us for not turning over more soil.

'Cheeky fella,' Grandad grinned as he watched the bird; then, stooping again, tugged at another clump of weeds. 'There you go, you rascal!' he said to the bird. But as he made a small heap of dandelions on the side for me to drop on the compost heap by the back of the cemetery, I noticed his face cloud over and knew he was thinking of Mum. We went over to Derek's plaque in the cremation area later, and tidied up his small piece of earth. Grandad split off some of the flowers on Mum's grave and placed them on Derek's.

Auntie Win and Tess came up when they could and tidied up the graves, but Win was getting on and Auntie Tess had her own family to look after, and with me away there wasn't anyone else who could do it. Except Dad, of course, but Dad said he found having Derek there and now Mum was too much for him; his heart was broken and he couldn't face coming back.

Now I was on my own on the number fifty-one, clutching flowers, and I remembered Grandad's words to me as I tried to get him to go out shortly after Mum had died:

'Nay, lad, don't grieve for me,' he said, 'when your own child goes before you like that, then happen it's time to go yourse'n.'

The sergeant had called me into his office almost as soon as I got back from leave. Auntie had gone round her Muriel's to borrow her phone to make a long-distance call to my barracks, and had left a message to say Grandad had passed away peacefully in his sleep last night. The sergeant gave me three days' leave to go home. It made me smile when he stamped my pass 'compassionate leave', as Grandad always used to call it 'passionate leave'.

'Isn't it time you were due some of that passionate leave, Neil lad?' he'd ask me, then wheeze as he laughed at his own joke.

Now, as I stood between Mum's sisters over Grandad's open grave in my uniform, I could just imagine what he'd be saying if he could see me: 'Look at ya' in that get up – England's last hope!' and rasp with laughter. Although, inwardly, I think he'd always been proud of me.

Auntie said they'd given the cause of his death some fancy medical name on his certificate but in reality we all knew he had died of a broken heart. And, in a way, I was glad he'd gone, because if such a thing were possible, he was now with Mum where he wanted to be.

After the funeral tea, Auntie Tess took me aside and said there was something she thought I should know.

'I've been wrestling with my conscience for some time now,' she said, 'and I've decided to tell you what I know as it might help you to come to terms with your mum's death. It's about your mum's trips to bingo,' she warned, 'but you're not going to like it.'

I wondered what she was could possibly say that would shock me after everything else that had happened. But when she did tell me, it was so ridiculous I started to grin.

'You've lost it Auntie,' I said, unable to be angry or even disappointed in her. 'Someone's been pulling your leg.'

But Auntie still looked serious.

'Neil lad, I've given it a lot of thought and I now accept it as true, and I think ,it's best if you did the same.'

Rather than going to bingo, Auntie told me, 'Your mum had been soliciting on the night she died.'

I waved Auntie away. 'Don't tell me any more,' I said, laughing at her. 'Mum would *never* do such a thing!'

In truth, I began to wonder if Auntie wasn't ill.

'It's the shock of Grandad dying,' I told her. 'You'll feel better in the morning.'

I'd overheard Auntie Tess telling Win at the tea just a few minutes earlier, that every time there was another Ripper murder, it was like going through what happened to Mum all over again. It brought me up sharp. All I'd done since I'd been away was to think about myself, but it made me realise that other people in the family were suffering just as much as me. Changing into my civvies, I decided to call round to see Dad at his new home in Bramley before I set off back to camp.

*

Although there hadn't been any rows between me and Dad, things had been strained between us when I left Churwell and I hadn't seen him since he'd moved, which was almost a year now. Despite this, I felt sorry for Dad, having to bring up Chris on his own and trying to start again in a new place, and I knew it must be difficult for him. But when I arrived at his new house, he seemed to have settled in.

'It's not so bad round here,' he said. 'I'm getting used to it now and I've got meself a new business partner.'

With Mum gone and me in the Army, Dad said he found it difficult to manage the business on his own and had recently brought Harry into it. Harry Renton was known in the trade as an honest man and a skilled roofer; he also had his own transport and did the books, so, just as with Mum, all Dad had to do was to turn up and do a good job, which he always did.

'Don't you think it would be fairer if you did the books, Dad, or at least gave Harry a hand with them – as he's got to drive everywhere?' I asked him.

'No,' Dad shook his head, 'Harry likes it that way; it suits us both.'

Many years later I was to find out the real reason why Dad preferred this arrangement, and the effect it had on my mother's life – and her death.

Dad asked me how the funeral had gone.

'Grandad had a sending-off that did him proud,' I told him.

But I didn't tell Dad I was relieved he hadn't turned up, which I feared he might, as Mum's sisters were fuming when they read the card on his flowers and realised they were from him.

'That's what I think of them!' Auntie Tess said, flinging them on the compost heap at the far end of the cemetery.

Dad seemed pleased to see me. 'We got your card,' he said. The postcard of Clifton Suspension Bridge I'd sent him and Chris when I'd first arrived at camp near Bristol was now propped up against the clock on the mantelpiece. He gave me all the news about Chris and how he was getting on at his new school, and what my little sister was up to at Auntie's.

As he was talking, I noticed the cushions on the settee had been plumped, and the backs on the armchairs were clean and ironed. Through the open door to the kitchen, I noticed a pot of fresh flowers on the windowsill. Dad never bothered about any of that when just me and him were living at Churwell.

'Dad?' I asked him, 'you expecting visitors?'

'No,' he said. 'I've met someone – she gives me a hand wi' the place from time to time.'

'What, you mean you've got a cleaner?' I didn't like the way this was headed.

'No,' Dad coughed nervously, 'not a cleaner; I'm courting again.'

Courting? I felt my jaw drop. I definitely didn't like the way this was going.

'I'm going out with a lady.'

'I know what courting means, Dad.'

'Her name's Betty; she's a widow; lives up th' road in Beeston.'

I couldn't take it in: Dad had a *girlfriend?* It was ridiculous.

'You'll like her,' Dad said. 'She's got three girls; I'll introduce you to her next time you're home.'

I remembered how Dad was with Mum one Boxing Day afternoon up at Wortley Working Men's Club just before we all set off for Auntie Win's for our annual get-together. Dad had nipped out the back and used the landlord's phone to call the public phone in the bar. When it rang, me and the barman took it in turns to pick it up. 'Call for Mrs Jackson,' we'd say. Mum rushed to the phone and there'd be no one there. After a couple of times, Mum worked it out and wagged her finger at us while Dad and the other customers burst into laughter. 'Emily love, you're priceless,' Dad said, slipping his arm round her waist. 'I'll never find another 'un like you!'

But now there was Betty. And, as nice as Betty might be, Dad had always been married to Mum, and I couldn't think of it any other way.

'Well, aren't you going to say summat?' Dad asked, with a coy smile on his face like a love-struck teenager; I'd seen that look on some of the younger lads in the barracks and suddenly I had a head full of steam.

'How could you, Dad?' I turned on him. 'How could you betray Mum's memory like that?'

He looked hurt.

'Well, I know there's some'll say it's too soon—'

'Too soon?' I scoffed. 'Mum's not yet cold in her grave!'

'It's been over a year.'

'That long? How *have* you managed?' I couldn't bite my tongue.

Dad stared at the floor a moment. 'Aye, well I don't expect you to understand, but life's lonely on your own when you get to my age.' Then, looking me straight in the eye he said, 'We all deserve to be happy, don't we?'

Happy? Had I heard that right? I wasn't even sure what it meant anymore and here was Dad talking about being happy like he was *entitled* to it.

Yes, I'd had a few moments of happiness when I'd had a laugh with the lads back at camp, or when Auntie Win and Grandad Woody had the occasional barney over him leaving his bag of boiled sweets in his trousers for the wash – but happy? It wasn't even something I thought about, never mind believed I 'deserved'– not since Mum had gone in the way that she had. Was he *mad*?

'Mum's dead,' I raged at him. 'Murdered! Don't you get it!'

'Oh, I get it alright,' Dad said. 'It's you that doesn't! Life moves on! You surely didn't expect me to become a hermit for the rest of my life?'

I walked out, slamming the door behind me, without looking back.

I caught the bus back to the railway station. There was a heavy police presence in the area, causing the traffic to come to a halt by a road-block just short of City Square. I knew if I waited any longer I'd miss my train back to camp and risk a night in the glasshouse, so I hopped off the bus and took the back way to the station. The waste ground to the side was used by commuters leaving their cars for the day, and a group of police officers were taking down the registration numbers of the vehicles parked up there. The endless hunt for the Ripper seemed to bring me out in another attack of hysteria for, as I stopped to watch them, I began to wonder what a group of police officers might be called. Like the *gaggle* of geese Mum had once

said she wanted on her smallholding or the *school* of fish
that had swum silently past me and Derek as we'd paddled
in Churwell beck that first summer. Would this group of
officers in front of me, all busy with their pens and pocket-
books, be called a *team* of policemen? A *unit*? A *plod*? I
laughed hysterically; what was the matter with me?

Whatever they were called, at least the local bobbies
were trying to do something to find the killer, but what
was taking those higher up the chain of command so long?
Mr Hoban had promised to find the bastard responsible,
and I believe he might've stood a chance if he hadn't been
packed off to Bradford. Mr Hoban was undoubtedly flamboyant in his style of dress and his car, and he was brave.
And I'd since learned that as well as defusing the bomb in
Woolworths on a busy Saturday afternoon with nothing
more than a fire hose beside him in case the whole thing
went up, he had a reputation as a detective who 'always
got his man'. He'd solved every murder he'd worked on
and I liked to think he'd done it properly, even though he'd
been the first to say Mum was a prostitute. I couldn't
understand why they'd taken him off the case a few months
after Mum's murder, but then I didn't know at that time
how such things as clashes of ego and the internal politics
of an organisation worked.

As I started off again for the station, I bumped straight
into a couple of officers coming from the opposite direction. I think they must have seen me laughing and wanted
to know what I was doing here.

'What's your name, son? Where are you travelling to?
Where have you been?' And so on. Wanting to get away
before we were joined by the plod of policemen that were

now approaching from the stationary cars behind us, I blurted out, 'I'm Neil Jackson. That's my Mum!' pointing to the second picture in a line-up of six on the clipboard he was carrying.

'Em'ly Jackson?' he said. 'You taking the Michael out of me?'

'No, officer,' I said. 'I've been stopped and asked that question so many times now, I've lost count.'

I was now aware that the other officers were standing behind me and eyeing me up suspiciously. Once more, I don't know what got into me but, grabbing the clipboard from the officer's hand, I turned to the others and addressing them directly said, 'In case any of you missed what I just said, *that* is my mother.' I pointed to the picture of Mum. 'And she is *not* a prostitute!' *And Dad*, I thought to myself, *is already forgetting about her*.

Very quickly, the police realised I was telling the truth and, expressing their sympathies, let me go. I can honestly say that there wasn't one police officer, uniformed or plain-clothes, who didn't treat me well during the inquiry, although because of the state I was in, I may not always have been pleasant to them.

As the train pulled out of Leeds station, I sat back in my seat and closed my eyes. Grandad had gone, Dad had a new girlfriend, and Auntie had told me something so ridiculous I hadn't once thought about raising it when I was rowing with Dad.

24

The Duke of Wellington's moved back to our own barracks at York in the autumn and there was a buzz going round that we were about to be sent on our first spell abroad, to Minden in northern Germany. A lot of the older lads had told me about it there; I hadn't been to Germany before and couldn't wait to go. Apparently it was a city with mediaeval buildings on the river Weser; a picture postcard sort of place with a famous market square and lots of bars, though near nowhere I'd ever heard of. The funny thing was, I'd only joined up to get away from home; never in my wildest dreams had I thought about being a soldier. But as time had gone on I found I really enjoyed the life; it suited me and I decided that when my four years were up, I wanted to stay and make a proper career of it.

Over the next few weeks we were busy getting prepared to go abroad when Dad suddenly contacted me out of the blue. I was taken aback by this; not just because of the row we'd had the last time I was home, but because he'd never been a letter writer for as long as I could remember, and had certainly never replied to any I'd written him in all the months I'd been away. In truth, I didn't even know what his handwriting was like, and when I was away in Benfleet it was Mum who wrote. But now I'd got a letter with a Bramley postmark on it and knew it could only be from him. Despite the bad feeling between us, I was chuffed to hear from him.

But if I was surprised to receive a letter from Dad, I was shocked when I read its contents. In spite of the bitter words between us, Dad wanted me to go home to live with him and was actually offering to buy me out of the Army. He said he was worried about Chris, who was now twelve; he was worried he was getting to that age where lads some-times get in with the wrong set and go off the rails. Even though Chris had always been a good kid, if a live wire and full of cheek, Dad was especially worried about him with what had happened to Mum. So he thought, me being Chris's big brother, it would be a good idea if I came home to keep an eye on him. On the one hand it made good sense – but on the other, I was now intent on making a career for myself in the Army.

I don't know what Chris and Bubs went through losing Mum like that and at such a young age, but can only imagine it must have been terrible. Since the family had split up on that fateful day, I'd managed to see my little brother and sister at the occasional family get-together, and I'm sure Auntie and Uncle in Farnsley would've broken the news to them in the best way they could and tried to protect them from what was now constantly in the news. That, however, didn't alter the facts of Mum's death or the lies that constantly appeared everywhere about her, and I realised that as time went on, and with the Ripper still at large, Chris and Bubs were certain to find out more about the circumstances and details of Mum's murder for themselves. And that didn't bear thinking about.

What I hadn't bargained on was other kids hearing about

it on the news or overhearing adults talk about the children newly moved into the area, whose mum had tragically died, and them putting two and two together, which, of course, was bound to happen. In fact, Dad told me it had all long since got back to Chris, and that he'd taken a lot of stick about it at school but had quickly learnt to stick up for himself. Poor Chris; no kid who'd been through what he had should have to put up with that. I knew from my own school days that children could be cruel, and felt guilty that I hadn't been there to look out for him or Bubs like my big brother Derek had for me.

I felt torn when I heard about this: of course I wanted to go home and be with Chris and, despite the seven-year age difference between us, we'd always got on well and I missed him. But I also wanted to stay in the Army and work my way up to Corporal and then Sergeant.

'But what would you do in Civvy Street?' Eddie asked me, when I told him about my dilemma.

'Go back to roofing,' I replied, 'that's what I'm trained in after all.' Although, in truth, I knew the much-talked-about recession in the building industry had finally arrived, and that going back to roofing was going to be difficult.

'It seems daft to me, that, when you've got a good career here,' Eddie pressed on. 'And you never know your luck, they might even make you up to Corporal one of these days!' he grinned, shoving the recently acquired stripes on his shoulder in my face.

'Yeah, well, some things are more important than career,' I replied, trying to convince myself that if I did go home, I'd be doing the right thing.

*

A few days later, our unit was sent out on night manoeu-
vres on the north Yorkshire Moors. Me and some of the
lads finished early and as soon as we got back, went off
to the mess for a pint until the canteen opened. I hadn't
eaten much that day and as soon as I'd sunk a couple of
pints of Tetley they very quickly went to my head. Then,
on the TV in the corner, I caught sight of a programme
about the Ripper. It included a clip of Jayne MacDonald's
father talking soon after her murder. The poor man looked
sick and broken as he said, 'He has murdered our whole
family you could say.'

I sobered up in seconds. That's exactly what he'd done
to my family too: Grandad had died; Mum's family no
longer spoke to Dad; I was here; and Chris and Angie had
been split up.

No, I told myself later that night, *the Ripper might've
killed Mum, but I'm not about to let him rip our family
apart as well. The Jacksons belong together and if Chris
is coming home, there is every chance Bubs will do too and
we'll be reunited again.*

That winter, I signed on the dotted line and was relieved
of all duties; my career in the Army was over. Returning
back to the barrack room with my papers and rail pass, I
found Eddie sprawled on my bed.

'So, this is it then?' he said, buffing the buttons on his
uniform, as he watched me clear the contents of my locker
into my battered Army hold-all.

'Looks like it,' I shrugged, as I tried to stuff all my
clothes and personal belongings into my bag with my collection of newspapers, failing to get it all in.

'Yeah, well, I'll be looking you up when I'm home on leave; you won't be getting away from us that easy!' he laughed, then shook my hand. 'Good luck, mate.'

Eddie and the lads had given me a good send-off the night before and even though I'd only been in for eighteen months, we'd grown up together in that time and I knew, for my part, that I'd miss the camaraderie and the mates I'd made there. After the set-to in the barrack room that night when the other private had taken my newspaper, no one had made any comments about Mum and had just accepted me for myself. As time went on, I realised Eddie was right in what he said – quite a few of them did have problems in their lives too and, while some were orphans, quite a few had been in care. I started to realise I was one of the lucky ones. I'd had my mum up until I was seventeen and I still had my dad and my family – although I didn't know then that it wouldn't be for much longer.

'Here, have these.' I threw my torch and aftershave to Eddie then, bashing the papers down, I pulled the drawstring tight at the top, and was homeward bound! Since I'd made my decision to leave, I was looking forward to going home and being with the family again – our first Christmas together since Mum had died. Although it wasn't quite the homecoming I expected.

25

I stepped off the train and walked through the centre of Leeds, where the Salvation Army were playing 'Once in Royal David's City' in City Square. City Hall was lit up with a string of red and white lights, and there were lights the length and breadth of the Headrow, right down to the bus station, and across the Merrion centre on one side and Schofields on the other.

I'd almost forgotten how few days were actually left before Christmas until I saw busy shoppers bustling past, loaded down with parcels and rolls of wrapping paper, and stopped off at Lewis's to pick up some presents for the family.

If, despite all the tinsel and baubles everywhere, I'd forgotten how soon Christmas would be upon us, it was impossible to forget the inquiry. Even if you failed to notice the increase in street patrols, house-to-house enquiries and the posters appealing for information on walls and in shop windows, you couldn't miss the climate of fear that suddenly struck at the heart of the city each evening as it began to get dark. Since the murder of shop assistant Jayne MacDonald, in the summer, women and girls in the city often went around in groups together or were chaperoned or simply disappeared from the streets altogether after dark. The feeling was that if he'd mistaken sixteen-year-old Jayne for a prostitute, there was every chance he could do it again – if he wasn't going after just any woman now.

But despite this, and the heavy police presence in the city, particularly in the red light areas, the Ripper decided to show the people of Leeds he could still carry on with his bloody business as usual, striking again just days before Christmas. This time the attack took place behind a disused factory used by prostitutes in the Chapeltown area. The attack with a hammer was so brutal and so vicious that it was nothing short of a miracle that twenty-five-year-old Marilyn Moore managed to survive. The next young woman, however, was not to be so lucky.

It was good to see Chris again too; he looked like he'd grown another foot and was nearly overtaking me.

'I can see you're going to take after Dad,' I said to him, as Dad was six foot six and Chris was headed that way.

'We'll be able to run the England flag up him now!' Dad laughed.

I hadn't seen Chris for a while but noticed he'd changed. As well as being tall for his age, with his dark hair and striking features, he was fast turning into a kind of boy who Mum used to say would be a right heartbreaker when they grew up.

I realised the Action Man I'd bought him for Christmas wasn't going to do now, and so I promised to buy him something more suitable after Christmas.

'Can I have a Chopper bike,' he asked, 'in tango?'

'I'm not sure me severance pay will run to that,' I said, 'but we could get you a new football and some keeper's gloves and go up the park for a kick around.'

His face dropped; he wasn't too impressed.

'Tell you what, we can go up Elland Road beforehand and see a game, if you like?'

Chris nodded and snuggled under the bedcovers. Most nights I popped in to see him before he went to sleep and we'd get talking a bit. It was usually about sport and United, and pop bands, and girls at his school, but we never once spoke about Mum. Not even acknowledging she was no longer with us. I think we both avoided it in the same way that me and Grandad avoided mentioning the house at Churwell as we passed it on the bus, both painfully aware it was always there between us, but just so big and so awful it was impossible to talk about.

I was happy being home again with Dad and Chris, and asked Dad when my sister would be joining us, so we'd be a family again. Dad shook his head.

'It's best lass stays where she is; she's settled with Auntie,' he said.

'Well yes, but she was settled with Mum,' I said, 'she can settle again.'

'Look, I'm telling you, she's alright as she is – no more upheavals,' he said, refusing to hear any more about it.

I couldn't believe he was dismissing it like that.

'But don't you see, Dad, if you let t' Ripper split us up permanently then he's won?'

'It's too late for that,' Dad said, 'he already has.'

I was bitterly disappointed that Dad had given up so easily, and wrapped up Bubs' present and decided to take it over to Farnsley that afternoon.

As I stood across the road from Auntie's, wondering if I shouldn't have rung first to let her know I was coming to see Bubs, the front door opened and my little sister stepped out. Like Chris, Bubs had grown a few more inches since I'd last seen her, and now looked quite the young lady. I was about to go over to her when Auntie and Uncle came out of the house and, taking a hand each, Bubs skipped along in between them, smiling and happy.

I stopped in my tracks and shrank back, hoping they wouldn't see me. They crossed over and went off up the street in the opposite direction. Dad was right; my sister was happy and it wouldn't be right to unsettle her again, not after everything that had happened.

I dropped the present in the waste bin and went back the way I'd come, passing a sign daubed in gloss paint on the street corner which read, 'Hang the Ripper', in large red letters. But hanging was quick and painless and too good for the bastard who had split up my family.

Over the years there'd been other attacks and murders of women in the Leeds and Bradford areas, and further afield, which were included in and then ruled out of the Ripper series, or the other way around. Quite often, after the initial report, you didn't hear much about the attacks again, but this evening as I watched the news while Chris was asleep, I found the bastard had done it again. This time he'd taken the life of an eighteen-year-old lass, Helen Rykta, in Huddersfield.

When I read about it later I found out that Helen had been brought up in care for most of her life, where she'd been shuffled from pillar to post never finding a loving, permanent home. When she left care, she shared a spartan bedsit with her twin sister in Huddersfield. Helen had dreamed of being famous and in a girl band with her sister, but ended up dead under a pile of rotting timber in a wood yard instead.

Her new life with her sister was ended when the Ripper decided to change his area of bloody operations. With four murders in Leeds and another down the road in Bradford, the monster had no doubt done this in order to avoid being caught in the police operations going on there, and had since travelled across to Manchester and now Huddersfield.

Helen had lost her job at a sweet factory shortly before her savage murder and had joined her identical twin on the streets only a few days before she was attacked. The police said that because she was, 'new to it, she was naïve, that's how she was caught'. I couldn't believe it: these were the exact same words the police had said to Auntie about Mum soon after she'd been killed.

I think I was in shock as I sat in the darkness in front of the television as I had no idea what was on the screen for the rest of the night. Dad had gone round to see Betty, and I barely noticed him coming in later that night.

'Got a power failure?' he asked, switching on the table lamp.

I didn't reply but watched as he took off his cap, then emptied the loose change from his pockets onto the coffee table.

'You heard the news?' I managed to mumble.

He nodded, then hung up his coat on the hook on the back door.

'How's your brother?' he asked, as sat in the armchair opposite.

'Asleep.'

Dad nodded, then he pulled the coffee table and the money towards him. As I watched him, I thought back to Grandad's funeral when Auntie Tess had taken me aside and, as she put it, tried to put me out of my misery. 'It's about your mum and her trips to bingo. But you're not going to like it,' she'd said.

She told me the police had come round her house after Mum's death to try to explain things – that they'd received information from call-girls who regularly worked the patch around the Gaiety. They had seen Mum working there for the past three weeks after Christmas.

Tess said she and Auntie Win hadn't wanted to believe it either, and had made some investigations of their own. They'd discovered the business was in trouble and about to go bust, and there were other big bills that Mum and Dad couldn't pay.

'The truth of the matter was,' Auntie told me, 'your mum had turned to prostitution to try to pay them off and save the business.'

When I'd laughed at Auntie Tess that day, Win had come over and tried to soften the blow; she said Mum had always wanted to give us kids a good life after our Derek had died, but she and Dad had been spending beyond their means until it finally caught up with them.

When I thought it through, I began to realise that while business had been good, there'd also been long periods where we'd have to sit around waiting for a gale to do some damage or for the rain to stop so we could get to work again.

On the other hand, Mum and Dad had always been resourceful. Mum had the fruit and veg round, which brought her in some pin money, while there was always the odd perk in the roofing trade. One year, me and Dad been asked to remove six tons of lead from the Leeds Dispensary roof in North Street and felt it over. The owner didn't care what we did with the lead as long as we removed it. Dad couldn't believe his luck and stashed it in the garage. Mum complained she had nowhere to store her fruit and veg as Dad waited for the price of lead to go up. The minute the price went up, Dad sold it and made enough to take us on holiday and keep us going handsomely through the next rough patch.

'Mum didn't have to go on the streets then,' I'd practically laughed in Auntie's face.

In the back of my mind, though, I knew that if Auntie believed this, then it was probably true, as she'd always strongly defended Mum against what she called 'the lies' about Mum being on the game.

And I remembered how Mum had looked like she'd seen a ghost when she saw Wilma's death on the television news that night. Perhaps Gwen was right when she asked Mum if she'd known Wilma, as according to everything I'd read since, they went to the same places around the red-light district in Roundhay Road.

Then I thought, if Mum was doing this on the streets while Dad was in the pub, what was his part in all this? Auntie Win had scoffed at the mention of his name since Mum's death. 'If he were on fire, I'd pour petrol over him,' now I remembered it was her saying that at Grandad's birthday party; it was quite clear what she thought his involvement was.

Despite this, for two years now, another question had

been eating away at me. And I suddenly realised I hadn't asked Dad about it before as I was too afraid of what his reply might be. But now, as I watched him separating his silver from his coppers, I couldn't wait a moment longer.

'Dad?'

He looked up.

'What *were* Mum doing up at Chapeltown on her own that night?' I asked him.

Dad looked thoughtful for a moment, then started counting his coppers, putting them into neat piles on the coffee table in front of him.

'Were she doing her veg round?' I carried on, but he still didn't answer me.

'Dad! I need to know!'

I was desperate for him to say, 'Yes' – willing him to say it – but he just kept on stacking up his coins into ever taller piles.

I always knew Dad had a fondness for money; I think it stemmed from his impoverished childhood. He watched every last penny and didn't like Mum doing favours for anyone, making sure she charged for the veg and the eggs rather than give anything spare away. And then it struck me like a slap in the face that while Mum had worked her fingers to the bone, Dad had been happy for her to do it – the fruit and veg round, the animals, the business, us kids – Mum did it all. But I'd never once heard him say, 'Sit down, love, take it easy,' like my friend Ian's dad did, or 'Go and treat yourself to something nice.'

When Mum had asked me to babysit while she went to 'bingo', Dad had practically bribed me to stay at home. 'She'll give you some of her winnings,' he said, giving Mum a look. Suddenly the mist was beginning to clear: Dad had been only too happy to escort Mum to her new part-time job and even pressed some of her earnings on to me each week.

I looked over at Dad; he was counting his silver now.

'You knew, didn't you, Dad? You knew what Mum were doing, but you didn't try to stop her!' I blurted out.

I saw Dad flinch, but he didn't reply.

'How could you, Dad? How could you! You should've been looking after her, she were your wife!'

'Leave it, it's past now,' he said, and then went back to counting his cash.

But I'd waited this long, I wasn't going to stop now.

'Past for you maybe, with your new life and your girl-friend! But not for me and Chris and Bubs, it's not!'

'I'm telling you to leave it!' he said, looking up from the cash. 'There's things between your mum and me, things you wouldn't understand!'

'I understand I'd rather have me mum here than all this!' I said, slamming my fist down on the top of the latest, largest colour TV that Mum had bought before she died.

I could hardly believe that the dad I admired, the dad I looked up to and wanted to be like, had been taking Mum out to pick up men while I babysat Chris and Bubs.

'I thought I had a magical childhood! The perfect family!' I yelled at him. 'The Ripper may have taken me mum, but *you've* robbed me of everything else!'

'Nothing's perfect,' he said, then lost where he was up to and had to start counting his ten pences again.

'Perfect? Perfect doesn't even come close!' I spat the words out.

'I said let it be!' I could see he was fuming now.

'What? Like you did, you mean? Your wife were on t' game but you enjoyed living off the proceeds, so you didn't complain! In fact, you even went with her and waited while she did it! You've got blood on your hands, Dad!'

Dad's face went white as a sheet but he didn't reply.

'What's the matter? Can't bear to hear the truth?' I said, goading him.

'The truth? Oh aye, I'll tell you the truth,' he said, suddenly exploding in rage. 'You thought you could just run away the moment things got tough, and then come back here and change things to how they used to be when your mum were alive! Well you can't, and no amount of raking up t' past or blaming anyone is going to make that happen! While you've been away, me and Chris and Bubs have had t' face up to what happened every single day of our lives – and still try to get on as normal! But as you're obviously not willing to do 'same, then you can pack up your stuff and get out!'

I was stunned.

'But you asked me to leave the Army.'

'You can see the week out,' he said, as he started scraping the coins into a bowl.

'See the week out?' I couldn't believe he could be so casual about it. 'Don't worry, Dad, I've got no intention of staying here a moment longer!'

There was not a chance in hell I could ever live under the same roof as Dad now I'd found this out. I kicked the coffee table in my anger; my foot caught beneath it, up-ending it. All the coins Dad had been counting flew up into the air, before cascading like a fountain down onto the floor.

I went upstairs and packed my bag, trying not to wake Chris in the next room. Dad was scrabbling around on the floor, picking up the coins and putting them in a bowl when I came back down. Stepping over the money on my way out, I suddenly knew what it felt like to be 'betrayed', as they said in the boys' comics like the *Victor* and *Valiant* that me and Derek used to deliver for Mr White; but worse than my feelings towards Dad was the confusion I felt towards Mum. The bitterest pill I had to swallow was that the Ripper hadn't torn our family apart as I'd believed; his terrible deeds had instead exposed a shocking secret in our family that made me question everything about my past and, worse, left me disappointed in Mum.

26

'Filled? Well what about in the future?' I asked the voice on the other end of the phone, but the phone line was burring, already dead.

I crossed out the last job circled in red on the 'sits vac' page of the paper and left the phone box.

A year had passed since I'd left Dad's; I was living in a bedsit in Leeds, and still trying to find work. It was the winter of 1978-79, or the 'Winter of Discontent' as it became known, and the bin-men, railway workers and others were taking industrial action across the country. The country was headed into a major recession, and things had been bad in the building trade for quite some time now.

I was going for any job I might have been able to do – from bottle washer to labourer – anything. I wasn't proud, I just wanted a job like all the rest in the queue behind me, but the answer was always the same: the job had gone and they'd got a list of others ready to fill the next vacancy as soon as it came up. I screwed up the sheet of newspaper and chucked it into the overflowing bin outside the phone box. Then, remembering what was on the other side of the page, I fished it out again. Smoothing the page out against my coat, I folded it up and shoved it into my pocket to add to my collection at home.

*

They'd been two more Ripper murders in 1978 and the Ripper had now become known as 'The Yorkshire Ripper'. Despite this, while one of the murders was in Bradford, the other was across the Pennines, when he struck in Manchester again. No doubt the Ripper bastard was still feeling the heat in Leeds, coward that he was. Yvonne Pearson was actually killed before Helen Rykta in Huddersfield, but her body had lain undiscovered for several weeks before it was found. There was a picture of Yvonne in one of the papers, with a small photo of my mum above it in the victim line-up; but it still wasn't Mum.

Yvonne had lived in a back-to-back in Bradford with her two small children. The press reported she had convictions for prostitution and, once more, she had been killed in a red-light area where she worked. Yvonne was a twenty-one-year-old single mum who liked to keep her house clean and her children 'just so', working on the streets when she had to in order to earn money for them. The neighbours said she lived for her children and as soon as she'd gone missing, they knew something dreadful was wrong. Yvonne's body was found under an old settee on some waste land; horsehair protruding from the settee had been stuffed into her mouth and throat, and her skull was shattered into tiny pieces.

At first, the police weren't sure it was an attack by that animal as the injuries were different to those made by his trademark hammer, but later they changed their opinion. The killer had been back and moved Yvonne's body to make it more visible so that his handiwork would once more be discovered, just as he'd done with Helen Rykta and Jean Jordan earlier. He'd also put a copy of the *Daily*

Mirror, dated 21 February 1978, under Yvonne's hand, as if to show the police how clever he was, knowing a post mortem would date her death the month before.

A special Ripper Squad was set up at Millgarth police station in Leeds, where me and Dad had been questioned after Mum's death over two years ago now. I couldn't even read the name of it in the paper without my stomach turning over. A dozen or so top detectives were assigned to the squad to bring the killer to justice, but shortly after, in May 1978, and as if to rub their faces in it, he struck again.

'Normally a murder victim knows their attacker, often it's someone in the family and there is an obvious motive,' I remembered Mr Hoban saying. 'But serial killers choose their victim like prey,' he'd said.

This time his quarry was Vera Milward, a forty-two-year-old, who was found brutally murdered on some waste land within the grounds of the Manchester Royal Infirmary, where prostitutes were known to take their clients. Vera was murder victim number nine.

Detective Chief Superintendent Jack Ridgeway, who was still investigating Scotch Jean's murder, came down to see the body. No doubt when he saw poor Vera's intestines protruding from a huge slash across her stomach and the massive blows to the back of her head, he knew immediately it was the work of that animal again. Although 'animal' was too good a term to use for him because most animals killed out of necessity, to eat, whereas he seemed to have something to prove, or so it was beginning to seem to me.

I couldn't help wondering whether, if the tabloids hadn't used the word Ripper, as they had for the first time when Mum was killed, maybe he wouldn't have started trying to live up to his name, like that of the Victorian murderer who ripped apart prostitutes in East End of London. But then, of course, he would still have killed, as he obviously got some kind of perverted pleasure from it before he inflicted the horrible injuries that he did.

Vera was an older victim, the same age as Mum when she died. Although Mum was the only victim to have a husband at home, Vera lived with a partner and their two small children; she also had another five older children who were either grown up or no longer living with her.

Vera had come to Britain from Spain after the war, looking for work. With no family here to help when she fell on hard times, she also turned to prostitution, which she had convictions for but had given up later in life. I read that Vera had always been very poorly and slipped out that night telling her partner she was going to get some medicine from the hospital pharmacy for her stomach problems. Her partner had no idea she still picked up men on the very occasional basis if the family needed the money.

Her partner was stunned by Vera's death. He said the killer had ruined his life and that seeing her in the mortuary had broken his heart. I knew what he meant; the Ripper had broken many hearts and ruined many lives. Not least, all the children like Chris and Bubs who had lost their mums at his hands. I'd lost count of how many when the number got into the mid-twenties, and wondered how Mrs McCann's children were getting on – the four little ones Mum had worried about when she saw them on television after their mum's death. I wondered what all the little children had been told when their mums didn't come home again, and if whoever told them had managed to say something better than 'summat's happened' as I had when Bubs asked me where Mum was.

It was obvious, like the police had said earlier on, this monster had a deep-seated hatred of women he regarded as prostitutes – whether this was women with convictions for it, 'good-time girls', 'women of loose morals' or any woman who had the audacity to make their way home alone in the dark at night. His twisted view of women, and his killing for pleasure, seemed to be his only motives to me. I'd heard rumours that Mr Hoban, before taking over at Bradford, had gone to all the doctors in Leeds and asked them if they had a patient that could've been so ill as to do these terrible murders, but had drawn a blank. But someone must know him, whether a doctor, a friend or a mother. Whoever he was, he was a psycho who needed to be caught before he caused suffering to another family. Yet despite the now lengthy police inquiry, constant appeals for information and the reward to help 'Catch the Ripper' going up from £10,000 to £20,000 as the press chipped in, still no arrests were made that I heard of.

If Mr Hoban, who was well known for catching murderers on his patch, thought the killer was local and probably a lorry driver or engineer, then that was good enough for me. I hoped that the new head of the Ripper inquiry, George Oldfield, who'd taken over in 1977, was making sure his officers kept an eye out for this type of person, but if he wanted advice from Detective Chief Superintendent Dennis Hoban now, he was too late as, by the spring of 1978, Mr Hoban had died.

It was rumoured Mr Hoban had always been in poor health with diabetes when he sadly suffered a heart attack.

I'd missed Mr Hoban's actual service that day but remembered the respect he'd shown Mum, and was glad to see on the news that night that many people had turned out to pay their last respects. All the great and the good turned up to his funeral and the streets were lined with officers in plain clothes and uniform all the way to the crematorium. Many mourners had to stand outside the crematorium chapel as there wasn't enough room inside for them, and they listened to his service over the tannoy system. Even the crims came out to see him off, taking out an ad in the Hatched, Matched and Dispatched column in the *Yorkshire Post*, to 'the copper they were proud to be nicked by'.

I was surprised when a mutual friend in the roofing trade passed on a message from Dad, inviting me to his wedding. Soon after our row, I'd heard Dad had given up the house in Bramley and he and Chris had moved in with Betty. Now Dad and Betty were tying the knot. I thought about it long and hard, and despite everything that had passed between us, decided to go. He was my dad after all; he'd brought me up and he'd taught me roofing, but more than anything, I'd always carried around in my head this picture of him nailing up the back door in his grief after our Derek had died. And I hoped me and Dad could find some way of at least having a relationship from a distance, even if we could never be properly reconciled again.

Dad and Betty got married at Leeds Registry Office with a reception afterwards at Craven Gate pub. It was a small family 'do' with a just handful of relatives on either side, including Betty's girls and Chris, Bubs and me. Dad was the life and soul of the party at the 'do' and spoke to me as if there'd been no bad blood between us, but, in reality I knew things could never be the same again and by the end of the evening, he made it quite clear I had my own life now and he had his.

That said, and despite my earlier resentment of him getting together with Betty so soon after Mum died, they were obviously happy and I was pleased for them both. Although I couldn't help thinking, as I walked back to my bedsit that night, they wouldn't be together if it wasn't for that evil bastard. I left my phone number for Chris and Bubs with Dad and hoped to see them again soon, not least to have that kick around up the park I'd promised Chris and to catch up with Bubs.

By the time I'd gone down to Albion Street, my head was full of the Ripper and I was beginning to feel ill. Although I was nowhere near the abattoir, I thought I heard pigs squealing as they went to their death. Rumours were always circulating about what the police were up to, to find the killer. In a close-knit city such as Leeds, there was always your girlfriend's dad who was a policeman at Millgarth or a mate's sister who was a typist on the inquiry, and I'd heard a rumour that with pig's flesh being similar to human's, the police had hired a butcher's somewhere and were bludgeoning and stabbing some poor pigs to death with various instruments to identify the weapons the evil bastard was using on his victims. I just hoped that, like Mum, the poor animals hadn't survived the first blow.

Much later I heard that the Ripper's weapons of choice were a ball-pein hammer, knives and a long-handled, sharpened Philip's screwdriver, which he'd used on Mum, and a hacksaw. Thankfully, though, he hadn't raped the victims, but I didn't want to think about that. As I carried on down the road, I noticed a mobile police unit displaying small black and white pictures of all the victims with a phone number to ring beneath. I almost waved to Mum in a moment of hysteria, but quickly put my hand back in my pocket. I had to get a grip.

When we'd lost Derek, I'd see him everywhere I went – or, at least, think I did – in a crowd, out shopping, or just walking to catch the school bus. Then I'd catch the boy up and realise of course it wasn't Derek; it couldn't be. But since Mum had gone, I really did see her everywhere I went – or at least her picture. And I think it was making me ill.

Despite the thousands more man hours spent on the inquiry, and the heavy presence of officers in Leeds and Bradford, or probably because of it, the killer once again looked for his next victim where he had less chance of being caught.

In the spring of 1979 he drove to Halifax, where he ended the life of a young clerk called Josephine Whitaker who lived with her mum and step-dad in a nice area of the town. It was said that Jo, as she preferred to be called, had a row with her teacher mum that night and had gone off to see her grandparents, not least to show them the new watch she'd recently bought. The Ripper had attacked her as she took a shortcut across a park on her way home. He was obviously changing his tactics, as this was, to my knowledge, the first attack outside a red-light area.

Jo had been killed on a football pitch, and I couldn't help thinking how Mum's brother, Uncle Smiler, had died on a football pitch too – but at least he was doing what he loved best. Not poor Jo. Her young brother had seen her pitiful, mutilated body lying there surrounded by police as he went out in the morning to do his paper round. He'd run back home and told his parents. The distress this must have caused was unimaginable, and I hated the bastard Ripper.

Eddie was on leave at the time of Jo's murder and came round to see me and told me about the lads' tour of Minden and that there'd been another once since. I have to admit I was envious of him.

'The lads said you'd moved. Why didn't you get in touch?' Eddie asked.

'Been trying to get on mi' feet first,' I said.

I could see Eddie looking round at the shabby state of the place and the pile of newspapers heaped up in the corner.

'You're still doing it then?' he said.

On top was the paper I'd rescued from the bin, with a picture of Jo Whitaker on the front. 'Ripper Murder Sensation' the headline said.

'She were nineteen, Ed! Just nineteen!'

'They'll get him, mate.'

'Aye, but how much longer? When?' I was beside myself. He shook his head.

'I don't know, mate, but it stands to reason they're going to – sooner or later.'

Mr Oldfield told the press this murder was similar to Jayne MacDonald's and that the lass was also 'perfectly respectable' this time. Now that the Ripper was no longer seen as confining his grisly and barbaric antics to the slaughter of mere 'good-time girls' such as Mum, but was a threat to all women, rumour had it that information was suddenly pouring in from a public now eager to assist the police. But I didn't raise my hopes.

Soon after Jo's murder, the vicar at her local church mentioned not only prayers for the victim's family but also for the Ripper's family who might be protecting him. I'm not sure it required prayers and the last time I stepped inside a chapel was when Grandad Woody died, but I thought the vicar had got a point: surely this monster had people who knew him, and someone somewhere must have seen him coming home covered in blood? If not this time, then on one of the many occasions he'd struck. How was he getting away with it?

Jo's stepfather, Mr Haydn Hiley, said that if anything good were to come out of Jo's death he hoped that it would contribute to the Ripper being caught, then she wouldn't have died in vain. I admired his strength but I also felt great sympathy for him as he tried to make sense of it all. I was not yet twenty-one but was already aware of how bitter and cynical I'd become, and I certainly knew enough by now to realise that one more murder wasn't going to make any difference. Jo was murder victim number ten, and it hadn't made any difference up until now. Instead, it had become no more than a numbers game between the police and the monster who kept on killing and getting away with it. It was going to take something else, like catching him red-handed or someone turning him in. But then Mr Oldfield came up with another idea, which the whole of the country was soon to hear about it.

27

Donna Summers' 'I Feel Love' was playing on the jukebox in the bar, and at last I had something to celebrate. In fact, I'd been celebrating the past few months, ever since the elderly chap in the flat next door took a phone call for me while I was out. They wanted me to call back about a job at a warehouse I'd filled in an application form for. I dropped ten pence into the tin by his phone and called them back. The job was packing and shifting orders around, was I interested? 'Interested?' Bloody hell, was the Pope Catholic? I nearly swore, then said, 'Yes, yes, definitely interested,' in my most calm and considered voice, while inside my head I'd already picked up the elderly neighbour and danced round the room with him in my happiness.

I'd recently seen my old friend Ian, who had got a job at the warehouse himself and recommended I try there too. I had to turn up at the warehouse at eight every morning, but I always aimed for half seven, in case there were traffic and things; I didn't want to be late. I can honestly say that just as the Duke of Wellington's had saved me at that time, so my new job at the packaging warehouse and the friends I made there, did now.

Every Friday night since I'd been there I'd meet Ian and another pal I'd met there, Mick, and we'd go out for a pint. I did a bit of overtime this particular evening and by the time I got to the pub Ian and Mick were waiting for me, grinning like Cheshire cats as I took out my pay packet. Three months ago I'd forgotten what it felt like, getting a pay packet in your hand at the end of the week, but now I enjoyed the little bit of power and freedom it gave me. I also felt as if I'd got some self-respect back at last.

It was impossible to ignore the pair of them as they deliberated over their empty glasses.

'Oh, go on then, what are you having?' I asked. It was the least I could do. During these past few months, when I got depressed about things and needed someone to talk to or even a sub, they'd always been there – even if they were a couple of cheeky sods at times! Because they'd been such good mates, I felt able to talk to them about what had happened. Ian knew most of it anyway and Mick was supportive when he found out. Sometimes it would all get me down about Mum, and as soon as they recognised the signs this was happening, they'd tell me to pack it in and sort myself out.

'Mine's a double!' Ian called from the table as I went up to the bar.

'Yeah, me an' all, wi' a chaser!' grinned Mick.

'Yeah, yeah, and I suppose you want the same?' I said to Ian, as I got the barmaid's attention.

'Well, if you're buying,' he grinned.

'You're like Tweedle bloody Dee and Tweedle bloody Dum, you pair,' I told them as they carried on taking the mickey.

Fighting my way back from the bar, clutching the pints in my hands, I'd hardly settled them on the table when the landlord turned off the jukebox and rang the chucking-out bell.

'Listen up everyone! This is important!' he bellowed across the hubbub of chatter and laughter in the bar. Gradually the bar fell quiet as, through the speakers on the wall, we heard a tape recording of a man's voice. He was speaking in a soft Geordie accent: 'I'm Jack . . . I see you are still having no luck catching me. I have the greatest respect for you, George, but Lord you are no nearer to catching me now than four years ago when I started . . .'

The Ripper was taunting the police and the victims; my head nearly exploded with rage.

'Quick, let's get him out of here,' Ian said, trying to propel me to the door as everyone in the pub shushed us.

'No, I want to hear it,' I protested. 'I want to remember his voice, so if I ever come across him . . . so help me, I'll kill 'bastard wi' me bare hands!'

I got shushed again and in my anger shushed them back and got some queer looks. And so the tape went on for a few more sickening minutes.

'I reckon your boys are letting you down, George. You can't be much good, can ya? I can't see myself being nicked just yet . . . Well, it's been nice chatting to you, George, Yours, Jack the Ripper . . . Hope you like the catchy tune at the end. Ha! Ha! Ha!'

I think the song by Andrew Gold, 'Thank You for Being a Friend,' played at the end, but I can't be sure. What a sick bastard.

The minute the tape finished, Mick and Ian were on their feet.

'Come on, Neil, let's go.'

But as they bundled me out of the door, a man going by the pub thrust a charity box under my nose.

'Catch th' Ripper! Come on, son, dig deep! Every bit helps!'

'Here, mate, take it and go!' Ian said, pushing a fiver into his tin, while Mick tried to shove me up the street, out of the way.

'You don't have to do that.' I was short with them both.

'Do what?' Ian asked.

'You know what – try to spare my feelings like that!' I blurted out. 'I don't need molly-coddling!'

At this point the collector, obviously impressed by Ian's generosity, ambled back over with his tin.

'Ta, mate,' he said to Ian. 'Most kind of you.' Then, as if to give him his money's worth, he added, 'Lass were perfectly respectable this time.'

Perfectly respectable this time? I felt my blood boil, and although I knew he was well-meaning and only repeating what continued to be in the papers and on TV since the police had said it, I couldn't stop myself going for him.

'Aye, poor lass, and so were all the others too – whether they were on t' game or not!' I could have cheerfully throt-tled him if Mick and Ian hadn't pulled me away.

'Alright, mate, alright! I were only saying!' The collector was shocked and started backing off, but I couldn't stop now.

'Aye, that's t' trouble, they're all *only saying*! And every other word is flaming "prostitute"! Well I'll have you know most of them girls on t' game wanted to provide summat better for their kids the only way they could, including my mum!'

I'd finally admitted it to whoever was listening: Mum

had been on the game. And by telling them, I was telling myself and beginning to come to terms with it.

The Ripper tape, as it soon became known, was played everywhere: at bingo halls, football matches, and even at the warehouse where I worked. Mr Oldfield put a great deal of store by it, as well as the letters with a Sunderland postmark that he'd received from the same person.

Billboards and posters everywhere now carried a sample of the Ripper's handwriting, giving a number to ring if you recognised it, and there was a number to dial to listen to the tape again. I didn't ring it, I didn't need to, I had that voice in my head and although I'd never been an aggressive person, I was in danger of decking anyone who spoke with that accent. On the other hand, and I don't know why, I wasn't convinced that the man on the tape was the right man. As the first five or so attacks had all been in the Leeds area, in my head he was a local man with local knowledge and a local accent, and I was surprised when Mr Oldfield suddenly put all his eggs in one basket and redirected the inquiry to the north east.

I remembered Mr Oldfield appearing on TV some time after Helen Rykta's murder. Making an appeal directly to the killer it had made the hair on the back of my neck stand on end.

'We are getting nearer and nearer . . . I am anxious we catch you before you add another death to the grisly catalogue that you already have to your credit.'

Credit? How can you credit someone with murder, as if it's an accolade to go in the trophy cabinet? But more importantly, Mr Oldfield seemed to be taking it personally, as if the Ripper in the tape had a vendetta against him because he'd called him by his first name in the recording. From the little I knew of him, I don't think Mr Hoban would have reacted like this. On the other hand, I'm sure Mr Oldfield had his reasons, which he couldn't disclose publicly, and I had to put my faith in him: he was lead detective on the case, after all.

As the inquiry ground on, it was impossible to go anywhere without seeing appeals to catch the Geordie Ripper. And while thousands of men were having their handwriting checked out on Weirside, men from the north east who worked in Leeds came under suspicion too. Sometimes the police came along to the warehouse and interviewed the Geordies we had working there: married men who went home to their families in the north east at weekends. The police never arrested anyone. I knew they wouldn't as I'd already listened carefully to these men, making a point of engaging them in casual conversation so I could check out their voices – none of them sounded like the man on the tape.

As I continued to read and watch news reports about the inquiry, I began to feel like I knew the victims and their families. Of course I didn't, but the little things I learnt about them and their families made them real instead of the number in a line-up of Ripper victims, Mum being number two.

I learnt that Jo Whitaker liked horse riding; Jayne MacDonald loved dancing and roller skating and her father, Wilf, had died soon after of a broken heart and been buried next to Jayne in the cemetery; Wilma was clever at school; and Helen, who'd been in care all her life, had written a poem which included the sad and telling lines: 'they put you in care, there's no love there'.

I started to think about all the things that Mum liked to do, like singing along to the car radio when we went to the wholesalers or cooking a pie for Mrs Stone with the apples she brought round every week after Derek died – even though Mum got her own apples from the wholesalers by then – and how she wouldn't let Dad get the butcher in to slaughter the pigs after the first year as she'd got so fond of them. I also remembered how Mum liked to treat us, like when Mr Rawlinson had taken us to the head office of the *Yorkshire Post* in Leeds when I was in a competition for selling the most papers in my area. After I just lost out on a place in the final, Mum took us to tea in Schofields instead. That all seemed light years away now, but I had to hang on to these memories as, in most people's eyes, Mum was just another Ripper victim, and a call-girl at that.

That said, reading about the victims who were 'call girls' helped me to understand why Mum had perhaps done as she had. None of the women were bad people: some were desperate, some had done it for their kids, and for others it was a way of life; and so I began to come to terms with what Mum had been doing.

When I came back from London, Mum had seemed determined to give us everything she couldn't afford for Derek when he was alive; and she had done so until she died. If this is what led to Mum and Dad getting into debt as Auntie Win had told me, or if it was just the business having problems separate to that, I don't know, but I couldn't change any of it. There was, however, something I thought I might be able to change.

Mum had died in 1976, over four years ago; since then there'd been another nine Ripper murders and countless attacks. If the police weren't going to catch the Ripper than I decided I'd give it a try myself. I couldn't do any worse.

28

It was the summer of 1980. Almost a year had passed since a young lass at Bradford University, Barbara Leach, had been brutally murdered as she left her friend's birthday party at a pub. Barbara was from Kettering and had been studying Humanities. I saw a picture of her little dog, Monty, in the paper, with his party hat on looking so sad. Barbara's brother Graham had listened to the Ripper tape with her when she was down from college. Now, tragically, Barbara was the Ripper's next victim: the eleventh. She'd been in her final year at college when the Ripper cut short her life and her promising career.

Again, the murder had been bloody and brutal but I no longer read the details, such as were given to the public, as I was becoming immune to it – even blasé: another frenzied attack, another bludgeoning, another tragedy and another terrible aftermath for the family.

As time went on, I hardly dare hope the Ripper had crawled away and died in case he suddenly surfaced again, as he had during the long gap between killing Mum and then Mrs Richardson a year later. As each day went by I began to feel a little more hopeful, although I spent all my spare time these days keeping an eye out for him.

Whatever route I used, whether to work or the pub or anywhere else, I made sure I always looked out in alley ways, dark corners or anywhere else the Ripper might hide to pounce from, once even stumbling upon a lass, about my age, soliciting. I wanted to say to her, 'Don't stay here, this is too dangerous, go home to your kids,' but I knew it wasn't that simple and, not wanting to scare her, I quickly left.

During the summer of 1980, a forty-one-year-old civil servant, Marguerite Walls, was savagely killed up at Farsley in Leeds. Marguerite had been working late at her office and been killed as she made her way home. Her murder was ruled out of the inquiry, however, as Marguerite had been strangled, which wasn't the Ripper's style, as they put it. There were also two attacks on women in West Yorkshire at this time, in Leeds and Huddersfield, and although both were savage and in the areas where the Ripper operated, these were also ruled out on the grounds of not being typical.

If none of these were the Ripper, then maybe I could stop looking for him everywhere I went, but if it wasn't him then surely another psycho was on the loose; or maybe the police just weren't saying what they knew to be the case.

Then, one November day when I got back home from work, I turned on the TV and saw a black and white photo of a young girl in glasses smiling out and knew this was going to be the latest victim of the Ripper. Jacqueline Hill was a twenty-year-old student at Leeds University. Her handbag had been found on waste ground the previous night and handed in, but there was no sign of poor Jacqueline.

Jacqueline had been put through a most terrible ordeal

and, despite believing I'd become immune to the attacks, this hit me as bad as all the others. As I watched the news report, the sweat started pouring off me as what had happened to Mum nearly five years earlier felt like only yesterday. I saw Mum's pinny hanging on the back door when I returned to the empty house that day, her lips imprinted in red on the tissue, and smelt the smell of death that still clung to my coat for days after I'd come away from the morgue. But now – worse than this even – there was the guilt. Since I'd accepted Mum was working as a prostitute and, more importantly, *why* she was doing it, I felt I'd let her down. She'd been my best friend after Derek died; I should have noticed she had money worries. Never mind that the horse and the cars had all gone back in front of my very own eyes, Dad was always going on about us getting a new van to replace the blue Comma, but we never got one. We couldn't even afford a new tyre when one had burst on the trip back from Ripon and Dad had to get a spare from a scrap yard in order to get home. All the signs were there, why hadn't I seen them and said something to Mum about it?

Despite my looking for the Yorkshire Ripper, he'd struck where students lived in Leeds this time and, as I kept an eye out for him there as well, I noticed on the wall by the university a sign daubed in black paint, 'Men are the Enemy', and further along a noose had appeared with Ripper written beneath it. This had been a recent topic of discussion between local MPs in Leeds and Bradford, responding to calls from their voters to reinstate the death penalty for the Ripper. Me, I couldn't say I was worried what they did with him: they could hang him or lock him up in a dungeon for all I cared, I just wanted him caught.

As I came out of a side street, a group of women clutching banners with 'Women reclaim the night' written on them were marching ahead of me. Some women's groups in the city had started campaigning to get all men put on curfew; I didn't have a problem with that. Mum was a working-class lass but I reckon she was a women's libber the way she lived her life, and with the way things were at the moment, I think she'd have agreed with them. Of course, the police, who'd been warning women not to go out on their own or to accept lifts from strangers, were right to do this, but why should women be stopped from going out and have to live in fear of being attacked by some psycho who was undoubtedly a man?

Suddenly the women turned round with their placards and, seeing me behind them, gave me a look. I broke out into a cold sweat and kept my distance in case they thought I was the Ripper. I knew if Mum had been with them she'd have charged after me and given me a whack with the sign for frightening the women. I went back to Auntie's demoralised; how could another man look for the Ripper without being threatening to women? This wasn't going to work.

I'd rushed out to the news stand soon after the last murder had happened; scouring the papers like a man possessed for further leads on the murder and who the poor lass who'd lost her life was. I learned that Jacqueline was a former Sunday school teacher from Middlesborough. She had been to a lecture on the probation service and was planning to be a social worker when she left college.

Her mum had given an interview on television soon after. I don't remember much of what she said, as my head started swimming with it all, but the poor woman looked totally distraught as she urged people to help find her daughter's killer – 'Please think,' she kept saying. 'Please think. I want everyone to help us find him. Perhaps he lives in your house . . . or in a block of flats. He lives somewhere, please think.'

Mrs Hill's plea had been heart-wrenching. But I had thought, and I'd looked and I'd thought again, and I knew I couldn't take much more.

As soon as the interview ended, I turned the TV over to the other side where the newsreader was in mid-flow: '. . . the brutal murder of the Leeds student brings the grisly total to twelve.'

I turned on the radio and heard, 'Jacqueline had been out to a lecture run by the probation service . . . she wanted to help under-privileged children . . .'

My head was full of news reports in between hearing: 'Please think! Please think!' All the news reports I'd ever heard over the past five years seemed to be scrambling around inside my brain and it was beginning to hurt. Would the hunt for this evil man never end? Auntie Win came downstairs and ripped the plugs from the wall: 'I told you when you moved in here, there'd be no more of this!'

I didn't know what to say. I'd moved in with Auntie earlier in the year when I'd gone down with flu. I hadn't been able to get up for two weeks. Mick and Ian did what they could to help, but I think, in truth, the whole inquiry was beginning to get to me.

'Aye, you can look at me like that an' all, young man!'

she said, as I looked at her sheepishly, then she started throwing my newspaper collection in the bin.

'Auntie? What you doing?'

'What's it look like I'm doing!' Auntie said. 'And don't think of fishing them out again, 'cos I'm going to give them to Mr Garner down the road for his bonfire!'

Auntie told me I was making myself ill, and I knew, deep down, she was right, but this thing had been haunting me for the past five years, and I think I'd finally reached breaking point.

'You can't keep staying out, looking for him like that. It's up to police to catch 'im, not you! And happen if you took more notice of me, we'd both get some sleep round here an' all.'

I knew I'd been shouting in my sleep again. I'd woken up some nights with a start as the nightmares returned, but unless they caught the Yorkshire Ripper, I'd resigned myself to living with them now.

Auntie put on her coat, knotted her headscarf under her chin and put her purse in her coat pocket.

'Auntie, you're not going out?' I asked her, alarmed.

'Shopping won't get itself done.'

'Wait a bit, I'll come with you.'

'You'll do no such thing,' she said. 'I'm only going down to corner shop and so far t' coward's not struck in daylight.'

I couldn't help worrying every time Auntie went out. I wasn't alone, as women's groups began setting up self-defence classes, and others began taking to the streets of Leeds in force as never before to protest. I don't remember them turning out when my mum and Maureen and Yvonne and the other prostitutes had been killed and attacked;

maybe if they had, something might have been done to stop him sooner. The huge public outcry, since Jacqueline's death and Mrs Hill's public appeal, gathered pace as the press united with them, demanding action. And with concerns also being raised in high places, it looked at last as if we were to get some action.

It was just before Christmas when a language expert at Leeds University wrote a letter to the local paper saying how he believed the Ripper tape was a hoax. A Mr Lewis, I think he was called, said the man who'd made the tape would have been interviewed and eliminated by now in the colossal inquiry that had been going on in the north east. I wasn't surprised, as I'd never been completely convinced by the idea of a Geordie Ripper; but it was terrible news indeed, given that it taken the police focus off where it was most needed, allowing three more murders to take place. Whoever was responsible for it, they too had blood on their hands.

Mr Oldfield was taken off the inquiry soon after Jacqueline's death, and it now had a new boss heading it up: Detective Superintendent Jim Hobson, one of the detectives who interviewed me when Mum died. I cannot remember whether I read it afterwards or if I heard him say it at the time, but Mr Hobson still seemed to believe that the tape was genuine, just as his predecessor, Mr Oldfield had. I was really worried by this; surely he wouldn't continue going down the same road they'd followed for the past eighteen months with no result?

The Chief Constable, Mr Gregory, also seemed to be resisting calling Scotland Yard in, which local MPs, as well as the press and public, had been calling for. All I knew was that we needed help, and this was no time for the police chief to be proud.

I later heard that the Prime Minister, Margaret Thatcher, who had a daughter Carol the same age as Jacqueline, was so incensed that the police still hadn't caught this monster, she threatened to take over the inquiry herself. The Home Secretary, Mr Whitelaw, came up to West Yorkshire police headquarters to sort things out. Soon after his visit it was announced that there was to be a review of the investigation led by a former Chief Constable and that a super squad of experienced detectives was going to be formed for the sole purpose of tracking down the beast. Surely *now* he'd be caught?

29

New Year 1981. Me and Auntie had a quiet Christmas with Auntie Tess and my cousins coming round for Boxing Day tea. We were all trying not to think about the inquiry and whether the recent developments would help, as there'd been too many disappointments in the past.

I didn't have to go back to work for a few days yet as I'd taken some time off to have a bit of a break and try to recover from how I'd been feeling of late. It was a few days into the New Year when Auntie dragged a dining chair across the front room. She was fussed about getting the decorations down before the sixth, not least because she didn't like all the dust collecting on them.

'Hey, come on, out the way, I'll do that,' I said.

'Would you mind, love? I'll put the kettle on.'

Auntie was clutching her back as she went into the kitchen; it had been hurting her a bit of late and she was unsteady on her feet.

I got on the chair and started removing the pins from the paper chains when there was a knock at the door.

'Auntie!' I called, 'I'll get it!'

Auntie came bustling out of the kitchen with the kettle in her hand. 'No you won't, you'll stay as you are, I may have a bad back but I'm not an invalid yet!' Going over to the front door, she grumbled, 'Happen it'll be those Jehovah Witnesses again.'

I heard Auntie talking in hushed tones to someone on the front doorstep, but I couldn't see who it was. As I carried on taking out the drawing pins from the ceiling and dropping the decorations onto the floor, Auntie shut the front door and came back in, followed by a policeman in uniform.

'Lad, t' officer needs a word wi' you,' Auntie said, but before he'd even opened his mouth I knew why he was here.

I got off the chair and, side-stepping the heap of paper chains on the floor, said: 'You've got 'im?'

'Aye,' the policeman nodded.

'Thank God!' Auntie cried, throwing her hands in the air. 'At least another family won't have to suffer now!'

I stood there for what must have been a full minute, unable to speak or to believe it was all over.

'Where?' I finally managed to ask. 'How?'

The super squad surely hadn't had time to get going yet? What was suddenly so different?

'A young rookie caught him in the red-light area of Sheffield with false number plates,' the policeman said. 'The lass in his car had a lucky escape.'

Sheffield? So he'd moved his cowardly, gut-wrenching acts into South Yorkshire too.

'Who is he? What's his name?' I wanted to know.

'Sutcliffe, Peter Sutcliffe,' came the reply.

Peter Sutcliffe? I repeated to myself, as if I expected the name to mean something to me, which of course, at the time, it didn't – although he was soon to become well known as one of the world's most notorious serial killers.

'He's a lorry driver from Bradford,' the policeman added. 'Works for an engineering haulage firm.'

So Mr Hoban had been right all along; if only he'd been here now to see the monster caught.

'We'll let you know when the case comes to court, so you can attend.'

'You'll do no such thing,' Auntie scoffed. 'Lad's been through quite enough, he'll not be going anywhere.'

I couldn't argue with Auntie because I was just too tired of it all, but when I did think about it later, I decided not to attend the trial at the Old Bailey as I didn't want to hear any more of the terrible pain and indignities he'd inflicted on Mum or anyone else for that matter.

'Aye, well, Sutcliffe's not far away,' the policeman said. 'They're holding him across the road, in Armley Jail.'

After Auntie saw the policeman out, we both stood on the doorstep looking across the road at Armley Jail, the prison casting a long shadow in the afternoon sun over the house.

I was so overwhelmed that the Ripper's reign of terror had finally ended that I couldn't stop shaking, like I had that day when Mum gave me a glass of hot milk after Derek died.

Soon after the families had been told, the news of the Ripper's capture was broadcast on TV and radio. People took to the streets singing and dancing. That night the church bells rang out across Armley and the nearby parishes, while news of his capture was transmitted around the world in different languages and on scores of different news programmes. All this, but I couldn't celebrate and I couldn't let go – not until they'd finally banged up this animal called Sutcliffe.

Auntie patted my arm, there were a tear in her eye. 'Come on love, let's go in and have a cup of tea. You can put the television on today if you like.'

I switched the TV on for the first time in six weeks; Auntie wouldn't even let us have it on over Christmas in case there were any more reports about the Ripper. As soon as the TV warmed up, the first words I heard were: 'the serial killer dubbed the Yorkshire Ripper has been caught in Sheffield . . .' and then Sutcliffe's face loomed up, filling the screen. The frightening thing was he looked like just an average man of average appearance, like someone you'd just pass in the street and not even notice. Then a small black and white photo of Mum appeared on the screen – a photo that I'd see so many times in the past five years as one of the victims – and I hated him.

30

Sutcliffe was charged with thirteen murders and seven attempted murders. He admitted all the attacks, including those on Maureen Long and Marcella Claxton, along with the murder of Marguerite Walls, the civil servant from Leeds. There may well have been others but, if there were, he wasn't saying.

He was a married man, wed to a teacher. They had no children but lived in a nice detached house near Bradford. He had it all and I couldn't fathom why anyone could do what he'd done unless he was seriously mad or plain evil.

Sutcliffe soon claimed he was mentally ill and hearing voices from God that told him to do it. He denied murder but pled guilty to lesser charges on the grounds of diminished responsibility, which both sides agreed on. This meant, as I understood it, that if the judge agreed, Sutcliffe would be rubber stamped for Broadmoor and the case over and done with without any need for a jury or a trial. It also meant there was a chance he could get out sooner than if he went to prison, if the psychiatrists there thought he was fit enough.

I couldn't see that he was mad or how could he have held a job down as he had, and keep his wife from finding out what he was doing for all that time? And surely, I thought, if you're mentally ill, you can't conceal it from people – like Granny Jackson couldn't when she lost the plot before she died? Also, hadn't he gone out equipped every time, and with his different screwdrivers especially sharpened for this purpose? When Granny Jackson started talking to herself and wandering off up the road, she didn't stop to take her purse or her shopping basket.

In the event, the trial started in April 1981 at the Old Bailey, where the Crown was asked to accept Sutcliffe's plea of manslaughter on the grounds of diminished responsibility based on psychiatric reports. Sutcliffe claimed he was hearing voices from God telling him to go on a mission to kill prostitutes – voices which he hadn't apparently mentioned to the police at the time of his arrest. However, as the psychiatrists had formed their opinions of the state of Sutcliffe's mental health based only on what he was telling them, that wasn't good enough for the judge, Mr Justice Boreham, who wanted Sutcliffe to go before a jury.

I was thankful to the judge and hugely relieved. Even though I knew this meant that I and all the other families of the victims would not now be spared the horrific details of the attacks, which would no doubt come out in court and would cause further distress, it also meant that this evil monster would have to face up to what he had done in a court of law. The whole nation would now see what he was about and I was certain that 'justice', as they say 'would be served'.

Auntie Tess came round to see me just before the trial began and said she had something she needed to tell me, to prepare me in case it came out in the trial. Although I intended to avoid the media as much as possible once the trail started, I knew this was easier said than done and so I listened to Auntie. The police had been round to see her

a few days earlier and told her that Sutcliffe had picked
Mum up from the roadside where she was soliciting, and
driven her to a quiet spot where he stopped the car, making
out it had broken down. He'd lifted the bonnet and said
he couldn't see the engine without having some light on it.
Mum, being the friendly person she was, offered to help
and struck her cigarette lighter above the engine so that he
could see. He'd crept up behind her and smashed a hammer
into her skull or, they believed, may even have slammed
the bonnet down on her first.

Keith was right all along: Mum had been taken unawares
and from what I'd seen of Sutcliffe, she could easily have
defended herself against this little creep – had he not been
the coward he was and attacked her from behind. Poor
Mum; she'd only been trying to pay off the debts and give
us kids a happy childhood after Derek had died. She didn't
deserve that.

I worried about my brother and sister finding out all the
terrible details that the trial would throw up, but heard
from Dad that they were all doing their best to protect
them. But if, of course, Sutcliffe had just pled guilty to
murder in the first place, he could have saved the families
going through it again anyway – but this was the Ripper,
he wasn't about to get brave.

It was a warm spring evening in May, when I came rushing
in with some fish and chips and a bottle of plonk for me
and Auntie.

'Auntie, get th' plates out, we've got summat to celebrate!' I told her. 'I've changed me job at the warehouse
and I'm getting a raise.'

'Oh aye,' Auntie said, absent-mindedly as she sat watching television, 'that's nice.' I looked over and saw the Old Bailey on the screen. I sat on the arm of the chair by Auntie and realised the jury were about to deliver their verdict. A reporter outside the court said that the jury had thrown out Sutcliffe's plea of guilty to the manslaughter, and announced that Sutcliffe had been handed down twenty life sentences – thirteen for the murders and a further seven for the attempted murders.

Outside the courtroom there were scenes of jubilation, but me and Auntie just looked at each other, stunned that after all these years it was finally over. Then, as the reporter read out a list of names of the victims, I heard Mum's called out and, for the first time since it had happened, I burst into tears.

'Let it out, lad,' Auntie said, tearful herself.

We picked some flowers from my cousin's garden, white chrysanths, which were Mum's favourite, and went down to Cottingley Cemetery on the number fifty-one. I split the flowers and put some by Derek's plaque and the rest on Mum's grave where I quietly told her, 'They've got him, Mum, they've bloody got him!'

At last I could look forward to the future and I could start to grieve. Or so I believed then . . .

31

Soon after the Ripper began life, and despite the deepening recession and people being laid off, I was lucky enough to hold onto my new job at the warehouse and was working alongside a man called Jim. Jim was older than me but we got on well, and at weekends we went fishing together.

One evening, after a hard day on the river bank pulling out little more than tiddlers and getting the line caught in an abandoned rusty shopping trolley, Jim suggested we cut our losses and turn in early at the pub.

We hadn't been sat at our table more than five minutes, when a pretty blonde lass, about my age, came in on her own. She caught me looking at her and smiled; I smiled back then felt myself turn red and quickly looked away, embarrassed. Even though I was now twenty-two, I was still shy with people, never mind the opposite sex. Jim copped all of this and, grinning, called the girl over to our table.

'There's someone I want you to meet,' he said. 'This is my niece, Diane. Diane, Neil.'

I immediately coloured up, but as soon as Diane sat down and we got talking, it felt like we'd known each other for years. Diane was waiting for her mate, and we spent the rest of the evening chatting. By chucking-out time her mate still hadn't turned up, but I'd plucked up enough courage to ask Diane out on a date.

'OK,' Diane smiled, and we agreed to meet up the next night at a pub in town. That evening she told me the previous evening had been set up, she wasn't waiting for a mate at all. Her Uncle Jim wanted us to meet: he thought we'd get on like a house on fire, but she wasn't so sure and wanted to check me out first.

Just a few months later me and Diane got wed at the registry office with a buffet after at the social club. All the family came except Dad; we didn't invite him as, like Diane said, we wanted it to be a happy occasion and this would've put a strain on things. In truth, I still couldn't forgive him or even understand his part in what Mum was doing.

Auntie Tess made a speech and said she was pleased I'd finally got someone special to share my life with and that she hoped one day I might have my own little family.

'Hang about, Tess!' Mick shouted from the back of the room. 'He's not had his wedding night yet!'

Win came in all her finery; 'a vision in blue' as I joked to her. 'Ay, that's enough of that lad,' she said. 'I'll have you know I've been up best part of the night making this; happen you'll give me a bit more warning next time you decide to get wed.'

I hadn't seen Auntie for a month or so, since I'd moved into my new flat, but suddenly she looked older and frail and I could see that the Ripper years had taken their toll. Although Win was a strong woman, who Mum and all of us had depended on at certain times in our lives, I realised how it must've taken everything she had to keep going herself at times. While I'd been busy with my own problems, I hadn't paid enough attention to hers.

'Come on, Auntie, let's get you a seat, and I'll bring you some grub over.'

Win took my arm; her steps were faltering.

'We got through it, Neil lad,' she smiled.

'Aye, Auntie, we did.'

Auntie passed away soon after but I was glad she'd lived to see the Ripper brought to justice, and me settled at last.

Me and Diane had a honeymoon at Flamborough Head; a family friend of Diane's had a caravan there. When we came back, we got our own little council house in Armley and a year or two later our Andrew came along.

'A chip off the old block and no mistake,' Auntie Tess said when she saw him in the hospital, with his reddish-blond hair and Jackson nose. I sent Dad a message to let him know about Andrew; it was two years since the wedding and I'd had time to think. Maybe I would never understand Dad's part in what had happened, but I thought we could perhaps now bury the hatchet; he was Andrew's grandad after all – but Dad didn't reply.

Nonetheless, I was content with my own little family and, to add to my happiness, not long after Andrew was born, I managed to get a job back in roofing. I was pleased as punch; the money was good, which I needed with a wife and new baby to look after, and roofing was something I was skilled at and enjoyed. The only drawback was it was long hours in the summer and it meant working away from home at times.

At first, I was only away for short periods of time, but then it was for longer periods and more frequent, until I was away far more than I was at home. It was hard for Diane being on her own with a little one, but when she asked me to cut down on my hours or get a job back nearer to home, I just couldn't do it. In the back of my mind, I had this thing eating away at me that I had to be a good provider for my family, and do it the right way, not like Dad, so I just kept taking all the overtime I could get.

Diane told me straight, 'what happened between your mum and dad was nothing to do with you, you've got to forget about the past or else you'll just let it keep spoiling your life.'

There were also problems when I was at home, as I still fixated on any news there might be in the papers or on TV about the Ripper, and I never missed a documentary about him.

I just couldn't relax, and even though I knew that monster was securely locked up, I felt there was always the danger of there being others out there like him. I was over-protective and always worried every time Diane went out on her own or with Andrew. Diane was understanding and patient but I must have been driving her crazy as well as myself.

Worse perhaps, I found it hard to trust people. I thought if I got close to anyone I'd end up losing them, as everyone I loved had been taken from me. So I think I remained distant with the people who meant most to me.

In 1989, Diane took a phone call from DS Johnson at Millgarth police station asking me to call him. When I rang back, DS Johnson asked me if I would mind contacting Dad, as he had some news for the family. The satirical magazine *Private Eye* had appealed against the large sum of money they'd been ordered to pay Sonia Sutcliffe, the Ripper's wife, from her action against them. They claimed she'd negotiated with the press to profit from her fame as the wife of a serial killer. She said she hadn't, as she didn't want to benefit from what Sutcliffe had done. She was awarded a record sum of £600,000, which was reduced to £60,000 on appeal. *Private Eye* now wanted to distribute the large sum of money they'd won back among the families of the victims of the Yorkshire Ripper.

There'd been no help or support of any kind for the victims' families as far as I was aware of, certainly me and Chris and Bubs hadn't had any, and I felt genuinely touched that the people at the magazine had thought about us.

I rang Dad and passed on the message and the police went to see him. Now, at New Wortley Labour Club, we were meeting up again after all these years. I brought Andrew along with me; he was coming up to five. It was the first time Dad had seen our Andrew, or shown any interest in his first grandchild, since he was born. When Dad gave him a five-pound note to get an ice-cream, I couldn't bite my tongue. 'That's a pound a year for every year of his life,' I said, as I felt that bitter about it. Things went downhill from there.

Dad had been given a cheque for fifteen thousand pounds from *Private Eye*, a great deal of money at the time. I didn't actually want compensating for Mum's death; obviously no amount of money could have done that, but this had been kindly donated by the magazine and so, on that basis, I felt I could accept it. The money would no doubt be good for Chris and Bubs too.

However, Dad's idea of fairness wasn't mine and while he gave us kids five hundred pounds each, he kept the rest for himself, immediately booking a holiday to Mexico. I don't know if my brother or sister said anything to him about it, but when I got home that night, the more I thought about it, the more I thought it wasn't right that Dad should use the money to subsidise his own lifestyle, when it was, after all, for all the family. Even a little more could have helped give Chris and Bubs some kind of start in life, and I could have put something away for our Andrew for when he was older.

I rang Dad up soon after and said this to him and we had one last, bitter row. I told him if he wasn't going to give us any more money, he could at least buy Mum a headstone at long last, and forego one of the other holidays he'd got planned after Mexico. Dad ended the call by threatening to stop the £500 cheque he'd given me if I didn't like it. I was bitterly disappointed with Dad, and realised then that money was more important to him than his own kids, just as it had been when he accompanied Mum on her trips to pick up clients.

My only regret was that while I had hoped the meeting would have been a starting point to forging a relationship with my brother and sister again, it seemed to create a further gulf. And if that wasn't bad enough, cracks were now starting to appear in my marriage.

32

Some ten years later, in June 1998, I was walking down the Headrow past Lewis's when a young woman came backwards out of the doors clutching some shopping bags. I looked at her and did a double take: medium build, fair hair, early thirties – I was sure it was Bubs.

A lot of water had flowed under the bridge since we'd last met and I wasn't quite sure what to say to her, so I followed behind a little way, being careful to keep out of sight so as not to scare her.

My Dad had taken my brother and sister under his wing as they got older and I had tried to stay in touch, leaving my number for them, but since I'd never heard back, I couldn't help wondering if he'd said something to turn them against me or if they simply saw things from Dad's point of view.

I was friendly with other roofers in the business who'd kept me informed about Chris. Apparently Chris had been working in roofing with Dad for some years now, and I'd heard Bubs had got wed and had a young family of her own. I was pleased things had worked out well for them both; God knows they deserved it.

But now, as I followed behind Bubs in the street, I was thinking that if I stopped her and said hello, I could then ask her how little 'uns were and tell her about Andrew. Then, perhaps, we could arrange to meet up.

I was just about to call out to her as she stopped by the kerb, when she suddenly turned round and looked back up the street and I wasn't so sure it was her. I then realised it had been so long since I'd seen her, I didn't have a clue what she looked like anymore; I couldn't even recognise my own sister.

I turned on my heel and rushed back to my flat. Drawing the curtains, I sat there in the darkness staring at the walls. I'd got divorced some while back and now had my own place, and even though me and Diane had managed to stay friends and I still saw a lot of Andrew, the separation had been traumatic. And now, not knowing my own sister – it just felt like the last straw.

I sat in that armchair for what must have been days just staring into space, and I simply couldn't make myself do anything. I couldn't get washed; I couldn't go to work; I couldn't even be bothered to eat. It felt like everything from the past was building up in my head and I was even convinced at one point I heard police loudhailers outside appealing for information about the Yorkshire Ripper, as I had all those years ago when I lived at Auntie's.

Worst of all, and despite what I'd told myself, I hadn't actually put what had happened behind me at all, and I was bitterly angry at myself for still carrying it with me after all these years. At times my thoughts were so dark I almost thought of suicide.

I don't know how long I sat there, it could have been a fortnight or a matter of a few days, when I heard voices outside and the letterbox rattled.

'Come on, mate, move your arse!' Mick yelled through the letterbox.

'Get out of there and come for a pint down t' Star!' I heard Ian shout behind him.

I knew at least these voices were real, they were my mates, but I still couldn't move.

After a while they gave up and I heard Mick slam the letterbox down in frustration.

Ten minutes or so later I began to stir; yes, they were my mates and they had stuck with me through thick and thin. And here I was, sitting in the dark feeling sorry for myself. I had my mates, and my son and my mum's family; what the hell was the matter with me? Was I really going to let that evil killer destroy me too?

I got up and started madly stuffing the rest of the papers I'd managed to rescue from Auntie's into my old hold-all. Then I had a bath and, putting on my togs, set off in the direction of the river. I walked over the footbridge by the weir and, stopping in the middle of it, hurled the bag of papers into the water below.

It made an enormous splash as it sank to the bottom before bobbing back up. I watched as it was carried along by the current, until it was finally dragged under and disappeared from sight. I let out perhaps the biggest sigh of relief of my life, then set off down to the Star: buying my mates a pint was the least I could do.

When I got to the Star, the place had had a power failure and was in darkness. I was about to go home, when I lost my step and stumbled through the door into the lounge. I put my hand out in the dark and managed to grab hold of a table to steady myself, when the place suddenly burst into light to a rowdy chorus of: 'Happy Birthday, Neil!'

I just stood there completely stunned, as party poppers and whizzers went off all around me. It took me a moment to come to and I began to grin inanely while all the faces of all the people I'd just been thinking about – my best mates Ian, Mick and Sue, Mum's sisters, my cousins and my lad Andrew were all beaming back at me. Mick and Ian and their wives had put on a mammoth spread for my fortieth and decorated the entire room with balloons and tinsel. I didn't even realise it was my birthday, and I couldn't believe they'd done this for me. I could feel the tears rolling down my face, but I didn't care, I was so happy.

'We didn't think you were going to make it,' Mick said in my ear.

'Aye, I nearly didn't,' I replied. 'If it hadn't have been for you lot . . .'

The celebrations that night were second to none; my mates and my family had done me proud.

I was just making a wish and blowing out my candles when a smartly dressed lady in her sixties came over and said she'd known me since I was that high – indicating her knee.

'Go on,' I said, smiling sceptically. 'I'll fall for it . . .'

But to my surprise, she opened her bag and got out a photo of Mum standing with her arms wrapped around me and Derek when we were little kids, long before our Chris and Bubs were born.

Mum and Mrs Lloyd had gone to school together in Hemsworth but then she had moved away from the area when they were older and lost touch. Then, when they'd got married and had families of their own, they'd found they lived almost next door to one another in Leeds.

I looked at the photo of Mum, all happy and smiling, and thought if she'd worked the streets for three weeks, three months or three years, then she had her reasons – but she were the best.

That same night, I got out all the photos I'd kept hidden away in the envelope since it happened, and for the first time in Andrew's sixteen years, I showed him pictures of his Grandma Emily and Uncle Derek.

Our Andrew had been in on my surprise party from the start, though he'd not once let it slip.

'I'm going to have to have words with you later, young man,' I told him, trying to keep a straight face. He said he wanted a few words with me an' all; then asked me if he could move in round mine!

Diane had married again and moved to Hull with her new husband some time back, but Andrew hadn't really settled there. He went to school in Leeds, that's where his friends were and where he wanted to be. Fortunately, me and Diane had always seen eye to eye over Andrew, so when Diane agreed to Andrew coming to mine, I was well and truly over th' moon. I'd never really seen myself as becoming a single parent dad, but there I was with me own strapping lad at home, rushing back home to cook his tea and doing the washing for the two of us – and loving every minute of it!

Andrew did his share too and I appreciated what a bright and grounded lad he was, which I am grateful to Diane and her family for, but with his crop of reddish-blond hair and Jackson features, he's still a chip off the old block as Auntie had said when she met him that first time at the hospital.

I can honestly say my fortieth birthday was a turning point; with the help of my friends and family, I'd finally pulled through after evil. Even so, I still clung to the hope that one day I might be reunited with my brother and sister, and there were other secrets I was yet to discover, including what Mum and Dad's 'fresh start' had been about when we moved to Churwell.

33

Some time after my birthday I answered an advert in the local newspaper from Jane Carter Woodrow, at Cambridge University, who was trying to trace the children of the women murdered by the Yorkshire Ripper to find out what had happened to them. I met Jane at Leeds railway station with Andrew, and in getting together to write my story, found there were other secrets that I was yet to learn about my family, and questions I would finally find the answers to.

We spoke to my family, friends of the family and former neighbours as well as Mr White and his wife, the newsagent who me and Derek had delivered papers for when we first arrived in Churwell. All were amazingly kind and helpful, and everyone we spoke to spoke well of Mum, saying what a hard worker and lovely lady she was.

Sadly, though, one family I had known for many years and who, like us, had been in the building trade in Churwell, agreed to speak to us, but when we turned up at the appointed time, shut the door in our face. They said they'd spoken to Dad the night before and didn't now want to talk to us. Clearly the hatchet would never be buried.

I went with Jane again recently to visit several of my relatives, who agreed at last to tell me why Mum's family believed Dad was involved in what she was doing. One of my aunties said she hadn't wanted to tell me before as she didn't want to make things worse between me and Dad, but she said that Dad was the only man Mum was frightened of, and that although he could be charming one minute, he would turn the next, and was often violent towards her, especially when he was drunk.

I knew Dad well enough by now to know he always had to have his own way, which Mum used to make light of in company. I also remembered how Mum used to quickly make him a cup of tea to keep him happy when the kids were noisy or there'd been a problem at work. She'd look strained at times then, but if he did flare up, it was all over just as quickly as it started. I really had no idea he was violent to Mum and I was shocked.

But then I had no idea what was going on right under my nose with the debt Mum and Dad were in. I knew Mum was a strong woman who had learnt self-defence and could stand up to most men – she'd even lifted a man off his feet who'd insulted her mum. 'Don't you *ever* talk to my mother like that again,' she'd said. Never mind all the heavy rolls of materials she'd lifted. I knew then that if Mum daren't stand up to Dad, it followed that if he'd told her not to work on the streets, she wouldn't have done it.

My cousin Muriel said that Dad had hit Mum on many occasions, even striking her with a poker and breaking her collarbone, resulting in her going to hospital. My Uncle Paul asked me to leave the room while he told Jane that when he was babysitting me and Derek at our old house as a teenager, Dad had come back drunk and threatened to hit Mum. My cousin said Uncle Paul had been so frightened for Auntie Emily he'd grabbed a knife from the kitchen and got between them, pointing the knife at Dad to stop him hurting Mum. Mum was pregnant at the time. And to think I'd told the police he'd never laid a finger on Mum.

Auntie then told me that Mum had left Dad because of his violence towards her, but because me and Derek were only small at the time, I have no memory of it. Mum started divorce proceedings against him on two occasions because of it; the first time he talked her round, promising he'd never hit her again but he soon broke his promise and she left him a second time, eventually finding happiness with a labourer called Mick, who Auntie said had thought the world of Mum.

Mum and Mick lived happily together for almost two years. He'd treated her like a princess, but Mum wasn't used to this and had found it hard to trust him after Dad. Mum and Mick had been planning to get married, but, as fate would have it, when she'd gone to the court to pick up her divorce decree that day, she'd bumped into Dad there.

Auntie said if only Dad hadn't been there at the same time as Mum, then history would've been different. Dad managed to talk Mum round again, promising things *really* would be different this time, and that they'd have a 'fresh start' as soon as he could afford it. Our new house in Churwell was to be that fresh start.

But life is a funny thing, full of 'if onlys': if only Mum hadn't bumped into Dad at court that day, then we'd never have moved to Churwell and then Derek wouldn't have died and Mum would still be here – but if only this hadn't happened, then our Chris and Bubs would never have been born, and their children. And that too would be unthink-able. It was when I began to think about this, that I was at last able to put the guilt I'd felt for so long behind me.

But the story doesn't end there, as yet another secret was to come out when Jane asked why it was that Dad had never driven. My auntie told us that Mum had shared his secret with her: that Dad couldn't read and write but because he felt so humiliated by it, Mum had always covered for him, just as Auntie said she'd always tried to cover for Dad when he hit her.

At first I couldn't believe it: Dad couldn't read and write? Then I remembered how he'd have to have complete silence when the football results came on in order to be able to follow them on the coupon and get Mum to check them after. And I remembered how Mum had always got me and Derek to test her on the Highway Code, saying she didn't want to bother Dad as he'd been working hard all day, and why he'd held his hymnbook upside down in the church, as he wasn't singing from it but by heart.

Of course, Dad couldn't read and write; suddenly it all clicked into place and I felt sorry for him. That must have made life a lot harder for him, and Mum too who'd had to do the books and write letters for him. After police claims about Mum, Auntie said that she and Win had carried out an investigation into the business and found it was in trouble to such an extent that Dad was about to be declared bankrupt. I'd always thought the business had been registered in Mum's name too, but I realised this couldn't have been the case.

At the time, Mum wasn't going to be allowed to go into

the court with him to help him fill in the forms and he'd been so mortified at the thought of having to admit he couldn't do them himself, that one or other of them came up with a quick way of Mum earning money to pay off the debts to stop it coming to court. Hence, she believed, Mum had gone on the game to help Dad to keep his secret.

There may have been other reasons too. Going through back copies of newspapers in the library in Leeds, we came across an interview Dad had given the local newspaper the day after Mum's murder. I was surprised, as I had no idea Dad had spoken to the press, never mind let them in the house. There seemed no sadness or remorse in the article; it was more like someone trying to excuse himself, more worried what the neighbours would think when his and Mum's secret was out. It also had a photo of me and Chris and Bubs at the top saying 'today's picture of the three children made motherless by the sadistic killer', yet I have no recollection at all of it being taken.

Dad said in the interview he gave to the press, that he and Mum had realised life was short after Derek died, and had decided to live life to the full from then on. This confirmed what I had thought when I got back from London all those years ago: how Mum and Dad had changed and had started going out more. They had seemed to have struck a pact of some kind, not only about their own lives, but to make sure us kids had the best possible childhood they could give us after Derek's death. Sadly this may have cost Mum her life.

But now the fickle finger of fate – or fortune – was about to point at Dad once more, or at least at his wife, Betty, who was about to become a millionaire.

34

I was in the pub with Ian and Mick some time after my fortieth, when through the roofing grapevine I heard that my step-mum, Betty, had won a fortune on the National Lottery as part share with two others. Although it had been some years now since I'd last seen Dad, I was happy for him as I heard he'd not been well and in recent years had been confined to a wheelchair. Betty spent all her time looking after him, but now they could at least enjoy their twilight years together in comfort.

I also heard that Dad and Betty bought a bungalow like the Ponderosa near the sea at Brid', and that Betty's girls, as well as Chris and Bubs, were given a substantial sum from the winnings. With what my brother and sister had been through as youngsters, I hoped it was true and was particularly pleased for them. I wasn't of course offered any money, nor did I expect any, and after that last row I had not heard from Dad again. Despite this, me, Chris and Bubs were at last to be reunited, though when it finally happened it was neither in the way I'd hoped for nor expected.

It was around this time, two years ago now, that I got a phone call out of the blue from my Dad's former business partner, Harry, ringing to tell me my Dad had passed on. A week or so later, me and Harry set off for Dad's funeral in the East Riding, where I was finally granted my wish of being reunited with my brother and sister. As Chris and Bubs stood beside me at the crematorium, I thought of how all the years had taken their toll of us, but hoped we could at last be friends and start to make up for lost time.

But then something strange happened, for when my brother Chris said, 'We must keep in touch this time,' I suddenly realised why this hadn't happened before and why I hadn't pursued it more myself: we were all reminders to each other of a sad and tragic past. And remembering that past was just too painful. I believe it had taken this many years before it was actually possible to have this reconciliation.

Once I'd realised this and stopped baying at the moon, I felt, at last, a sense of closure and peace. I was no longer Neil the older brother, babysitter or boy soldier; I'd grown up and put tragedy behind me: there was life after evil. And with that new life comes hope for a future with me, and my brother and sister too.

I made a trip to visit Derek and Mum's graves recently. I am glad they are close by each other in Cottingley Cemetery and like to think they are keeping each other company. It was hard to find Mum's at first, as the grass and wild flowers had reclaimed it. I am intending to buy Mum a nice headstone, but in some ways I quite like it as it is now as it means the Ripper, should he ever get out, could never find her again. She's at peace. And although I still miss Mum, like at such times when our Andrew was born and when I got divorced, I remembered as I stood by her grave, her words to me all those years ago after Derek had died:

'Life's for living, son, and that's what your brother would want you to do.' And so would Mum.

I now have a new beginning with my partner Sue and I became a proud grandfather this year when our Andrew's partner Lisa gave birth to Harry Jackson, weighing in at nearly nine pounds!

I recently took a trip down 'Memory Lane' and went to visit my old secondary school, Bruntcliffe, in Morley. I hadn't been there since I left over three decades ago, but the chair dedicated to Derek's memory is still at the school, and now has pride of place in the office of the current head, Mrs Lynda Johnson, beside her desk, where, as she says, 'she can keep a special eye on it'.

In my heart of hearts, whatever the theories are about Mum working on the streets, I am certain now that such was her shock at Derek's death, and perhaps even her guilt at opening the door at that particular moment, that caused the back draft, she wanted to provide the best she could for us remaining kids, and this probably contributed to their debts. Dad certainly knew what Mum was doing and was not just complicit, but happy to go along with it.

I have often thought about the families of the other Ripper victims, including Wilma McCann's daughter Sonia who sadly hanged herself at Christmas 2007, and Wilf MacDonald who, like Grandad, died of a broken heart after his beloved daughter Jayne was murdered. I hope the surviving victims and the victims' families have at last, like myself, found some peace.

I have seen Sutcliffe in the press over the years: the attacks on him in Broadmoor, the money he won from the criminal injuries compensation board for losing an eye, which was far more than any of his victims or their families got, and about his being let out to scatter his dad's ashes – but these days I don't go looking for such reports. They will always be there, as long as he and I live, but Sutcliffe is my past now, not my present or future.

Although it has been a long haul, I realise I am one of the lucky ones and am making up for those lost years through my family, my grandchild and in my new relationship with Sue, and I couldn't be happier.

When I took the last trip back to visit Mum's grave, I got back on the number fifty-one and went through to Churwell, where I got off at the top of the road. As I turned the corner into Back Green, just for a moment I could hear Goldie's cowbell clattering and see him trotting down the middle of the road with the little ones on him as I ran alongside holding the reins; Mum was smiling at me as she waved at us from the front doorstep to come in for our teas. As I stood across the road from our old house, I was about to wave back, when Mum and the children and Goldie gradually faded from view and were gone. And, as I set off back up the hill to the bus stop, I knew I'd left my childhood behind.

Author's Epilogue

Author's Epilogue

The experience of writing this book has ultimately been healing for Neil who, like many victims at this time, had no access to counselling or help of any kind after the loss of his mother. Neil, now a man of fifty, has at last been able to draw a line under the past and to move on with his life. Neil and I both hope other such victims of the Yorkshire Ripper have also been able to find some peace.

As the Ripper case was so vast and complex, it is impossible to touch on all of it here. However, I now give a brief overview of the case to fill in the gaps in Neil's story, and to shed light on some of the main points and key players involved in it, including the police, Sutcliffe's family and Sutcliffe himself.

The discovery

On the morning of Wednesday 21 January 1976, the nightmare began for the Jackson family and seventeen-year-old Neil.

While most of the good people of Leeds were beginning to stir from their beds, a workman taking a shortcut across some waste ground noticed what looked like a shop dummy dumped by a ginnel. Going over to take a closer look, the workman clutched a hand to his mouth and rushed off to find the nearest telephone phone box.

Within minutes of receiving the call from HQ at his home, the Head of Leeds CID, Detective Chief Superintendent Dennis Hoban, was already donning his sheepskin and trilby and flying out of the back door.

Dennis, an experienced detective with dozens of solved murders under his belt, and whose many commendations from the courts had led to him receiving the Queen's Police Medal, had forgotten something. Quickly backtracking to the kitchen, he sprayed the insulin in the air, then drew back the hypodermic and thrust the needle into his leg.

Pecking his long-suffering wife Betty on the cheek, he then jumped into his brand new customised Daimler and the 'Crime Buster in the Sheepskin jacket', as he was hailed locally, was gone.

Betty wearily shook her head; she and Dennis had been married twenty years by this time and she knew well enough by now that her husband's job came before anything, not least his health and even, at times, the family.

Dennis rushed through the early morning traffic on his way to Manor Street, a former industrial site which he knew only too well was frequented by prostitutes and the clients they picked up in the nearby red-light district off Roundhay Road. It was the '. . . mucky end of town' as Dennis called it.[1]

Yet, despite all his years of experience, what greeted him that morning as he lifted the police tape and went over to view the body, made him 'almost paralysed with numbness'.[2] Lying on the rain-sodden waste ground, among the discarded heaps of rubbish, broken bottles and weeds, was the mutilated body of a middle-aged woman.

The body was partly covered by a checked coat; the woman's sling-back shoes were lying in the mud not far from her handbag, which still contained her purse. Blood near the roadway and tracks in the mud showed the woman had first been struck and then dragged to where her body was found. She had been turned onto her back; her leg and arm on one side had been arranged at right angles to her body, her dress had been pulled up above her midriff and a strip of old timber thrust against the vaginal area. A pool of blood had formed near the head, merging with the puddle beneath.

The police were immediately able to identify the woman from her name and address given inside her purse. Dennis briefed colleagues to break the news to the deceased woman's family; they needed the next of kin down at the morgue to make an identification.

What Hoban's colleagues found that day was that the victim, Mrs Emily Jackson, was a married woman with three children, the eldest being seventeen-year-old Neil, who agreed to accompany his reluctant father to the mortuary to identify the body. 'This is no job for a boy the same age as my youngest,' Dennis shook his head at a colleague.

Hoban, who was exceptional at linking cases, immediately recognised similarities between the attack on Emily and that on twenty-eight-yearold Wilma McCann, whose body had been found on playing fields near her home in Chapeltown just eleven weeks earlier. Just a few hours later, he was also to find out that both women occasionally had sex for money.

At the city morgue, Professor David Gee began the postmortem. Emily had sustained massive blows to the back of the head administered by a blunt instrument, probably a hammer. The outer clothing had not been stabbed through but lifted and put back – the latter becoming the signature trademark of the killer – and the breast area was covered in stab wounds, as with Mrs McCann.

The only difference between the two bloody deaths was the instrument used to inflict the stab wounds. Clusters of small star-shaped wounds were found in Emily's back, throat, neck and stomach. And, as if to show contempt for his victim, the killer had stamped on her body, leaving a muddy impression of a size seven wellington boot on her thigh. Sex had not taken place in either case.

Although the detective's suspicions that the two cases were linked were all but confirmed, Hoban remained circumspect. There was still one person who appeared to have a motive for Emily's death – someone who might have found out his wife was on the game and killed her in a jealous rage – that man was Sidney Jackson. Hoban brought him in for questioning.

He realised that if Sid Jackson could be eliminated from the inquiry, then he had a serial killer on the loose in Leeds.

The prime suspect

After his wife's appalling murder, Sid Jackson was taken in for questioning and had some fast talking to do.

Sid had a history of beating his wife. She had left him in the past because of it, although it is unclear whether the police were aware of this. Sid also knew that his wife was working on the streets; indeed, he had a hand in it – going with her to pick up men and travelling round in the van beside her. But rather than reveal himself to be the kind of man he really was, he told the police: 'My wife had an insatiable sexual appetite. I couldn't satisfy her, so she went out looking for other men.'

It took several hours of grilling for the truth to emerge.

'We had money worries, so she went on t' game,' he finally admitted.

Usually, Emily picked men up in the red-light area close to the Gaiety pub where she dropped Sid off; at other times she went out soliciting in the van when Sid would sometimes accompany her.

Emily had dropped Sid off at the pub on that terrible evening and he expected her to return before closing time. But when the chucking-out bell rang and she still hadn't appeared, he saw the works van was still standing in the pub car park and, assuming she was finishing up with a client, he left her to it and went home in a taxi instead.

Following the grilling at the police station, Sid went home a worried man: worried that the neighbours would believe he was the killer and worried about the reaction he'd get from the people of Churwell, who were about to find out he had been helping his wife to solicit men on the streets.

To the outside world the Jacksons had always been an ordinary family, which, to all intents and purposes, they were – except for Emily's trips to 'bingo'. Having suffered a tragedy when they lost their eldest son, this tragedy would lead to another, culminating in Emily's murder as she did her best to ensure her surviving children had the best possible childhood she could give them.

Shock waves went around the neighbourhood when Emily's occasional occupation became known.

'Never in a hundred years would I have thought Emily Jackson was on the game,' the landlord of the local pub in Churwell said at the time.[3]

But, once the shock waves had subsided, the tragic loss of Emily, particularly to her children, was incalculable as they and the rest of her family were left trying to pick up the pieces.

The Ripper inquiry begins

With Sid no longer in the frame, Hoban had bigger fish to fry than a man pimping his wife. Wearing one of his favourite Aquascutum suits and floral ties, he began giving more information to the press, although still understating the viciousness of the attack.

'In both this and the McCann case, the obvious deep-seated hatred of prostitutes manifested itself in the many stab wounds. While this man, who shows every sign of being a psychopath, is at large, no prostitute is safe.'

Thus, the biggest manhunt the country had ever seen was about to begin, as the police searched for the man now dubbed by the press 'The Ripper'. Posters of Emily appeared in shop windows, on buildings and on the side of police vehicles touring the streets. Appeals were also made over tannoy systems at cinemas, bingo halls and football and rugby matches. Prostitutes operating in the area where the attacks had taken place were interviewed about their clients, and anyone who had convictions for attacking prostitutes was also looked at.

Over the course of a year, officers checked out thousands of vehicles, took over eight hundred statements and made almost four thousand house-to-house enquiries.[4] Hoban even spoke to doctors about any patients they may have had who could have done such terrible attacks.

No stone was left unturned but, despite all this, and Hoban's extraordinary clear-up rate, the Ripper still eluded him. There was not even so much as a peep from one of his many snouts in the Leeds underworld – which Dennis knew meant they too did not have a clue.

On the night of the second murder, a dark-haired man with a moustache, and with blood on his trousers, went home to his wife where they lived together at his in-laws in Bradford. Dropping his bloodied 'work' clothes into the black bin liner he kept in the garage for such purposes[1] this quietly spoken and sensitive young newlywed, told his wife, 'Don't worry about washing those – they're just me oily work clothes, I'll do 'em meself.' He smiled, exposing the gap between his teeth.

'It'll be my contribution to t' household chores each week.'

Sonia was impressed by this man she'd married; he really showed he cared, so unlike other husbands. Her parents were also charmed by him, particularly his mother-in-law who warned her daughter that as Peter was so good-looking and well-mannered, she might lose him to another woman.

'Don't worry Mum, Peter will never look at another woman,' Sonia replied.[1]

As soon as his mother-in-law had finished washing the family's clothes, tea towels and other household items, Peter Sutcliffe loaded all the evidence of his gruesome crime into the washing machine straight from the bin liner. Then he put in the powder and turned on the machine, washing away all his sins as if the former altar boy at the Sacred Heart Church in Bingley was, once again, cleansed.

And there was a lot more washing to be done the following year.

Moved on

Hoban was promoted to Deputy ACC (Crime) and asked to take over as head of CID for the Western Area. This meant that Dennis, a Leeds man to the core, who knew the whole of the criminal fraternity there, had to move to a new office in Bradford. He was not happy about this, particularly as it meant his new duties would mean leaving the Ripper case for someone else to solve.

The man he had been struggling for weeks to catch had married fifteen months earlier. Since then he'd moved in with his wife's parents, who were Eastern European refugees, the Szurmas, in the Clayton area of Bradford.

Sutcliffe was now getting on his feet, having had a string of jobs since leaving school. In October 1976 he got a job as a lorry driver at Clarke's, an engineering haulage firm. Here he proved to be a model employee, and was chosen by his boss to feature, sitting in his cab, on the firm's large advertising poster.

Sonia was also doing well. She had completed her teacher training and was supply teaching in Bradford, when the young couple started hunting for their own home. They fell in love with a large, four-bedroom detached house, high up from the road, in Garden Lane, Heaton, Bradford. Sonia now had 'the house of my dreams'[4], and the young Sutcliffes moved in on 26 September 1977.

This upwardly mobile couple were on their way, and Peter, as ever the attentive husband, carried on giving a hand with his particular household chore, having some washing to do just five days after they moved in.

On 9 October Sonia and Peter threw a house-warming party for Peter's family. Peter, or Pete as he was known to them, wondered to himself why nothing had been reported in the press since he'd murdered Jayne MacDonald and attacked Maureen Long that summer; but he was worried for other reasons than that his recent barbaric handiwork was lying undiscovered.

The guests duly enjoyed the Sutcliffes' hospitality at the party, which included baked potatoes 'as hard as nails', that Pete had thrown into the oven when he realised Sonia had underestimated on the food. The guests were invited to admire the pottery Sonia had made and placed around the house, including a sculpture that stood on top of the piano. Baffled by the strange, cylindrical shapes, Mick took his brother's word for it that it was 'art', while his dad compared it to 'halfway between pottery and that bloke who does the sculpture with the holes, Henry Moore'.[5] Peter, sensitive to Sonia's feelings, had warned his family not to laugh at them.

At the end of the evening, Pete put a hacksaw in his toolbox in the boot of the car and took his mum and dad and siblings home to Bingley. He was gone some time, as he decided to stop off a little out of his way, by Southern Cemetery in Manchester, where he went back to the body of Jean Jordan whom he had killed nine days earlier, his first murder out of Yorkshire and his first since he had moved into his new home.

Sutcliffe pulled the body out of the bushes at the allotment by the cemetery; he needed to find the new £5 note
he'd given Jean from his wage packet so that he couldn't
be traced. Becoming angry when he couldn't find the note,
he slashed at the body again so hard that the intestines
spilled out. Then he got out the hacksaw from his toolbox
and began trying to remove the head in order to leave it
somewhere else to 'create a mystery'[6] and avoid detection
as he was later to tell the police, but the blade was blunt
and he couldn't manage it. The body was already badly
decomposing in the warm weather and had attracted flies,
which laid their eggs on the wounds, but this didn't bother
Pete who had previously worked in a mortuary.

Pete was surprised to find he didn't have much blood on
him when he eventually got home that night; he put his
trousers in the garage, burning them later, and wiped his
shoes clean. A day or so later, he read about the body of
Jean Jordan being found and 'sat back waiting for the
inevitable . . . line of enquiry about the five pound'.[6] Then
the knock at the door came.

The new Ripper head

George Oldfield was a former petty officer in the Royal
Navy who had taken part in the heroic D Day Landings in
France in 1944. Married, with three children, George had
taken over as head of West Yorkshire CID, ACC (Crime),
in the early 1970s.

Just a year into the post, in 1974, George had headed
up the investigation into the M62 coach bombing of Army
personnel and their families in which twelve people,

including two children, were killed. Despite his wartime experiences, the carnage that he had witnessed from this bombing shocked him to the core and he developed a phobia about ticking clocks.

In the 1960s, he had been brought in from the West Riding to investigate alleged corruption in the Leeds City Force, including the CID. He was rigorous in his approach and placed suspected officers under surveillance, making him unpopular with officers who were later to become his colleagues when the forces were amalgamated. He then took over as ACC from a former West Riding officer, which some former Leeds city officers resented, believing Dennis Hoban should have got the job.

In 1977 there had been three murders of so-called 'good-time' girls in Leeds and Bradford, and a fourth in Manchester – the killing of Jean Jordan. When sixteen-year-old Jayne MacDonald was found horrifically murdered on a children's playground in Chapeltown that summer, George Oldfield believed she had been mistaken for a prostitute as she walked home. He took the lead in Jayne's case while also heading up the Ripper inquiry.

Oldfield toured the streets talking to prostitutes, warning them to take extra care and to operate in pairs, taking down client car numbers. This was the fifth victim and while women's groups staged a march from the playground where Jayne was murdered, there were also calls to legalise brothels for the women's safety. Yet when a group of prostitutes began taking their clients back to a house in Bradford for their own safety, the police raided it on the grounds they were running a brothel.[4]

The public were more willing to help after Jayne's death,

but despite various ongoing lines of enquiry and police tactics, George Oldfield still had very little to go on.

Then, just before Christmas, there was another attack. The punter, who had a gap in his teeth and who stuttered when he was under stress said, 'My . . . my . . . name's Da . . . Dave.' Agreeing to have sex with 'Dave', Marilyn Moore was about to climb into the back seat of his car, when he clubbed her from behind. As she fell to the ground screaming, he fled in his car. Marilyn only just survived. She had a number of severe lacerations to her head and the neurosurgeon had to elevate the skull to relieve the pressure on it. Professor Gee, the Home Office pathologist, watched the operation and recognised Marilyn's injuries as being consistent with those of previous victims of the Ripper.[4]

Marilyn was able to give the first description of the Ripper: a man with dark curly hair and a Jason King moustache and beard. The photo-fit bore a striking resemblance to Peter Sutcliffe. It also resembled descriptions given by earlier victims of attacks, which had not, as yet, been attributed to the Ripper.

However, Marilyn thought she saw her attacker some weeks later and made a frantic call to the police with the number of the car he was in. The police traced the man but he was eliminated from the inquiry. Marilyn then thought she had spotted her attacker in the street, and again it turned out to be an innocent man. This caused Oldfield to have doubts about Marilyn's photo-fit, leading him to downplay its significance and all but withdraw it.

The £5 note enquiry

On 15 October 1977, Jean Jordan's handbag was found 200 yards from her body with the £5 note that Sutcliffe had given her inside. As the note was brand new, Detective Chief Superintendent Ridgeway of Manchester Police realised it was possible to trace where it had travelled from the Bank of England to the person who had given it to Jean.

The note was the sixty-fourth in a batch of sixty-nine brand new notes sent to the Leeds clearing bank from the Bank of England and then delivered to Midland Bank at Shipley.[7] Jean was murdered on 1 October and the note had been paid out two days before; the police therefore realised they had a good chance of finding the person who had given her the money. Clark (Holdings) of Bradford, where Sutcliffe worked, was one of the companies which drew their payroll from that bank.

A month after Jean's brutal and callous slaughter, Sutcliffe was interviewed at Garden Lane, Bradford. He could not produce any £5 notes from his wage packet and said he was at home with his wife on both 1 and 9 October, the latter date attending his own house-warming party.

Sonia, having no idea what he had done, confirmed his alibi, failing to remember that he had taken a very long time to run his family home later after the party, or perhaps not thinking anything of it. The police also recorded that he didn't have a car when in fact he had a Corsair.[7]

The police returned in the second phase of the enquiry, a few days later. Two different officers discovered Sutcliffe did in fact have a car, but they didn't examine it, or search the garage or the house, as they were given instructions to do. If they had done so, they would have discovered that the car had three tyres the same as those that had left tread marks at the scene of Irene Richardson's murder at Roundhay Park earlier that year, and at Marilyn Moore's attack a few months later in December.[7]

Profile of a serial killer

Sutcliffe was the oldest of six children and was brought up in Bingley by his father John and mother Kathleen.

John Sutcliffe bullied his wife and children, and ruled the roost with an iron rod, while exhibiting bizarre behaviour at best. He beat his children, stole from allotments, tried to grope his sons' girlfriends and openly boasted of his affairs. He also brought home a joint of meat each week which his wife cooked and the family ate for Sunday roast, believing it to be beef when in fact it was horse meat he'd obtained from a pet shop.[5]

Peter was unable to stand up to his father as his younger brother Mick did, and clung to his kindly and hard-working mother Kathleen. Kathleen was a devout Catholic whom he and his siblings idolised and Peter called the 'Angel'. The Angel brought her children up as strict Catholics and Peter, like his mother, shunned 'dirty talk' and 'smutty' jokes.[1]

However, in 1972 the Angel's halo was to slip when she had an affair with a police sergeant. John Sutcliffe, playing another cruel joke on his wife, rang her up pretending to be her lover. Arranging to meet Kathleen at a hotel, he told her to bring some suitable nightwear for their romantic tryst. Sutcliffe senior then got his unsuspecting children Peter and Maureen, to turn up at the hotel at a prearranged time. Once Kathleen arrived, she was shocked to see them all there. Her husband then opened her bag and produced a new nightie from it, humiliating her and embarrassing the children.[5]

Peter was in his mid-twenties at the time, but long before his mother's halo became tarnished, he seemed only to be able to see women in one of two categories – 'decent girls' or 'whores' – and by now he'd had plenty of experience with the latter, having visited red-light areas with his mates for the last three years. His growing obsession with sex and violence had also been apparent some years before. He had pushed his sister's little ten-year-old friend down a flight of stairs. The poor child was terrified and when she landed at the bottom of the stairs she looked up to see him standing at the top with a sickly grin on his face.[1]

When Peter was eighteen, he had gone on holiday with a friend Steve, staying in the family caravan in the Lakes. As he and Steve were getting ready for bed, his friend made a joke about sex. Peter went mad, slashing at his 'private parts' with a knife and raging, 'I'm going to cut your dick off, you bastard!' His friend ended up having to go to hospital for stitches.[1]

The early years

At school, Peter was always at the top of the class and was a skilful artist who enjoyed drawing and painting. However, despite being clever, when he left school at fifteen he drifted in and out of a series of jobs, until he found the one that was perfect for him: grave digging.

Although still a teenager at the time, as soon as the

mourners had left a burial, he would take the coffin lid off
and search the bodies for jewellery. Robbing graves was a
perk of the job for Peter, who was never short of money
down the pub with his gravedigger work-mates. If a ring
was stuck on the deceased's finger, this didn't present Pete
with a problem as he'd get a pair of sharp shears and snip
off the finger. He also prised open mouths to look for gold
fillings, yanking them out with pliers.[1]

Touching corpses appeared to give him great pleasure.
He examined almost every dead body that came in, before
sitting down with his work-mates to eat his lunch without
washing his hands. He even enjoyed going through bags of
flesh, which were all that was left of a person who had gone
under a train and which arrived for burial one day. At other
times he would don a hassock and, carrying a prayer book,
would begin conducting a service over the grave, swiftly
turning it into a rant of obscenities. He grabbed a deceased
magistrate hard by her face and screamed at her, 'You won't
be putting anyone else away, you bitch!' There were also
stories of necrophilia.[1] When Peter was offered twice the
wage to work at a local factory he turned it down, prefer-
ring to stay in his dream job, only moving on when he took
up a job which he saw as step up – working in a mortuary.

Peter particularly enjoyed post mortems, especially after
accidents. He loved washing the knives and went into gory
details about the job to his friends, but he was a mass of
contradictions. When he was grave digging, he wouldn't
take his shirt off, even if it was boiling hot, as he was too
embarrassed to expose his body. And later, when he worked
as a lorry driver, if his boss told him off when he had done
something wrong, he would burst into tears.[1] But this shy

and sensitive side of him was soon to come in handy when he met the love of his life.

The true love of a serial killer

Sutcliffe met Sonia in 1966, when she was sixteen and he was twenty, in a pub frequented by gravediggers in Bradford. Despite his forays into necrophilia at work, he was shy with women but went out of his way to get to know Sonia, 'accidentally' spilling beer over her. As she wiped herself down he suggested taking her home on his motorbike so that she could get changed; it was the least he could do.[5]

When they returned half an hour later, his gravedigger mates were shocked to see their shy friend buying her a drink and staying to talk to her. She told him she loved painting and was hoping to study this at college; he also liked to sketch and paint and said he wanted to be an artist or a musician. Soon he was taking Sonia home to meet his family at Cornwall Road, Bingley. Here, at first, she wouldn't speak, but only whisper to him.

Theirs was to be a fairy tale like no other. On one occasion, some years on, she pirouetted round in front of the settee and said, 'Guess who I am today? Cinderella.'[5] While they were going out together, her Prince Charming continued to visit prostitutes, contracting a sexually transmitted disease in the process, as he became 'Da . . . Da . . . Dave' by night.

Sonia went away to London to train to become a teacher and, under the strain of studying, she began to exhibit erratic behaviour, wandering into the street in her pyjamas, believing the world was coming to an end and that she was the Second Coming, with stigmata on her hands.

Peter joined her in London some time later, first camping in the grounds of her hall of residence and then getting a place to stay and working as an odd-job man, bringing his toolbox with him. When Sonia was transferred to a psychiatric hospital at Bradford for compulsory treatment for schizophrenia, he followed her home and did what he could to help her. After her discharge from hospital, Sonia became a voluntary outpatient but he felt she didn't look well. He worried that the medication his princess was on had robbed her of her personality, while Sonia thought she was an aeroplane.[5]

'I'm determined to pull her through,' Peter told her parents, the Szurmas, which made a favourable impression on them. And Sonia did begin to get better, even attending his friend's wedding later in 1972, although having occasional relapses, including tearing off her clothes in public. Peter had helped with her outbursts of rage at college, where her Prince Charming would gently try to restrain her, pinning her arms by her side.[5]

Theirs was a mutually supportive relationship, for, when Sutcliffe got overexcited, which he frequently did in telling a story to friends – stopping to laugh manically to himself – she would look over at him like a schoolteacher frowning at a naughty pupil. 'Peter!' she'd say, and he would instantly stop and calm down.[5]

Sutcliffe also appears to have been the nurturer of the two, for when his sister Maureen had a baby, Sutcliffe cooed over the child and nursed her, but when Sonia was handed the baby, as soon as she started to cry, she unfolded her arms, letting the baby drop heavily into the pram.[5]

But if she lacked maternal instincts, Sonia had aspirations

for them both and began by refining Pete's tastes. Just about tolerating his habit of visiting working men's clubs to see rock 'n' roll bands, she introduced him to classical music and the finer things of life. They even went to see Sonia's sister give piano recitals and to the opera and ballet on occasions.[5]

Yet, while the idea of 'going up in the world' had always appealed to Sutcliffe, his family didn't understand it. 'You mean you go an' sit for hours listening to her playing fucking concertos and stuff like that? . . . it 'ud send me crackers, like!' his younger brother Mick said.[5]

Some eight years after their first meeting, this bloody Prince Charming and his Cinderella got married, on her birthday in August 1974, at Clayton Baptist Chapel in Bradford and honeymooned in Paris. The night before the wedding, as the groom celebrated his stag night with his friends in the pub, he left them to go down to the red-light district of Bradford.

The demise of a detective

Deputy ACC Dennis Hoban had been a diabetic for most of his life, but he did not look after himself. The job and the anti-social hours he worked made this practically impossible. Dashing from one crime scene to the next, setting up large-scale inquiries, tapping up his touts and rounding up and interrogating suspects, meant he ate irregularly and his diet was frequently poor. He would also forget to take his next shot of insulin when it was due.

On top of this, Dennis had asthma and his eyes were playing him up, which became evident when he dented or scraped his beloved Bentley going round corners or when giving chase after criminals. In those who suffer from diabetes, sight problems, strokes and other conditions are not uncommon and in March 1978, Dennis was admitted to hospital with a chest infection. After an exploratory operation, Dennis suffered a heart attack.

Doctors told the family that Dennis's heart was badly diseased and that as his brain had been starved of oxygen during the heart attack, he would be left in a permanent vegetative state. The family had to make a heartbreaking decision to let him live or die, but because of Dennis's character, the decision was clear.[8] On 15 March, standing round his bed that spring morning, the family said their goodbyes to their flamboyant and loving father one last time; the machine was then switched off. Dennis was just fifty-one. Policing had been his life. His friend, Jim Hobson, who had by now taken over as Head of Leeds CID, said he had worked himself into an early grave. Although he was joking, it had some truth in it when Jim said the only way he could get Dennis to go to a rugby match was by suggesting they nicked some pickpockets on the way. His wife Betty, who had undoubtedly suffered because of her husband's job, remarked with some bitterness, 'He should never have got married, as his job meant so much to him.'[4]

All the great and the good turned out for Dennis's funeral, which was led by the Chief Constable of West Yorkshire. Crowds turned out to watch the procession go through Leeds up to Rawden Crematorium, where over thirty officers formed a guard of honour and six detectives carried his coffin. Many of those who came out to pay their last respects to the 'Crime Buster in the Sheepskin

Jacket' were the Leeds criminal fraternity, who sent tributes and flowers.

There was also a moving tribute to Dennis that night by his friend Richard Whiteley on *Calendar*, YTV's local news programme; as Dennis's son Richard said, 'Dad would have enjoyed that.' A Dennis Hoban trophy was also set up in his honour by his journalist friends, and is awarded every year to the best detective in the area.

Sadly, Dennis didn't live to see the Ripper caught. He had always believed that it must be a local man, and a lorry driver and/or possibly in engineering. When Sutcliffe was finally caught it turned out that Dennis had been right all along.

The red herring inquiry

Tyre tracks were the one positive clue from the Richardson case in February 1977. Jim Hobson set up a tracking enquiry, which found that over 50,000 cars could have made these tracks; he had eliminated 30,000 cars when Oldfield decided to abandon it as he was critically short of officers to investigate another attack that December.[7] As Detective Superintendent Dick Holland said, 'If you were warm and breathing, you were on the Ripper case.'[4] Hobson was furious and rightly so, as it turned out that Sutcliffe's Corsair was in the 20,000 still waiting to be checked.

By the spring of 1979, there had been ten murders and at least five attempted murders. After the last murder, that of a nineteen-year-old clerk Josephine Whitaker from Halifax, George Oldfield was to say she was, 'perfectly respectable this time' as he had also said in connection with the Jayne MacDonald murder.

Now that the Ripper was no longer seen to be striking at prostitutes alone, Oldfield began receiving greater assistance once more from the public. But he also had another line of enquiry to pursue when a tape and some letters arrived with a Sunderland postmark, personally addressed to him. The tape was from a man with a Wearside accent, claiming to be Jack the Ripper and goading Oldfield. This led to resources being diverted to the north east as the hunt focused on interviewing men in an area of Wearside, and checking their handwriting.

Oldfield believed in the tape and letters because the person sending them seemed to know facts of the case that were not in the public domain; but actually, this wasn't true. The details the sender of the tape appeared to know about the Vera Millward case had been given to the local press in Manchester by Jack Ridgeway in order to generate public interest and, thereby, information. The same was true of the Joan Harrison murder in Preston – George Oldfield did not know that a Leeds newspaper had actually published some time before the theory that there was a possible link between this murder and the Ripper. Joan, however, was not killed by the Yorkshire Ripper, and this case remains unsolved even today. The letter writer, who had licked the envelope, was blood group B, the same as the man who had killed Joan. Both Joan Harrison and Jo Whitaker (a Ripper victim) appeared to have been murdered by the same man, as both had been bitten on the breast by a man with a gap in his teeth. All this, however, was coincidental – but for Oldfield, it helped confirm his belief that the letters and tape were genuine.

The tape was a massive red herring, and arguably another

three lives might have been saved had the inquiry not gone off at such a tangent. The Ripper Tape inquiry reopened in 2005 and John Humble, an unemployed man in his fifties from Sunderland, was imprisoned for eight years in 2006 for perverting the course of justice. Certainly Sutcliffe, who had been interviewed by the police yet again in connection with the Ripper inquiry, would not have been discounted on the basis of his local accent and his handwriting not fitting the bill.

Had more attention been paid to what Marilyn Moore, an acknowledged Ripper victim, had told the police in December 1977 that the attacker had said, 'I know a right quiet place' [where we can go for sex] – a typical Yorkshire turn of phrase – Oldfield might not have put all his eggs so completely in one basket. But George Oldfield saw the tape and letters as 'a personal thing, between him and me,' and refused to shift focus.

However, not all those working on the inquiry were quite so blinkered. When a young Detective Constable, Andrew Laptew, interviewed Sutcliffe as part of an enquiry into cross sightings of cars in red-light areas, he was immediately suspicious. He found Sutcliffe had a record for 'going equipped', and despite his denials about using prostitutes, his car had in fact been spotted some thirty-six times in the red-light area of Bradford.

Laptew also noticed how Sutcliffe was a good match for Marilyn Moore's photo-fit and that he also had a gap in his teeth. Laptew's boss, Dick Holland, however, abruptly discounted anything to do with the photo-fit. Furthermore, because Sutcliffe had always lived in Yorkshire and his handwriting didn't tally with that in the letters received from Sunderland, Holland marked his report 'File'.[4] Yet again, Sutcliffe breathed a sigh of relief.

As it was, the inquiry was awash with information, so much so that the floors of the incident room that held all this paperwork were caving in beneath it and had to be reinforced. There were also inadequate indexing and cross-referencing systems, so that it was impossible to make links easily or to keep track of everything. (There were no computerised records, the technology still being in its infancy.)

Before 1980 was out, Oldfield had been replaced as head of the Ripper inquiry; a Ripper 'Super Squad' of experienced detectives was formed and a review of the inquiry was launched by the HMIC under Lawrence Byford's direction.

Apart from the person sending the tape and letters, there was one other person who knew the truth. When Carl Sutcliffe, Pete's younger brother, had mentioned the tapes to him in conversation, Pete had scoffed, 'They can't be from the Ripper; why would such an intelligent bloke who is getting away with it and laughing at the police, hinder himself by doing that? He's too smart.'[1]

Getting away with it

Sutcliffe was interviewed by the police a total of nine times in connection with the Ripper inquiry, from 1977 onwards,[7] yet he was never arrested. Despite being seen as a result of every major operation mounted by the Ripper Squad – the tracking inquiry, the cross-area and triple-area sightings in red-light areas, and in both of the £5 note enquiries – the police let him slip the net every time. For four of the murders he was given an alibi by his wife, though none of these were ever corroborated by anyone outside the extended family.

Clearly, as the inquiry ground on Sutcliffe had got to a point where he believed he had got away with it for so long that he would never get caught. As his young brother Carl said, when people would talk about the awful things that had happened to the Ripper victims, Pete would say, 'I'll bet it's nothing as bad as people think, though I don't suppose we'll ever know because they'll never catch him.' Carl was in no doubt about what they should do with him if they ever did and he told Pete, 'They ought to castrate him [the Ripper] without anaesthetic then hang him.' Peter agreed but quickly changed the subject.[1]

The sexual proclivities of a serial killer

As Pete and Sonia settled into their new home and Pete continued doing his own washing, he was also taking women back to Garden Lane with his mate Trevor Birdsall, when Sonia was away at her sister's. Hiding all the wedding photos, the four of them would get into bed 'for some fun' – despite Sutcliffe having told Carl earlier that he had serious erection problems.[1]

Sutcliffe was described by friends, family and others as either kind, charming and polite, or a violent, aggressive sexual pervert. Certainly, he appeared to have no interest in 'straight sex' or perhaps was not interested in sex at all. In 1979, in Lanarkshire, while making deliveries, he met a young divorcée. He told her that his wife had been killed in an accident. Theresa Douglas said that although she had met him several times, 'he was the perfect gentleman', and never once tried to have sex with her.[1]

Another girlfriend, who was just sixteen when he was in his twenties, said he was considerate, and 'the perfect gentleman'. They went out on and off for four years, and she said he never touched her apart from a chaste kiss goodnight. And at twenty-five, when he was with Sonia, he was going out with a fifteen-year old, Margaret Tovey, for three years, who said, 'He'd make love to me in every imaginable way . . . but we never had straight sex. He didn't like it; it used to disturb him even talking about it.' Margaret remarked that she was still a virgin at the end of the affair.[1]

On the other hand, his brother-in-law, Robin Holland, said, 'Prostitutes were always on his mind' and he would nip out for a 'quickie' with one. Robin stopped going out because of this. A male friend of Sutcliffe also recalled that he'd met Pete in his local and he'd said, 'Let's go down Lumb Lane for a jump and give a pro a good kicking instead of paying.'[1]

One theory is that because of his mother's strict moral views, he felt sex was wrong and disgusting. Instead, Sutcliffe gained sexual gratification from killing, ejaculating as he did so. This appears to have been borne out on his arrest when the police discovered his rather unusual, home-made underwear discussed here later. Sutcliffe may have been consumed by sexual guilt, killing the women to destroy his own lust.[9]

Captured at last

'They call me Da . . . Da . . . Dave,' the driver stammered nervously as twenty-four-year-old Olivia Reivers climbed into his car in Sheffield. Ten minutes later and still no erection, Olivia had the best piece of luck of her life when the police came along and interrupted them, finally arresting Sutcliffe for false number plates.

The gap in the teeth, the size seven shoes, the Jason King moustache from the Marilyn Moore photo-fit and the many sightings of his car in red-light areas started at last to add up. The arresting officer went back the next day and checked out where Sutcliffe had gone to urinate, finding a knife with a long blade and a ball-pein hammer hidden in a grate there. They'd got their man.

Dick Holland and a colleague went round to collect Sonia to take her to the police station and to search the house. Sonia was wearing an outdoor coat in the house and sat in the cold in front of the television watching *Kontakte*, a German-language programme.

Holland, clutching the ball-pein hammer and the knife in two plastic bags, told her they were holding her husband and making enquiries into murders of women in the north, but Sonia just kept watching her programme until he had to ask her to turn off the television. Shortly after, he went to the kitchen where he discovered a block of kitchen knives with the second largest one missing – the knife in the plastic bag fitting perfectly into the gap in the block.[4]

Sutcliffe admitted thirteen murders and seven attempted murders. Sonia was also taken in and questioned, and the police accused her of covering up for Peter. But as

Sonia said, 'I had no idea what he was doing', and finally, after a very long interrogation, the roles reversed and the police had to convince Sonia that her husband was the Ripper. They took her to see him and he admitted it to her.

That night, before going to Armley Jail, Dick Holland from Leeds and Jack Ridgeway from Manchester constabulary stopped off at Garden Lane, to pick up the clothes Sutcliffe had worn during the attacks. Sonia, however, insisted her husband could not go to prison until he'd had his piece of Christmas cake and a glass of milk. The serial killer looking harassed, raised his eyebrows as if to say, 'Oh, God there she goes again.'[4]

The police were frozen with cold and felt uncomfortable in this 'sterile' house but Sonia insisted and so Sutcliffe asked the sergeant with the two detectives if it would be alright. Sutcliffe sat at the table with his handcuffed officer beside him; every time Sutcliffe took a bite or a drink the sergeant had to raise his hand too, their arms going up and down in unison and Holland and Ridgeway barely able to contain themselves. Both said that if the circumstances had not been so tragic, it would have been hilarious.[4] However, and more importantly, the washing machine had completed its last grisly cycle.

Disbelief

'I just can't believe Peter killed thirteen women. Even if it comes from his own mouth I will never accept it . . . He was worried about the Ripper and he used to drive me about when I had to to go out at night so I would be safe . . . Nothing was too much trouble for him,' Sonia's mother, Mrs Szurma, said.[1]

Not everyone, however, was surprised when they heard of Sutcliffe's arrest. William Clarke, his boss at the haulage company, said that although he was hard working, they had been calling him the Ripper for years at work. 'He fitted the description to a T,' Mr Clarke said, 'and had been interviewed several times [at work].' This included over the £5 note traced back to the company. He was also taken away for saliva samples but, as his former boss said, 'as they kept letting him go, we assumed he must be innocent', then the Ripper tape came along which let him off the hook.[1]

Mr Clarke took down the poster in his office of his 'model lorry driver' Sutcliffe as soon as he heard.

*

When Sonia first saw her husband after he was charged, he told her straight so that she'd believed it, 'It's me. I'm the Yorkshire Ripper. I killed all those women.' To which she replied, 'What on earth did you do that for, Peter? Even a sparrow has a right to live.'[4]

During the few minutes they were allowed together what she particularly wanted to know was if he'd had sex with any of the women he'd brutally murdered.

'Only once,' he said, 'and that was mechanical,' referring to nineteen-year-old Helen Rykta, who had lain dying beneath him.

Soon afterwards, his brother Carl visited him on remand in prison and asked him, 'Why did you do it, Pete?'

He just smiled and casually replied, 'The women I killed were filth, bastard prostitutes . . . littering the streets, I was just cleaning up the place a bit.'[1]

On another of Sonia's visits to her husband, on remand in Armley Jail, she said to him, 'Whatever you have done, I will always love you. I'll sell up everything to move nearer to where they send you. I'll visit you by taxi and when I haven't got the money I'll come by train and if I can't afford that I'll come by bus. And when I've got no money, I'll walk. And if I run out of shoe leather, I'll come in my bare feet.'[1]

After such a remarkable piece of prose, her attention then seems to have turned to the more mundane – she turned up clutching the gas and electricity bills, complaining that they had shot up since the police had been coming round to search the house.

'For God's sake Sonia, what if they are a bit high? . . . I've got other things to worry about apart from bloody bills!'[1]

The neighbours, who described the young Sutcliffe couple as devoted, were shocked to wake up the morning after his arrest to find that the Ripper had been living next to them for several years. The Sutcliffes had only recently been decorating their home, and had talked to friends about plans to adopt a baby from the Vietnamese boat people, and to sell up so that they could use some of the money from the sale to open a pottery.

The trial

When the case came to the Old Bailey in April that year, Sutcliffe pleaded not guilty to murder but guilty to manslaughter on the grounds of diminished responsibility to all thirteen murders, and guilty to all seven attempted murders.

Counsel for the prosecution was willing to accept this plea on behalf of the defence based on the opinions of four psychiatrists whom Sutcliffe had seen and who had reached a consensus on diminished responsibility due to his suffering from schizophrenia.

But Mr Justice Boreham had other ideas. 'I have grave anxieties about Sutcliffe and his pleas.' He was not satisfied that the psychiatrists had based their opinions on what Sutcliffe had told them alone, and that his story of his hearing voices from God in Bingley Cemetery to go on a mission to kill prostitutes conflicted with what he told the police at the time of his arrest. Mr Justice Boreham adjourned the case until a jury could be sworn in to decide.

When the trial reconvened in May, his confessions to the murders were not in dispute, but the jury had to decide whether he was guilty of murder or manslaughter; in effect, was he mad or bad.

While the defence put forward the case of Sutcliffe hearing the voice of God setting him on his mission when he worked as a gravedigger, the prosecution countered that, with Sonia, he had a ready-made model for feigning schizophrenia.

The court heard how, when Sonia had visited him a few days after he was charged, he told her that he was guilty of what he was charged with, and that he had told the police all about the vehicles he'd used, the dates and times and what had happened and that he expected to get thirty years. But he was later overheard by a prison officer who testified against him saying, 'If I can convince people I'm mad, then I'll only get ten years in the looney bin.'

He was also said to be highly amused that doctors considered him 'disturbed', proclaiming, 'I am as normal as anyone', while in front of the jurors was a table bearing the Ripper's tools, ranging from hammers and a hacksaw to specially sharpened screwdrivers and knives.

Families of the victims were in court to see justice done while others could not put themselves through such an ordeal again. Sutcliffe could have spared them this had he simply pleaded guilty to murder.

This would also have been the case had a certain item of underclothing not been overlooked as evidence. Before being interviewed for a major crime, the police should have searched Sutcliffe thoroughly and removed all his clothes from him, bagging them up and sending them off for forensics. When he was finally asked to strip, it was after the interview, and he was reluctant to do so.

The police soon found out why: he had his underpants in his pocket and was wearing special, home-made woollen leggings. They consisted of a V-neck jumper which he wore upside down with his legs in the sleeves; he had sewn padding into the area where his knees would be to make it comfortable when he bent over his victims to do his grim deeds. He had also sewn a silk lining in the back to go across his buttocks and he wore the V neck at the front to expose his genitals, making it easier for him to masturbate.[4]

Perhaps, in the flurry of activity at the time of the arrest of one of the world's notorious murderers, these 'leg warmers', as Sutcliffe called them, were never in fact documented or presented as evidence. Had they been, it would surely have swept away Sutcliffe's plea of diminished responsibility. The leg warmers were, as Michael Bilton said, 'as important in terms of evidence as the actual weapons he used to murder his victims. It spoke volumes about his sexual motives and his state of mind during his attacks on helpless women.'[4]

They also clearly backed up Mr Harry Ognall's argument for the prosecution: 'This isn't a missionary of God, it is a man who gets sexual pleasure out of killing these women.'

Sutcliffe was found guilty by a majority verdict of murder on all thirteen counts. He received twenty life sentences with a recommendation that he serves thirty years. In February 2009, the Prime Minister said he could not foresee any circumstances under which Sutcliffe would be released, despite recent speculation that he would.

The aftermath

A year later, Sutcliffe was to tell prison doctors that Emily Jackson was haunting him in his cell and he could smell her perfume.[4] Psychiatrists then reversed the jury's finding, deciding that Peter Sutcliffe was paranoid schizophrenic after all, and in 1984 he was sent to Broadmoor. Sonia married again, but that marriage has since broken down and she is now alleged to be visiting her ex-husband in prison again.

The families of the victims were handed down their sentences on the day that Sutcliffe callously and brutally slaughtered their relatives, as in Neil Jackson's case. Like Neil, they are the forgotten victims, whose lives were damaged and, in some cases, completely destroyed by the Yorkshire Ripper. But I hope that in telling Neil's story, of how he has overcome all the odds to find happiness again, it has demonstrated that there can, after all, be life after evil.

Bibliography

1. John Beattie, *The Yorkshire Ripper Story* (A Quarter/ Daily Star Publication, Leeds, 1981).
2. Roger Cross, *The Yorkshire Ripper: The in-depth study of a mass killer and his methods* (HarperCollins, 1981).
3. Peter Kinsley and F. Smyth, *I'm Jack: The police hunt for the Yorkshire Ripper* (Pan, London, 1980).
4. Michael Bilton, *Wicked Beyond Belief: The Hunt for the Yorkshire Ripper* (HarperCollins, London, 2003).
5. Gordon Burn, *Somebody's Husband, Somebody's Son, The Story of Peter Sutcliffe* (Heinemann, London, 1984).
6. Michael Bilton, *Wicked Beyond Belief: The hunt for the Yorkshire Ripper*, Appendix A: Statement of Sutcliffe to Police, Crown Copyright, p. 659.
7. Lawrence Byford, *The Yorkshire Ripper Case: Review of the Police Investigation of the Case*, Report to the Secretary of State for the Home Office (London, December 1981) (The Byford Report).
8. Richard Hoban, Dennis Hoban's son, 2008.
9. John Beattie, *The Yorkshire Ripper Story*, p. 137.

Acknowledgements

With deepest gratitude to the family, friends and former neighbours of Neil Jackson, and to Richard Hoban, Deputy ACC (Crime), Dennis Hoban's son, for their help and support with this book.